Published by John Blake Publishing Ltd,
3 Bramber Court, 2 Bramber Road, London W14 9PB, England

First published by John Blake Publishing in hardback 2001

ISBN 1 903402 32 8

British Library Cataloguing-in-Publication Data:
A catalogue record for this book is available from
the British Library.

Typeset by t2

Printed and bound in Great Britain by
Creative Print and Design (Wales), Ebbw Vale, Gwent.

Pictures reproduced by kind permission of
Scope Features and Darien Davis/COBRA.

3 5 7 9 10 8 6 4 2

Papers used by John Blake Publishing Limited are natural, recyclable products
made from wood grown in sustainable forests. The manufacturing processes con-
form to the environmental regulations of the country of origin.

Contents

This book is dedicated to my mother. Thank you for the gifts of determination, passion and humour. Without these I would not be where I am today.

Foreword

I first met Louise at a party on a summer's evening in Hollywood some years ago. She was standing alone, by the pool, sipping a drink. We began to chat idly about this and that, and she at once impressed me with her intelligence and humour. Also, one could not help noticing that she was beautiful and spoke with a sexy English accent. And there was a serenity about her I found compelling.

She told me she was an actress and somewhere in our conversation casually mentioned the word 'accident'. It was then she told me, without a trace of anger or bitterness, her extraordinary story.

It is a story of a body shattered and rebuilt. A dream destroyed and re-born. There is despair and pain, both physical and mental, which ultimately leads to acceptance and action. It is also about the kind of hope which defies all human logic and reason. Hers is a courage that is truly awesome. Louise's heroic triumph over appalling adversity humbles and inspires, and teaches us the true meaning of Faith. I am honoured to know such a woman.

Gabriel Byrne

The Magic of the Mask

I first met Lou through mutual friends and my sister Kate. Whenever we saw each other, it always seemed to me that Lou shone very brightly, drink in hand, her raucous laugh filling the room; she was the archetypal life and soul, the person you wanted to be seated next to at dinner. I had no idea of the trauma she had been through, that she had been put back together piece by piece, that the big, outgoing personality masked an enormous amount of personal pain.

I remember watching Lou one night. Her face seemed to change somehow, as if it had grown weary of what it was projecting, and needed to settle for a while into sadness. I went and sat down next to her and, after having asked how she was, she told me. Her extraordinary story amazed me, not just because she was alive, having withstood unbelievable injuries, but that the internal damage she had sustained both physically and emotionally meant that this near-fatal accident would be something she would deal with every day for the rest of her life.

Her courage is inspiring; it is one thing to articulate pain in conversations that you can end if they get too much, it is quite another to write an entire book. Terrible things happen in our lives, and Lou is a fine example of how that doesn't mean life itself is terrible.

Minnie Driver

Prologue

---

4 October 1992, Los Angeles

The sound of the phone smashes into my unconscious, waking me up from my nightmare. My hand reaches out from under the cover to find the receiver in the darkness. As I pull it to my ear, I miss and hit myself in the head. I wish I had missed it ringing altogether and could still be sleeping through my jet-lag.

'Lou? What's wrong? You sound terrible ...' Emma's voice, as if from another planet, brings me closer to reality. I peer at the alarm clock. The room is completely dark. The fluorescent digits on the clock shine. It is ten past five in the morning.

'Emma,' I yawn, 'I just had the most frightening nightmare.'

'Really? What about?' she asks.

'Oh God,' I say, thinking back to my dream. 'It was horrible. I was in a car accident and I lost all my hair.'

Losing my hair would be a nightmare. Emma, I gather from the non-committal pause on the other end, fails to comprehend the magnitude of that concept.

I have been in Los Angeles for six weeks and am feeling more at home each day. My morning ritual, which thanks to the early wake-up call is earlier than normal today, is coffee first then a good long stare in the bathroom mirror. This is ruined by my discovery of an unseemly spot on the right side of my nose. I lean in closer, allowing the bright bathroom light to emphasise every blemish on my face. Every open pore is visible, as are the dark, tired circles around my eyes. I am tired. I have been frantically organising my new life.

California has made me obsessive about my imperfections. I remember I have a meeting with a casting director on Tuesday and any physical blemish is justifiable grounds for anxiety. Once you've been in Los Angeles for a short period of time, it becomes apparent that appearance is not just important here, it is critical. Height, weight, colouring, beauty, breast size, lip pouts – these are the building blocks of stardom.

I have an attractively symmetrical face framed by lush brown hair and punctuated by large blue eyes. The abundance of sunshine has turned my skin a golden brown. In fact, I look rather Italian. Of course, I could probably stand to lose a bit of weight, which I am determined to do post haste. If it weren't for the spot, I would feel better. I'm feeling positive and confident about my new life and finally following my dreams. I've no distractions and only myself to think about. For me, this is a new experience. A feeling of not having to worry about taking care of someone else and putting my life aside. I miss my family and most definitely my friends, but I can rely on the early-morning phone calls to keep me connected to London.

When I go out to my car, a rush of adrenalin adds to my good mood. Just looking at my new sleek, black Mustang convertible gets me high. It's new to me, but really a few years old. I feel like a star just sitting in it. Having a roof that moves up and down is enough to make me smile. I never put the top up, even if it were to rain, which is an event in Los Angeles which apparently calls for storm watch.

My friend George, another transplanted Londoner, is house-sitting in one of the most coveted neighbourhoods in Los Angeles – Bel Air. As I drive over, the wind whips through my hair and I wind up the hills, along the tree-lined roads where hidden mansions protect their celebrity dwellers. I can't help but feel that I belong here. A giggle of sheer joy tears through me as I pull into the driveway.

We sit on plush lounge chairs drinking freshly squeezed lemonade. George and I amuse each other by pretending already to be rich and famous. So far, much of my time in LA has been spent day-dreaming – about my acceptance speech at the Academy Awards; about my films in which I am a marvellous leading lady in both comedies and dramas, alternately hilariously funny and heartbreakingly poignant; and, of course, about my father's face, glowing with pride.

George, in the meantime, is nursing a ferocious hangover. That's another thing I've quickly discovered about LA, the people that *do* party, party pretty hard. George is no exception.

'Oh, Lou ...' George moans, gulping down three aspirin with his healthy organic lemonade.

'Headache?' I laugh, only to see his little face, which is already bright red from the sun, sag lower.

George resembles a mouse-man. He is small with mouselike features and even has tiny tufts of hair growing down his high cheekbones. He is very English and an extrovert, a characteristic of which the British are proud, especially George. I can rely on George. I feel relieved that I hadn't gone out with him last night. I'd hate to be feeling how he looks.

After we've toasted ourselves on both sides, we retire into the sitting room to watch videos and eat junk food. Sated and happy, I fall asleep.

I often wonder about what I would have done differently if I had known. Would I have called my father? Written my will? Would I have taken a taxi straight to the airport and left my Mustang where it was, to rot in a Bel Air driveway? Would I, could I, should I? Just words floating irrelevantly through space, waiting to meet with the inevitable impact that is my destiny. When Fate knocks on your door, you may not be ready. You may not even notice the signs that are pointing to your destiny. My fate crept up on me with naught but a whisper. I was entirely unprepared.

The Magic of the Mask

5 October 1992

This morning, Los Angeles is an annoying confusion of sounds. The horns, screeching tyres and zooming audio flashes of the traffic on Doheny, the unbearably intrusive air conditioner clattering on and off with little rhyme or reason, the neighbour who spent all night trying to convince the entire block that the best music in the world was ... Brazilian. Getting out of my warm comfy bed is painful but necessary.

Coffee, bathroom ... the mirror is not so kind today. Please don't let me become one of those obsessive women who stare at themselves in the mirror for hours to find any possible faults. Come to think of it, the spot does seem somewhat improved, thank God. I wander out to the living room, two steps from the bedroom, one-and-a-half from the bathroom. My apartment is small. The room is blindingly bright with sunshine, which shoots in through the uncovered windows and ricochets off the brassy furniture that apparently Mary Tyler Moore left behind 20 years ago. The answer machine flashes invitingly. Part of the fun of those machines is wondering whose disembodied voice will jump out from it at the press of a button. In this case it is Craig, Ian, Charlotte and Jason who are temporarily trapped in my little black box. Did I say *Jason*? A moment of silence, please ... His voice, slightly sarcastic, perhaps a bit tender, undeniably sexy, fills the room with promise. This is going to be a great day. My only question is whether to call him right back or make him wait. Clever girl that I am, I decide that making him wait is the winning answer.

I sit on the dark bar stool that is close to the wet bar and return my calls. As I make plans for the day, I glance around my apartment, searching for ways to make it more me. I could replace the plastic blinds with something else. How could I remove the permanent stains from the mirror. This search is in vain as I don't have the money to re-decorate. My wandering mind is interrupted by Charlotte's voice, which has now reached the other end of the phone.

'Please get me out of here tonight, Lou. My parents are driving me crazy,' she says desperately, itching to be rescued.

'I'll pick you up at four,' I promise. One would think I'd told her she'd won the lottery.

My secret lover, disguised in a suit of steel and rubber, has already made arrangements for our passionate rendezvous. And still, I know nothing.

Now it's 3.30pm and my date is waiting. Outside the day glistens and I wind east on Sunset Boulevard wearing a midnight-blue, long-sleeved shirt, spoils from a relationship gone awry, the best thing I got out of Adam. Charlotte's parents live in Los Feliz, one of the oldest neighbourhoods in Los Angeles, the houses immense and solid on wide, grassy lawns.

I wind around the narrow curvaceous street. Trust Charlotte to live in a street like this. She is a bombshell if ever there was one. I think of her as a smaller and British version of Marilyn Monroe. Her voice coos the same way Marilyn's did.

I spot the house on the left and honk my horn, while appearing to do a professional parking job. Before I have a chance to turn off the engine, Charlotte appears as if by magic on her balcony, waving down frantically. 'I'm coming, I'm coming. No need to come up.' Brian and Maureen, her rock star parents, come out to admire my car.

'Charlotte, when you make a movie you'll be able to get yourself a lovely car too,' they shout down at her. She rolls her big brown eyes at me, annoyed, as children often are at the most innocuous things said by parents. I take my cue and we drive away.

Charlotte pulls out a giant bag of tapes to play on my new car stereo system and, as she roots through them, she fills me in on some gossip on our friends back in London. I've known Charlotte for seven years (since I was 14) and she can chatter on for hours but, strangely enough, it doesn't bother me. Maybe it's the quality of her voice, smooth and soft, soothing like an incomprehensible lullaby.

'My new manager is English, which I somehow see as an advantage,' she says. 'Chris is in London and he misses me terribly, but we both agree that Hollywood is where I need to be.' She turns and looks at me seriously. 'We are going to be stars.' Then her seriousness turns to giggles and she pushes in her choice of music.

Swinging by Chin Chin, a trendy nouveau Chinese café on Sunset Plaza, I pick up the two white bags filled with healthy take-away. I jump into the car and turn back on to Sunset Boulevard; Charlotte is searching for a different tape. I wait for the light to change then turn on to my street. 660 Doheny Drive. Apartment 2. My place is mere moments away. Our stomachs rumble in anticipation.

Charlotte and I are discussing which video to watch first – *Who's Afraid of Virginia Woolf?* or *One Flew over the Cuckoo's Nest.* I notice the big American car approaching. It seems to be taking up much too much space on the road.

What I see on the road, now mere fractions of a second later, is the impossible. The 1982 brown Pontiac sedan is barrelling straight at us, on the wrong side of the road. It doesn't stop. It doesn't slow down. I turn the wheel to the right, as far as I can, as fast as I can, attempting to veer away from the juggernaut that is Fate. I am too slow, my reach too short ... I scream out curses. Curses old and new, for today and yesterday and all the tomorrows that will come. I meet my new life head on, screaming like a newborn baby. It is loud.

It is black.

It is done.

PART ONE
The Monster that Ate Hollywood

'Fasten your seatbelt, it's going to be a bumpy ride.'
Bette Davis in *All About Eve*

Goodbye

'You gotta have a dream.
If you don't have dream,
how ya gonna make a dream come true?'
Bloody Mary, from the movie South Pacific

August 1992, London

It is 3.30 in the afternoon and I have been staring into space, delaying the monotony of packing. I started early this morning, with enthusiasm, which has slowly turned into overwhelming exhaustion. I have packed the kitchen, the dining room, the kids' bedrooms and now I am in Mum's room. My mind is racing, as I'm careful to wrap the correct things in the correct boxes. Years of moving have taught me this. Every year we have to move, since the divorce. Mum would buy a house, do it up and then sell it. Just when it had reached a state of homeliness and completeness, it would be time to go. She wouldn't have it any other way. My mother the interior designer. My mother the perfectionist. Unfortunately, these qualities of hers had not been passed down to me. Abigail, my younger sister, had these qualities. It was my destiny to add the drama to our lives.

It was turning out to be the hardest room to do and I was pleased for the interruption of the phone ringing. Now, finding the phone was a task in itself. I followed the ring and discovered the device somewhere under a pile of clothes by the bed.

'Hello,' I breathe into the receiver.

'Louise, we have an audition for you tomorrow at 3.15.' Elaine, my agent, pauses and I hear a shuffling of paperwork.

'Great,' I respond, making room on the bed to sit down. 'What's it for?' Pen. Pen. Where can I find a pen?

'It's for a film for television on Lady Diana and Fergie. I don't know which role you're going for yet ... Can you bear with me a minute?'

As she looks for the information, I think about how I don't look anything like either Diana or Fergie. I survey the bedroom, which is filled with boxes and suitcases; some filled with Mum's old clothes and the others in the process of being started. It's a mess.

'Louise, hi, I'm back.' Elaine has returned to the phone. 'I was just looking at the notes and it just occurred to me that you might already be in Los Angeles. When do you leave?' she sighs.

'In ten days, August the twenty-third,' I reply, trying hard to hide the excitement I feel for the new life I'm preparing for myself. This is it. It is finally going to be my time. The last five years have been incredibly hard and concluded when Mum died last year. I need to leave now and get on with my life. I miss her and find it difficult living with the memories in this house.

'Oh well ... no, that's too early. You can't go for it then,' Elaine continues. 'It's such a shame you've chosen to go at this time. Things are beginning to happen for you. You've been working and it's only going to get better. Isn't this what you've always wanted?'

It *was* what I've always wanted. I realised my dreams as I was four years old taking an acting class at The Polka Children's Theatre in Wimbledon. The teacher turned to the class and said, 'Now, Louise is talented.' I had nudged the little Asian boy seated beside me and made sure he'd taken in the full import of her words: 'Did you hear that? Hey, she said I'm talented. Do you know what that means ...?'

Having failed to impress him, I chose to inform my mother when she picked me up, and then my father. 'I know what I want to be when I grow up ... I'm going to be an actress.'

Since that moment, I never swayed from my path. My determination has been resolute. Having been born in Australia while my mother was modelling and my father touring with The Seekers as their agent, I had done my first commercial. I was the Vegimite kid. Los Angeles has always been in my scheme.

I replace the receiver and return to my packing. Old dusty photo albums fall down from their hiding place on the top shelf of Mum's wardrobe, into the open case. I pick one up curiously, thankful for the distraction. I turn the glossy covered page and am immediately transported into another world as images of my childhood flash before me. I am only 21 years old. I turn the page and see pictures of me as a baby in Australia with my mother and father, when they were still together. Mum looks so beautiful. No wonder she was a model. Dad looks the rock star agent that he was, even then. Pictures told me of my journeys, not memories. The next page shows me at four years old as a bridesmaid at my mother's second marriage to my stepfather. I wonder if he is still my stepfather seeing as they divorced. I was so scared of him, but then I had reason to be, bully that he was. Look at Abigail as a child. And then Oliver.

Now, we were all to be separated. They were going to live with their father and I was going away. I had offered to stay and take care of them but he wanted them with him. It feels like the right time to go. I think about what I'm going to be leaving behind. The pains I am pleased to be rid of. Things going on around me made me believe that I was always in the wrong, that all were jealous of me. The thumps and the rage. The mixed messages. Sunday lunches at restaurants, me sitting alone at ten years old at a table whilst my family sit together. Was I that naughty? Did I deserve it? My mother too terrified to tell him to stop as then it would be her turn. Then she would sleep in the comfort of my arms. I would protect her. He leaves home. And then she gets sick. When she is at her lowest point, she has no one to blame any more but me. It is my fault she is sick, she says. Her disease is fearful and I'm the target. I talk to the doctors and they tell me it's not my fault, she is sick. I should not let the words affect me. But I do, because I love her more than anything. And now she is gone. And I feel calmer with my understanding and knowledge that she is no longer in pain. The pains are ours now. The loss is ours. But we have to pick up the pieces and move on. Separated from what we know. This is why I must leave. I shut the album and lean back against the chest of drawers, feeling the handles digging uncomfortably into my back. I hated the separations. Not waking up under the same roof. Not knowing what the other was doing.

When my mother told me she had cancer, I hadn't believed her. I trusted that she was always going to protect me. We had been in our favourite restaurant, at a table for two. Her beautiful glowing face had two exhausted eyes staring at me, searching for an understanding. Her small upturned nose wiggled as she spoke. She held my hand with her right hand. Her hand felt warm and safe. These were the hands that touched my face and wiped away my tears when I was sad. The hands that fed me with love and life. Her hands that expressed along with her words. The safe hands that felt warm that day as they clutched on tightly to mine. She took a deep breath, and then came back to my questioning eyes. She stopped and took a sip of her white wine, the fresh and crisp wine that would give her the strength to say what she needed to say. And then, once again, she came back to me,

'I'm sick,' she began. Those words were not what I had expected to hear at a mere 16 years old having just finished school. These were the words that took their time to sink into my mind.

'I have a disease called cancer. Leukaemia, actually,' she continued. Suddenly, nothing else mattered to me, no voices other than hers were heard. Even though I didn't know what leukaemia was, I knew by the tone in her voice and that it followed the word 'cancer' that it was sinister. It was just her and me in the restaurant. Everyone else had magically disappeared. My 16-year-old lips quivered as the lump that hid in my throat made itself known. I stumbled and tried to speak. I didn't want to. I didn't want to ask the inevitable question.

'Are you going to ... die?'

I stopped and decided that her glass of white wine had become very inviting. I picked up the glass and gulped down the sweet-tasting fluid. I needed her reassurance now more than ever. I needed to know that my life wasn't ending. If hers did, then mine would too.

The salty tears flow freely down my cheeks and the sound of the front door slamming shut catapults me back to resilience. My memories fade back into the pictures where their stillness holds them fresh.

'Hello, Lou, are you here?' Abigail's voice yells up the stairs.

'Up here in Mum's room,' I say, quickly wiping away any signs of smudged eye make-up. Her young freckly face appears, her cheeks with a rosy glow and her thin brown hair is tied back messily into a clip. She is 14. I am trying my best to be a good role model and take care of her. She is confused and scared but feigning as if she were fine. It disturbs me sometimes. Oli, my brother, is 12 and doesn't like to talk about Mum any more. Occasionally, when I pick him up from school and bring him home for the weekend, he'll ask me questions about life and death.

'I can't believe that I wanted to play tennis that day, Lou,' was the last thing he'd said to me on the subject. He was tucked up in bed and felt that he needed to talk about it. I was encouraging him to do so. We talked for a while and I reassured him that there is no right way to deal with grief. I think about how a 12-year-old should be protected from this fate. But it is exactly that, Fate; it is not in our control.

'Lou, what are you going to do with all your things that you don't take to America?' Abigail says as she settles herself into the bed and picks up the remote control.

'My dad's going to store them, I guess.' I pause. 'I'm going to come back a lot though, Abi,' I try to hearten.

'Sure,' she says, disbelieving me.

I get up and jump on to the bed, taking her into my arms. 'I love you. You know how much I love you.' I try to get a smile and then I do.

'I know,' she says, 'I just wish I could come with you. I don't want to stay here on my own. I don't know where my home is any more.'

We hold on to each other tightly, feeling the warmth of our shared loss. Together, we feel safe.

The next few weeks go by fast. Goodbyes have never been easy for me. Saying goodbye to the house and then to Abigail and Oliver was the hardest of them all. My stomach is tight with feelings of sadness and excitement. We cry heavily and then talk of plans for when I would be home at Christmas and what we'll do together. Then they walk away and I question whether I should leave or not. I don't know if Mum would want me to. Then I remember that I have the freedom to do what I want now.

I'm minutes away from saying goodbye to my father and leaving through the gates into the departure lounge. The airport is filled with Brits stocking up with reading materials and duty free for the plane rides that will take them to their chosen destinations. My ticket and passport are clasped tightly in my free hand. The other grips a case filled with belongings I couldn't fit into one of the three that had been checked in. Dad has managed to get me upgraded to first class and I feel that my life is turning a corner. I think about the trip we took to Australia after Mum passed away. I have never travelled with a more organised man. We had gone for six weeks. It was the longest amount of time I ever remember spending with my father. I hadn't wanted it to end. He stands there, all of 6ft 2in, and I rest against him as if he were a pillar. I grab one last hug.

'Listen, love, I want you to call me when you get there. Kathy is picking you up and I'll come over in a few weeks to help you buy a car and make sure you're settled in', he says solidly. 'Now go on, you better go through', he concludes with an extra squeeze.

'I'm going, I'm going, I stammer quickly, filled with anticipation of what's in store for me. It is the end of a chapter in my life, and I cannot help but feel that the new one is only a plane ride away.

Coma

6 October 1992
Intensive Care Unit, Days 1 and 2

There can be no greater mystery to a survivor than a coma. The first two days after impact are complete blackness. Hours that are filled with frantic travels of news and people, critical medical interventions, blood-soaked and fingers crossed, weeping and wailing and the gnashing of teeth – and I in blissful ignorance.

Those that are here – my father, my best friend Emma – are here to say goodbye.

Day 3

What on earth is that fleshy bauble, distended and looming, that's coming into my field of vision? Oh God, I think it's somebody's head. Christ, what the hell ... wait a moment. What a strange moustache! Isn't that Doctor Hofflin? The poor man. Someone's done something to his head. And anyway, what is Michael Jackson's plastic surgeon doing staring at *me*?

'Louise, can you hear me?'

I do. I do. I just can't discuss it with you at the moment.

Day 4

That voice. I know that voice. Emma. What's she saying? Hi, Emma.

'I'll be right here reading my book, Lou. Please, darling, please wake up ...'

I turn and look at her. Why isn't she looking at me? Why is she so blurry and vague?

'Is it a dirty book?' I'm curious. She seems very involved. It'd better be something exciting if she's ignoring me.

My God. What a reaction. You'd think I'd just popped out of my grave by the look on her face.

'Oh my God, Lou! You're awake! Oh God. Hold on. Hold on, I have to go find your dad. Oh Christ, don't sleep, stay awake ... NURSE!'

Wow. No need to scream, Emma. I'm right here. What nurse?

Dad? Daddy, what are you doing in LA? God, you look wretched, too. I look at him and realise that I'm only looking from one eye. My head is throbbing and I can feel bandages covering the circumference of it. My left eye is shut and sticky. 'You look like you haven't slept in weeks,' I want to say but no words come out. He always did have problems with insomnia, poor Dad. But he's gorgeous. Except for those big ears. Gave them to me, the bastard. But, thankfully, my hair covers them. I love my hair.

What a strange face Dad's making. Growing up, I was alternately thrilled and embarrassed by Dad's facial antics. He has what you might call an elastic face. He can pull it into any direction, that big juicy mouth of his contorting ... Why is he crying? Dad, you look absolutely awful. Haven't you bathed? The one thing I can usually count on is your hygiene, that and a sophisticated, immaculate style. Crisp white shirt unbuttoned revealing chest and gold chain ... very showbiz. British showbiz, that is.

Wait a minute, let's not get off the track here. Why are Dad and Emma in Los Angeles? I'm fine, really. I've only been out here for a few weeks. There's no need to rush over and check on me. Is it my birthday? No. That's in a few weeks, too early for a surprise visit.

Oh. Your hand feels nice, Dad. Big paws you have. Emma, why are *you* crying now? Owww. Fuck, my neck is stiff. Hard to see you over there ... Look at all these machines. Noisy little buggers bleeping and ... sucking? Oh my God! There are tubes coming out of my stomach. And my arms. And my nose. Look at that one coming out of my head, the one with that dark stuff shooting through it. I think that's blood. Is that coming from the back of my *head*? *Now* I'm awake!

'So you've decided to join us!' White coat. Kind voice. Huge glasses. It's a doctor.

'That's right.' My voice sounds strange to me, like I'm hearing it from the other end of a tunnel.

'How's your headache? On a scale of one to ten, ten being the worst, what is it?'

'Oh, about a two,' I lie. About a 200, actually. I'm not sure why I choose to lie. I feel very calm.

'Unbelievable!' He chirps, looking at my dad. 'Unbelievable!'

A nurse has been busying herself around me, checking the various tubes. She needs to empty them, she says. The doctor, his name turns out to be Dr Kalb, notices my father turning pale and suggests that they go outside for a chat. Emma, valiant soul, offers to help the nurse. And does. What exactly they're emptying is beyond me but it sounds a bit grotesque. I notice one of my favourite handbags sitting on a chair in the corner.

'Hey, Emma, is that my bag?' I try to piece things together.

'Yes. I borrowed it as I didn't want to bring my huge one here and that's all I brought with me. I hope you don't mind,' she smiles.

'No, not at all. Would you just pass me the mirror?' I ask.

There is a dense split-second of silence. A moment that almost could go by unnoticed except for the strange attendant energy surrounding it. Something was off. Way off.

'Unfortunately, there's no mirror in the bag,' she says almost too quickly. This was a lie that, if I felt less rigid, would have broken me into convulsions of laughter. Louise without a *mirror*?! That would be the day.

'Don't be silly, Emma, give me the mirror,' I demand. If I could move, then I might be able to get it myself. I try just to reach for the cover and move my legs. A move that is hopeless. My whole body feels weighted down with bricks.

Quickly now, 'Honestly, Lou, there's no mirror in the bag.'

'Oh.' Not believing her for a second, I turn my attention to the nurse. 'Would you lend me a mirror?'

What the hell is going on? Emma and the nurse are trading

glances as if they were secret agents on the same mission.

'I'm sorry, Miss Ashby,' the nurse demurs, 'I don't happen to carry a mirror either.'

'So no one has a mirror here. Oh, come on.'

This is met with no response at all.

I am beginning to feel a bizarre undercurrent in this room. For the first time I notice that the walls are literally covered with modelling and acting photos of me. I feel something stirring inside of me. A slight movement deep, deep below the presages ... I still don't know what. All I know is that my pictures are everywhere and mirrors are nowhere. The combination sends a minuscule electric current through me.

'Why are all my headshots on the wall?' I ask, confused.

'Less antiseptic, don't you think?' Emma avoids my eyes.

'Oh, yes, very beautiful and warms up the room,' the nurse concurs.

I sense the falseness in this exchange. There must be another reason. Maybe the doctors need to know what I look like. Looked like ... This train of thought is taking me towards a dark and unknown station. I don't think I want to go there now. I think I'll take a little rest ...

I wake up and Dad is sitting beside me on the bed. I'm expecting him to crack one of his dry, sarcastic jokes, he generally can't stop himself, and I brace myself but, surprisingly, it doesn't come. I find this unsettling.

A new doctor enters the room. On his forehead, a helmet with a light makes him look like a coal miner although, with the spotlessly white lab coat, it's a funny combination. I giggle involuntarily. This seems to please the doctor and he looks down at me with piercing blue eyes.

'Hello, Louise.' He turns to my father. 'Mr Ashby. I'm Doctor Alessi and I've been helping to take care of Louise. I'll introduce you to Marshall Grode who was one of the neurologists who helped with the 12-hour brain surgery the night Louise arrived. He'll be up here soon and then we'll go over the arrangements for tomorrow.'

'Hi.' I stare at the complex examining equipment that hangs from around his neck. 'Who had brain surgery?'

I must have drifted away for a moment because now Dr Alessi and my dad are deep in conversation. I strain to hear and, from what bits and pieces I gather, they are discussing pictures. Pictures of me?

'Perfect!' Dr Alessi winks at my dad.

Hello? Anyone want to let me in on this perfection? I don't suppose we're setting up a photo shoot, are we? *Harper's Hospital Spread* perhaps? I feel left out of the loop.

'So, Louise,' the Doctor finally turns to me, 'you have a very big day tomorrow.'

Sounds good. I'm always partial to events of which I'm the centre.

'We are going to be taking you in for a big operation which will help put you back together.'

Stop. Rewind tape. Put me *back together*? Oh, no. I have a doctor clearly on drugs. Come to think of it, that's not such a bad thing; maybe he'll give me some of whatever he's on.

Wait a moment. Why is Dad handing him my headshots? The ones I took in London with that lecherous photographer who kept trying to undress me.

'Do you have any questions? Is there anything you need?' he finishes.

Oh, yes. Yes I do. 'I need a mirror,' I say firmly, in that don't-mess-with-me voice that never fails to get results.

Dr Alessi looks at my father. My father looks at Dr Alessi. I look at them both. Quickly, subtly, my dad gives his big head a sideward shake. No. No? Something stirs deep inside me again, like a warning bell going off. There is something I don't know here. Something big.

'Let me see what I can do,' Dr Alessi says carefully. I'm not going to get one. *I'm not going to get one.* I'M NOT GOING TO ...

But before this sentence can build itself into a shriek, it suddenly vanishes. Everything falls through my fingers in a flash. What sentence? What did I want? I can no longer piece together the demand. All that's left is a sense that something is missing and I don't feel quite right. I blink. I think I'm thirsty.

Kathy leans in the doorway like Joan Jett after a long tour. Her black spiky hair ignores the occasional flash of grey and her eyelashes strive to match her hair in length and brittle pointedness. I love Kathy. Coming to Los Angeles would have been unthinkable without having her here. Helping me get myself together, acclimatised, helping me build a new life. I can't believe she's in here now. They don't allow smoking and I don't think I've ever seen her without trails of cigarette smoke coming out of her facial orifices.

'Can I come in?' she asks quietly.

Before I can respond, my father does. 'Of course you can, Kathy. She's awake.'

She comes over to the bed and grips my hand tightly. I've never seen her like this. Kathy's not really the sentimental type.

'You had us all so scared. I love you, baby girl,' she punctuates her words by mashing my hand.

This is just great. I really must have done something extreme. Everyone is so happy to see me and, I must admit, it's making me feel very special.

Kathy pulls a little black box from her pocket. I think it's a Dictaphone. 'I have to play you something,' she says.

She presses a button. A hiss. A crackle.

I hear the voices now, coming from the little black box. These are the voices of my friends, voices I've heard many times in many places. But more than that. These are voices that I have heard exactly thus. Exactly these words, exactly that series of diphthongs and consonants with that exact pitch and hue. I can repeat these words. And I do. Along with the tape.

The room falls still. A sacred hush descends as I prove that, yes, in that darkest pit of nothingness, Louise was here. Louise, lying in that hospital bed with tubes like Medusa's snakes spewing forth from every inch of her body, with sentient technology beeping and monitoring her every neurological function, Louise in her vast and penetrating absence ... *that* Louise was, in fact, here and present and listening and waiting and alive.

Kathy cries. Dad is dumbstruck. And I continue reciting the play called *Friends in and out of the Waiting Room*.

Craig, his beautifully well-formed mouth the vessel for words of encouragement, of support. 'Wake up, Lou. It's time to get up. Wake up now. Open your eyes. We love you, Lou.' I chant his words with him, as if I remembered him saying them when I actually don't. They are just somehow there and I know them by heart.

I cannot explain this to them. And I do not question it much. Questions are missing from my mind right now. And I thank God for that.

For now, I just look at Steve, Kathy's husband, who stands, serious, crushing his hands into each other and looking as usual like Richard

Dreyfuss. He is grave and concerned as he wishes me well.

Dr Kalb enters the room, pushing his big glasses up on his nose and smiling broadly. 'I have come to wish you luck,' he says. 'Luck for tomorrow.'

Dad must see the slight wave of bewilderment pass across my face because he softly shoos everyone out, out ...

'Listen, my little girl,' his paw strokes mine, 'I don't want you worrying about tomorrow. I'll be with you when you go in and I'll be there when you come out.'

My eyes fix on him. He is my lifeline and I will not let him out of my sight. I'm not even sure why, but I know that it is so.

'You don't look quite the same as you used to and Dr Alessi is going to work on that. Now rest and sleep. That's all you must do.'

'But, Dad, I thought you told me I've been sleeping for four days,' I wonder. 'I know that I've always needed my beauty sleep but this seems slightly ridiculous.'

'Very funny,' he says almost choking on the frog in his throat. 'I love you,' he says with such tender passion that my heart aches.

'Don't leave me. Don't leave me now' I plead. And he complies, waiting for me to fall asleep to take his leave. But I cannot sleep and so I watch him as he falls sweetly into oblivion, drained with what has passed and what lies ahead.

Day 5

It is cold this morning. Dad holds my hand. It is thick and sweat drips down our conjoined wrists, the sweat of not-knowingness. His voice cracks with the pressure of trying to remain normal, of not letting on what he knows or fears or prays will not happen.

'You may not look the same for a little while, Lou,' he strains.

'That's OK, Dad, I haven't gotten lucky in six weeks anyway.' If he can do it, so can I. I will myself to stay here and I'm feeling the necessity to make jokes to change the atmosphere that seems so deadly serious. To laugh off the myriad tubes and hanging bottles that chase alongside me on rolling metal stands. These are my accessories now. Not mirrors.

The gurney slams into the two broad doors at the hallway's end. As I enter the operating room my mind takes on a pastel tint and everything seems quite lovely and somehow it all makes sense.

Moments later

I am in the land of unconscious where there is no dream state and no reality, just darkness. This state lasts for 22 hours as they saw and sew and sponge and suture and excavate the damaged twitching greyness within my skull. Major reconstructive surgery along with brain surgery. Dad and Emma popping Valium and mainlining caffeine. Dr Alessi, hawk-like, overseeing the team of specialists as Louise is remade.

Dad recalled later what he was going through:

'I didn't feel good, it was totally horrific how I felt, and you think, My God, what is happening? And when people say things happen for the best, you think that's a load of rubbish because that sort of thing never happens for the best.'

Dr Alessi also eventually told us what he'd gone through during the operation:

'Louise's life was in danger at every moment during the surgery. A head injury of that magnitude causes the brain to swell and the increasing pressure can, in itself, be fatal. We placed a shunt in the back of her head to drain some of the fluid and release pressure. This shunt had been placed on the night of the accident when we performed the first neurosurgical procedure; however, the situation was still critical.

'We were concerned that the sinus could have shut off from the rest of the brain and she could have easily developed meningitis. Viral or bacterial meningitis is a lethal condition. Therefore, the surgery was structured around the protection of the sinus and the reconstruction of the roof of the left eyeball. As it was, it was completely unprotected; the brain was resting on the eyeball due to the complete shattering of the bone above it. This trauma had caused severe swelling in the area.

'The eye itself is pretty resilient. It's very difficult to rupture an eyeball. You would have to whop it very hard for it to actually rupture. The roof of the orbit is weak, all the bones are meant to expand and break. The inner tissue surrounding the eyeball is paper thin, very, very weak. In Louise's case, the area surrounding the eyeball was completely crushed, much as if someone had taken a jackhammer to an eggshell and completely crushed it.

'I'll never forget lifting up Louise's brain. This was easy to do as there was nothing in the way of access. Before she went into surgery, you could see the brain and eye pulsating abnormally. The blood supply to the brain was so great that every heartbeat would cause a marked pulsation and expansion. This expansion of the brain caused a chain reaction in the eye, which was pulsating along with it, reacting to whatever communication the brain was giving it.

'I have to admit, although as a surgeon you must become somewhat of a technician, this was one of the worst cases I have had. Louise was a beautiful young woman and I wanted, to the best of my abilities, to restore that beauty. I do the best I possibly can with every one of my patients, but Louise affected me deeply.

'She had no eyebrow, no eye area at all. We used some cranial bone to rebuild the top of her eye socket. We used bone from the top layer of the back of her skull (we have three layers), reshaped it and applied it to her face. If you were to rub your hand along the back of her head now, there would be a dip where that bone was removed. The bones were re-attached to her face using tiny metal plates. Louise and I joke about her remarkable ability, given how much metal is in her head now, to pick up AM radio by tilting her head to the side. Louise has a miraculous spirit and has maintained her irreverent sense of humour through this tragedy. She was an inspiring patient.'

Day 6

My head aches.

Day 7

Worried eyes peer into view. Am I hallucinating or is the room full of people? There's my aunt Sally, her little round glasses perched on her nose, her entire frail frame bent towards me in concern. Her voice, as always, is quiet and gentle. 'Louise, how are you feeling?'

I can't seem to talk. Uncle Don, his shape a massive rock behind his bird-like bride, resonates deeply. 'Hello, love.'

I guess I am awake again. Dad leans in. 'It went very well, Lou, you did very well.' I must be smiling because I see his eyes soften in relief. The room clears except for Emma who, seemingly, has no need for food, no need for rest. I remember when Mum died and Emma rocked and soothed and listened to my sobs for days and weeks on end. And here she is again. Here absorbing my pain, alleviating it by her very presence ... I think I'm falling asleep ... but there is something important, *what is it?* Something I need ... mirror ... mirror ... that's it. I must see now, see Louise. We haven't seen each other for so long. But when I manage to murmur the request, she is clear and flat and there must be a damn good reason.

'No, Lou. Not today.'

I am tired, my head aches, but I am able to ask the obvious. 'Am I ugly?'

The words fall leaden to the ground and don't move. A nurse coming in, wheeling an extra chair, which she situates, beside me, breaks the awkward silence. She is carrying something in her hands. A plastic bag.

'Hi, Louise!' She seems happy to see me. 'How are you feeling?'

'Tremendous!' I match her tone and fake a quiet, sleepy chuckle. She is fiddling with the bag in her lap and I see her desire to say something. It must be a surprise because she is bursting with excited pride and I know she means well. She holds up the sealed freezer bag. In it is a matted mound of brown hair clumped together with blood and flesh, still sticky.

'Look, Louise, before the operation yesterday they had to shave your hair off. I kept it for you in case you wanted to have it.'

My stomach tightens and heaves. A scream begins to build in my guts and I push it down. I can't – I will not. I WILL NOT SCREAM – but it's my *hair*. My fucking hair.

'Why would I want it, am I to glue it back on my head?' I say, trying to make it into a joke although I'm quite aware she doesn't understand. I grit my teeth and pat myself on the back because I pulled it off. Emma throws the nurse a sideward glance as if to say, 'Louise's sense of humour is a bit warped, you must excuse her.' The nurse, somewhat discomfited, removes herself and the bloody bag and I wonder if Florence Nightingale would have offered an amputee his gangrenous leg on the battlefield.

And so it begins. That is how I will win. I will take the bloodied remnants of Louise Ashby and I will put on a brave face. I will not let anyone feel uncomfortable in my presence and, most of all, I will not feel afraid. I will greet the crowds and wave my poised hand and tell them that I am here, I am just fine. I am, in essence, unchanged. I will lie and they will be at peace.

It is late at night and I cannot sleep, alone with a Louise no one will let me see. I try to watch television. The nurse rolls one in and tries to find a plug that isn't in use keeping me alive. It is hard watching TV with one eye covered in bandages, my face inflated like a balloon, tender as a vicious bruise. But it is harder being alone with Louise.

When the whisper comes, I am floating between dreams and video and it takes me a moment to recognise Emma in the doorway.

'Lou, you must be very quiet – I'm not meant to be here.' She looks behind her conspiratorially. 'I have a surprise for you ...'

Karim Halwagi – 'Wagi' to his close friends – is one of my oldest London friends. When I see Wagi, I know everything will work out. And even if it doesn't, we'll giggle about it. When his big balding head pops out from around the corner and his soft blue eyes light upon mine, we both start giggling and my heart races with excitement. Wagi!

'My God! What are you doing here?!'

Beep ... Beep ... Beep ... BEEPEEPEEPEEPEEEPEEP ...

Total uproar as my monitors go into overdrive. Wagi dives under the bed. Emma hides behind the door. A nurse rushes to my side, another to the machines.

'What is it, Louise? Are you all right?'

'Fine,' I manage. 'This show on the television has always made me laugh,' I reassure her. The nurses exchange a look. One checks the monitors sceptically and the other glances at the drab weatherman on the TV screen looking for a clue.

'Well, please try and keep calm, OK?'

'Sure.'

They leave, questioning my sanity, no doubt.

Wagi emerges from under my bed and, when he stands up, I am dismayed by what I see. His expression is mirroring enough for the moment. And although he tries to disguise his emotion by joking and making his love for me known, it is painfully clear to me that just looking at me has sent him into shock.

Wagi said later, 'I was horrified. I had a lump in my throat. My heartbeat rose by 25,000 per cent. I couldn't believe that this was Louise. I didn't recognise her. The tubes, the machines, all that medical equipment ... it completely overwhelmed me. Her head was twice the size it used to be and her beautiful face was ... well, I couldn't even tell if it was still there, it was almost completely covered in bandages. There was this big tube coming out of the crown of her head filled with blood ... I was completely freaked out!

It didn't take a brain surgeon to tell me that things are looking pretty bad for me. I just wasn't aware how bad.

Monster

'A woman is like a tea bag;
you never know her strength until you drop her in hot water.'
Nancy Reagan

I am told that I'm out of critical danger. Somehow that makes real for me the fact that I could have died. I suppose that being surrounded by love hid the shadow of death lurking right over my shoulder. When the nurses come to move me into a private room, out of intensive care, I suddenly feel sad. I have become attached to these valiant people who have looked after me and listened to all my jokes and stories. They say that in Hollywood it's not *what* you know, but *who,* and this proves to be the case when I am relocated to the 'VIP' ward. Apparently, Kathy knows someone important at Cedars Sinai, the hospital where everyone who's anyone comes. I am whisked to the top of that dubious hierarchy of the ill and famous to my own quiet, white room with couch, refrigerator, television and, most valuably, private bathroom and telephone.

I am carefully wheeled over – walking is still a goal out of reach – and when Dad and I arrive, Kathy and Wagi are already waiting in the room. Flowers are exploding everywhere, their colour bleeding on counters and tables, filling the room with life. These are from friends who have not been allowed entry into the heavily guarded Intensive Care.

Almost before I am comfortably manoeuvred into my new bed, the phone rings. I pick it up excitedly.

'Louise Ashby? This is Sergeant Davies from the Los Angeles Police Department.' The voice is stern and official. This is a long sentence for me to comprehend at the moment as my brain is only letting in simplicity.

'I would like to ask you some questions about the accident that occurred on October 5th 1992.'

I feel a bit hazy. 'What accident?'

Kathy springs into action, furious, and grabs the phone.

'This is a bad time, Officer. Please give me your number and I'll get back to you.' She is curt and her face is pinched with disapproval.

'What accident?' I repeat.

I hear the intake of breath, as the room becomes an exchange of worried looks and I wait for an answer. It feels like the mirror incident, which, I may add, I am still waiting to be cleared up.

'Sweetheart,' Kathy is delicate, 'you had a very bad car accident. You were with your friend Charlotte ...'

'Is she OK?' My mind leaps to the dreadful possibilities, unaware that the worst has occurred, but not to Charlotte.

'Yes, baby girl, she's fine.'

'I want to speak to her. Can I speak to her?' I quickly say.

Kathy looks at my father for an answer. Dad argues, 'Not now. Please relax. You have time to deal with this later. You must take it easy. It's too soon.'

I know that he's trying to protect me from something. I didn't want to be protected from the truth. I want to speak to Charlotte. I have no recollection of a car accident. What else has been misplaced or lost for good? I want to know. I'm getting upset. Kathy's head is bowed down and I can sense she is trying to avoid my eye.

'Kathy, please call her for me,' I say. She looks at my father with a look of 'I'm sorry', and promptly dials the number.

The phone rings a few times. I hold the earpiece to my tilted swollen head.

'Hello,' I hear faintly. It is Brian, Charlotte's father.

'Brian, it's Louise,' I begin.

'Oh my God, Louise. How are you feeling? We've been so worried. Poor Charlotte has had a terrible headache and feels like she has still got the flu.'

I try to comprehend what he has just told me. Me, who is in hospital with my head in bandages, hooked up to machines and unable to move. I manage to tell him that I'm doing all right but need to speak to Charlotte. Before he passes over the phone, he says, 'Well, just think about all the money you're going to get!

What is he talking about? What money? Now I'm really confused. Confused at how the statement was thrown away. Confused about the money comment. Generally very confused.

'Charlotte. It's Louise ... How are you? ... Yes, my head is aching, too ... Can you tell me what happened?' I hold on tight. 'Please, Charlotte ...' I need to come out of the dark now.

She begins. 'You can't remember anything? Anything at all?'

I am silent, ashamed to admit that I ran off with my marbles and left her there to record the events. She continues.

'We had arranged to watch videos that night because I had the 'flu and didn't want to go out!' She takes a breath and a sip of something, preparing herself to continue. 'You said you would pick me up because you wanted to show me your new car. I had some new tapes and we were listening to them on the way to Chin Chin to pick up the Chinese take-out!'

Sudden flashes like images caught in a strobe light. White bags. Picking them up off the counter. The young cashier smiling. Placing them in the back seat of the car.

'We turned left on Doheny. A little way down, another car was coming towards us. A big brown American car. It didn't stop. I thought it was going to turn left but it just kept heading straight for us. Next thing it was just chaos. You were trying to turn to avoid him but it was too late. He hit us and our car lost control. We were pushed to the right, over the pavement and into a palm tree. His car was still embedded in the front of ours. I was completely winded. My head was all the way back against the seat. All I could see was hazy sky. I couldn't breathe. I didn't know how hurt I was. I could hear a dripping sound to my left!'

My mind races to keep up and unravel. There is something disquieting about the dripping sound, I'm not sure what, but I don't like it. Charlotte is still talking and I try to catch up.

'A homeless guy came over to the left side of the car. He was acting crazy. I looked over at you. Your body was completely upright but your head was totally bent over in an odd way. This guy was losing his mind, over by your side. Another man had stopped and approached the car. He kept asking, "Are you OK? Are you OK?" I couldn't really speak. The man looked at you and suddenly the crazy homeless guy started screaming at him, saying, "Get away from this! It's got nothing to do with you! It's none of your business!" I was confused, I couldn't really figure out what was going on.' Charlotte hesitates. 'Lou? Do you want me to carry on?'

I feel like I'm hearing a scary story around a campfire. A story I've never heard before. A story that is a complete fabrication and has absolutely no bearing on my life. At the same time, part of me realises that this *is* my life. This is why I'm here.

'Yes. Yes. Carry on.' I am stammering, with dreadful anticipation as all the pieces of the puzzle are falling into place. Still nothing makes sense.

'OK.' Charlotte takes a deep breath. 'I was starting to be able to breathe more easily and so I undid my seat belt and looked at you more closely. That's when I saw the blood dripping from your head. You were unconscious, struggling to breathe. I couldn't tell where the blood was coming from. It looked like it could have been a nosebleed. Either that or it was coming from somewhere else and blocking up your nose. Then you woke up and you turned your head to face me and it was then that I saw. The left side of your face was gushing blood. Completely covered in blood. I couldn't see your face at all. I started screaming. Someone tried to calm me down, telling me it was going to be OK. Then you started mumbling. You were complaining about your ankle, how it was stuck. You didn't say anything about your face. I had no idea what to say ... what to do. You wanted to touch your head. I think you wanted to scratch it. I remember that we kept pulling your hand down. Then I saw your eyebrow. It was hanging off the corner of the windshield. There was flesh attached to it. I realised where all the blood was coming from and what had happened to your face. I went into shock.

'The next thing I remember there were lots and lots of people around us. The sun had gone down. It was dark except for red and blue and white flashing lights. Paramedics, cops, fire engines everywhere. The crowd was huge. They needed to move me out of the way. There was glass all over the place. I was lifted on to the sidewalk and I watched them try to get you out of the car. They were very very careful and it took quite a while. I don't suppose they knew what your injuries were yet. You were screaming profanities at them as they tried to cut you from the car, "I just want to go home and eat my fucking Chinese. Leave me the fuck alone." Finally, they put you in the ambulance. They put me in the front and I could hear you in the back screaming and screaming. You kept telling them not to "put that near me" and cursing at them. I guess they were trying to get you hooked up to something and you were very unhappy about being poked by it. I could hear you struggling. Maybe they were trying to undress you. I couldn't really see.

'When we got to the hospital, you were put on a stretcher and held down because you were still struggling and screaming. They took me in for X-rays and even from that room I could still hear your screams. Some doctor came into the room, a really young one, and told me that your neck was broken and that you would be paralysed. Before I could even take that in, another doctor came in and told me that your neck wasn't broken but that you were in critical condition. He told me to prepare for the worst.

'I got to a phone and called around to find your father's number. Then I called my dad and told him to make the call. I couldn't stop crying. They wheeled you past me. You were unconscious and covered in bandages.'

I am silent. The phone has dropped from my ear although I still have it in my hand like a used-up piece of garbage that I haven't thought to throw away yet. Kathy notices and she gently removes it from my hand as I stare into space.

'Charlotte? It's Kathy. I'll call you back in a bit, honey, Lou needs to have a rest now.'

The days that follow

The loneliness of night-time is the most difficult aspect of my stay here. Outside my room, I can hear occasional noises in the corridors, the footsteps of nurses and doctors, maybe a beeper going off. I cannot sleep. Neither during the day nor night. But it is at night, when everything in the hospital settles into whispers and silence, that my thoughts become loud and intrusive and I need to escape them.

A man, I think he is next door, is screaming in pain. I hear quick footsteps then soothing murmurs and he quietens. I call out quickly and the nurse enters my room.

I love the nurses here. They give me solace, relief and company during these dark hours, which I exchange with my imagination and sense of humour. I ask this nurse whether she'll sit with me. She sits down.

'Are you in pain, Louise?'

It is my nature to endure. I cannot afford to complain, my bruised head won't allow it. Or maybe it is my mother standing by my side willing me to be strong. Only when compelled, do I complain in these weeks.

'No,' I venture, 'but there's something on my mind. Can I talk to you?'

She settles in gracefully, realising that this, too, is part of her job.

'Is your mother alive?' I ask her.

'No.' There is so much in that word.

Neither is my mum, I tell her. I am serious, tonight, for the first time since the accident. Perhaps it is the first time that I feel safe enough to tread waters where the sand is not clearly visible.

'Do you think that I went up to Heaven and my mother sent me back here?'

She considers carefully. Then, 'Yes, Louise, I do. You're alive and you should be dead ... it is a miracle. I have no doubt that you are here to do something important and special.'

This is the first night that I can sleep and I do, deeply. The generosity of these nurses is not limited to appeasing my soul; they also indulge my friends. My friends who have decided to move the local bar into my refrigerator, who sneak in after hours for an illegal hit off my oxygen tank, my friends who occasionally come by and vomit upon looking at me. Hangovers notwithstanding, I know that I'm not too pretty.

It's very early now. The dawn is threatening to break and Dr Alessi is already in my room. I'm still drowsy, only vaguely aware of the tools in his hands. He begins to remove my bandages. I'm immediately frightened. I need some warning. I need some protection. These bandages have become a security blanket. I haven't had the strength to contemplate what lies underneath them. Please stop.

'What are you doing?' A feeble cry, already too late.

'I'm taking the staples out of your head.' Matter of fact. Like 'I'm taking the dog for a walk' or 'I'm going out for some milk.'

Staples? First I try to wrap my mind around that image. Staples in my head. Wait a minute ... STAPLES *IN* MY *HEAD*??! Complete and utter panic.

'Wait, wait, wait ... hold on, what staples? You can't be ...'

He just carries on. Doing his job. Doing it well. Click. Ssssliiide. Click. Ssssliiide. The sound is monstrous. Repellent. Disgusting. The metal, thick with sharply pointed ends, pulling out of my skin and skull. Their job is done and they are once again foreign objects removed and discarded from that which is Louise. The staples are bizarrely long and when they exit there is a brief sensation of vacuum, of tiny spots of emptiness that are quickly filled by my flesh as it closes ranks. What the hell is going on? The panic builds in my stomach, making me queasy.

I try not to think. I try to go with it. Maybe it will be over faster this way. But I'm cold. I feel a chilly breeze drift over my head. My mind tries to figure this out. Suddenly it clicks into place. I am bald. BALD.

I flash back to the freezer bag, my hair in it. Until now I didn't really understand the truth of that horrible image but now it slaps me in the face. To put it mildly, it is *not* a good feeling. I HAVE NO HAIR. I have to keep saying it, calmly, because if I just sit with the idea it will explode out of me in unstoppable amounts of rage and sorrow. I HAVE NO HAIR.

After Doctor Alessi and the staples have said their goodbyes, I pick up the phone.

'Hello, Kathy ... I HAVE NO HAIR.'

A brief pause. 'Yes, baby girl, I know. Shall I bring you some turbans?'

'Turbans? Like Indian turbans?' I try to picture myself with a high, white turban, wrapped in tight intricate layers like I've seen on Hindu men in the Indian restaurants in London. I balk. Somehow I feel this is not exactly my style. I must try to retain *some* Louiseness through all of this, for God's sake.

'No, silly, they call them turbans but they actually look like thin little scalp caps.'

Scalp caps? Christ. I have been scalped. I have no hair. I have to start wearing *scalp caps*. I start moaning. This is all too much. I'm turning into my mother. She, too, wore these same pieces of cloth to hide her unfortunate loss. I now shared her tears.

Craig comes to visit me at lunchtime, his lovely silver hair thick and glorious around his beautiful face. His deep-blue eyes, framed by lush black eyelashes of an impossible length, see into my battered soul and I feel his oversized heart open to me. But I greet him with the only sentence I can now form: 'I have no hair.'

It isn't just that. I know by reading people's expressions that there is something else wrong. Something worse. I think something is wrong with my face. When I reach back to gingerly touch my skull there are lumps and I can feel a scar slicing viciously across me, from ear to ear. On either side of the scar are holes from where the staples dug their sharp metal points in deep, forming tunnels to the centre of my skull.

Craig tries to comfort me. 'Don't worry, Lou, your hair will grow back. And I'll be back to see you later. Please. Please try not to worry about it.' I can feel his heart breaking.

'But, Craig.' *Why doesn't he understand?* 'I've got *no hair.*'

When Craig returns, he, too, is bald. His shimmering mane is gone. I laugh and cry. I am deeply touched.

Until now I have had an old dish cloth on my head. Not very elegant but certainly more acceptable than having my baldness naked to the world. Emma, Wagi and Dad are here with me when Kathy arrives bearing a small selection of turbans – sorry, skullcaps. I look through them with only half of my attention. The inevitable moment has arrived. I can feel the mirror through the door that separates us. It pulls at me like a magnet.

'Emma? Will you come into the bathroom with me?'

All talk ceases. The tension in the room is thick. Emma helps me out of bed. I can feel the anxiety of my loved ones pressing in on me. I throw them a look. *Calm down. Stop staring at me.* My ankle is badly sprained and I limp the few steps to the bathroom leaning heavily on Emma's solid frame.

The lighting in the bathroom is explosive, unforgiving. I take a deep breath and ask Emma to close the door behind us. I stand before the mirror. My head still bowed. I feel as though I am at the pearly gates, waiting for the ultimate judgment to be passed. I try to breathe again, pulling oxygen deep into my lungs and belly to give me the strength to look up. My head raises itself.

You cannot be prepared for what you cannot imagine. In a fraction of a second, an abyss opens before me, a black gaping hole that is widening at the speed of light. What I see in the mirror cannot be real. The woman who stares back at me from that simple silver piece of glass is not, *cannot* be me. She is a MONSTER. A sideshow freak. A creature so deformed that the universe itself recoils in disgust.

Her heart is going to explode as she stares, searching for some sign – help her, God help her. Tears are burning salty tracks down her face … *that's not my face, that's not my face* … this isn't me, oh, Christ, please God – fear overtakes her like a freight train with no brakes and she will surely die here in this cold white place. Get her out of here, get me out of this nightmare. This face, this life, I have got to get out, GET OUT, GET

OUT, SOMEBODY GET ME OUT OF HERE. I can feel a scream building.

'That's not my head!' I turn to Emma, wanting her to bring me in on the joke. It is a joke. Any minute I am going to wake up and say 'What a horrible dream', but then at that moment I remember I had already had this dream. I look again – don't do it, Louise, don't look – and nothing's changed and it's all changed and I don't understand. She is still there. Her ugliness makes me nauseous. Again, I look at Emma – WHY ME?

The floor is cool and safe. I have fallen and my collapse is a relief because I cannot see that thing, that mirror. I thought you were my friend. *I thought you loved me.* I will stay here, down here and I will not move and I will stay here quiet and little. Please, God, make her GO AWAY. My fingers pet the cold tiles.

'It's OK. It's OK, everything is going to be OK, Mummy loves you.' HELP ME, MUMMY – WHERE ARE YOU? HELP ME.

I can see Emma through my tears, crouching down. Her face is beautiful. She has perfect eyes, a perfect nose, a perfect mouth, no dents ... no bruises ... no visible scars. She must be ecstatic. She must feel her perfections. She strokes me on the back, too afraid to touch the bulbous head. Why would she touch it? The woman who lies on the bathroom tiles is a monster. My breath is short and tight and my sobs are like strange music, with a ring of Quasimodo. They echo in this room. I cannot look again, it is too much, I am a monster, an ugly *monster*. Outside, Dad is trying to get me out. 'Please leave me alone,' I want to say, 'I cannot ever come out and show this face.'

Dad's voice cuts through to me where I lie, still hugging the bathroom floor. I can feel the pain overflowing from him as he speaks. There is nothing he can do and he knows it and it's killing him. I have to get up. I cannot have him see me in pain. There is nothing in his power that will turn back time and make things all right like daddies are supposed to be able to do for their little girls and this is a new and horrible feeling for John Ashby. Daddy, I'm so sorry, so sorry – Get up, Louise. I don't want him to hurt like I am hurting. All right. I will get up. Emma places the turban on my head solemnly. I recoil without meaning to. Oh, Emma. How can you even touch a creature such as myself? I will have to leave this room. I will have to face the world. I can't. I will. *I can't.* You will, Louise. You will forget the chill across your scarred skull. You will ignore the pus and blood seeping from the corner of your left eye, swollen shut, purpled and angry. You will not let your right eye see the dents and bumps, the foreign shapes that are now a part of who you are. But my head is the size of a ripe watermelon! I don't care. My skin has become plastic wrap. It's not about you now.

My mummy loves me. My mummy who never forced her leukaemia, the pain, the fear, the dread of it, on any of us. My mummy who put on a brave face. My mummy who never complained. Think of the little boy in *The Mask*. He went outside. He was brave. He was loved. All right. The lump in my throat is hard to swallow. But I do it.

All eyes are on me. Don't look! Please. Don't look at me. My eyes meet my father's. He is disgusted. He is crushed. His daughter is deformed.

'What other colours do you have, Kathy?' I break the ice and try to concentrate on the sound it makes when it shatters.

Visitors

'The battle to keep up appearances unnecessarily,
the mask – whatever name you give creeping
perfectionism – robs us of our energies.'
Robin Worthington

My room is crazy with people coming, going, eating, drinking, socialising. My fridge is the bar at a cocktail party. I am just watching. I am not even here. Finally, I must say it.

'Hi. Remember me? I'm tired now and I'd like to rest.'

I give my lunches to Julian, who could use the free meals. He's been wandering all over the world and I'm never hungry. I call him at night and we go over the following day's menu. I order his choices and watch him eat as I sip the chicken broth off the top of the soup Wagi has once again brought me. I can manage only a few sips.

My self-consciousness has become unbearable. I am convinced that people can barely stand to look at me. My legs are grotesquely hairy. Maybe I can do nothing about my face, but my legs ... I call Wagi. The answer machine clicks on and I hear Dad's voice, serious and factual.

'Hello. This is John Ashby. Louise has been involved in a car accident and is presently at Cedars Sinai Hospital. She is unable to take calls but we'll pass on any messages. Thank you.'

A shiver goes down my spine. It is real. This isn't a dream. A gruff 'Hello' interrupts my thoughts and I'm so happy that my voice bursts out, gushing, 'Wags?!'

'Lou?'

'Hey ...' Suddenly I'm hesitant. 'Are you sleeping?'

'Yes, Lou. It's seven in the morning. Are you OK?' Wagi is

31

immediately worried.

'No.' And I'm completely serious. 'My legs and armpits are hairy.'

There is a confused moment on the other end of the line.

'I need you to shave them,' I whisper.

Wagi starts giggling. Come to think of it, it is a pretty funny request. I start giggling, too.

'You are calling at seven in the morning to tell me you have hairy armpits?' He tries to talk through the giggles.

'Yes. Can you please come over and shave them? I know it's early, but you're only here for a week.' My logic is somewhat twisted but I don't care. My woolly limbs must be shorn immediately.

'Lou, the phone has been ringing off the hook all night. Everyone in London has been calling to see how you're doing.'

'Pleeeeeeeeeeease?!' I know I cannot be refused.

'All right. I'll be in as soon as I can.'

'Thank you. I love you.' I replace the receiver, satisfied.

Wagi enlists the nurse to stand guard outside my door in case someone should approach. He couldn't stand the idea of someone catching him in the peculiar act of shaving my armpits. Who could blame him? It would ruin his image. Wagi applies himself to the task with intense concentration that would make me laugh if I wasn't afraid I'd jog my arm and he'd slice into me. Once done, the nurse instructs him to take me for a walk. My ankle is badly sprained and must be worked on. The fact that Wagi would have to 'take me for a walk' as if I were a poodle or a toddler makes us both crack up so hard that it takes us 20 minutes just to get me out of bed. It really hurts and after a couple of baby steps I start the 'OK. That was great, now let me get back into bed' routine. Honestly, I feel as weak as a kitten and the door to my room looks a million miles away.

My private phone rings constantly. It seems like everyone that I've ever known, and some that I barely do, is calling to ask how I am. Frankly, I know how I am. I am much more interested in what they're up to out there.

'Hello?'

'Hi, Lou. It's Louise Golley.'

Shit. Who the hell is Louise Golley? Oh! Christ, Louise *Golley*!

'Louise Golley? My God! How are you? I haven't spoken to you in *years*! How *are* you?'

'Em ... uh. I'm fine. How ... how are *you?*' She hesitates, clearly unsure whether she should be asking that question.

'Great, great! I'm so excited to hear from her. We were great friends in school. It's been four years since we've been in touch.

'So what's going on?' I continue. 'How are your parents? Are they still together or did they split up? I remember you were having trouble at school.'

There is a long silence. Then, 'Lou, are you OK? I heard about the accident and I was really worried.'

'Oh, don't worry about me, worse things happen. I'll be fine.' I don't want to dwell on the tragic. I'm not in a wheelchair. I'm out of danger. I want to enjoy these talks, not drag myself back into depression and self-pity. I've made a choice. I made that choice when I came out of the bathroom and faced my father. And that choice is that I am fine.

★ ★ ★

'Hello?'

'Lou? It's Abi!' My sister sounds upset.

'Abi, how are you?'

She starts to cry. When my little sister cries, unless I'm in a particularly sadistic mood, it brings out protectiveness in me. My sister lost her mother just a year ago. I lost my mummy, too. I will not add to her pain.

'You aren't going to leave us like Mum did, are you?' She is sobbing now.

'Are you crazy? It's not my time to go anywhere. Don't you worry about that.' I try to lighten the mood. She continues to cry, unconvinced.

'Abi, please don't cry. It's going to be OK.' I comfort her.

'Tell me about things with you and your father.' I try changing the subject.

'I don't know any more,' she sniffles.

'Tell me!' I am pleased to get her on to a new track.

'Louise? It's Ian!' Ian is one of my new LA friends.

'Hi, honey, how are you?'

'How am *I*? My God, Louise, I've been so worried about you. What happened? I was supposed to come over that night. I'm so sorry ...'

I can tell that he is truly upset. I deflect, I evade, I coax people on to new paths, usually themselves, their lives. It always works. I console Ian as he tells me what's been going on in his life, that he's been fired.

'I can't believe you. You're the one in the hospital and you're making *me* feel better. I'm sorry.'

'Don't be silly. What else have I got to do in here?'

What else indeed? I don't want sympathy. It makes me feel pathetic and it solves nothing. The fact is that I'm in a hospital bed and I have to deal with it. Full stop. I am not paralysed. I do not have leukaemia. I will be strong and I will cope and that is how I will make it through this. At least I can still talk! Although sometimes I wonder if people would have preferred that I be struck dumb. I do love to talk.

Kathy and I are alone and gazing at the television set in silence when my door is opened to reveal an older-looking man who resembles a cowboy. He is in his early fifties and has a full head of white-grey hair with a large moustache. Dressed in a suit and large cowboy boots, he strolls over to Kathy and gives her a warm hug. He then turns and stares at me.

'Well, you must be Louise.' He leans forward to get a better look. 'Wow,' he says as he searches my disfigurement. 'I'm Harold Levy and my law firm will be representing you in the law suit.'

Law suit? What's he talking about? I wish someone would tell me what exactly is going on. I had heard the word 'money', 'Sergeant Davies' and now 'law suits' and had no comprehension as to why. Have I done something wrong? Could I please have my life back and my face? I moved here to be an actress. I didn't leave London for this. This was not the plan. This was not in the dream I had.

Kathy moves over to the bed where she sits down and holds my hand. I stare into her face. Her face which makes me feel loved. Her hair which she colours to hide any traces of grey. I wish I could colour my hair. Maybe I will one day when it grows back.

'It's OK, Louise, he's Steven's lawyer and just needs to take some pictures of you as proof of your condition.'

Proof of my condition? Look at me – what fucking proof do you need? Then I remember Kathy doesn't mean to upset me. She is not the enemy. I manage a smile.

'Well if you say it's all right then ...' It is then that I feel overwhelmed at what has happened. I am doing a photo shoot in

Hollywood, except it's not the kind that had been in my dreams. I lie there patiently as I'm approached and told not to smile.

'Great, this is terrific. I have found that, by me standing over here, I get the worst angles and you look terrible. Actually, wherever I stand, that seems to be the case', Hal says.

Oh terrific, I think, as long as you're happy.

My visitors from England are ecstatic that Cedars Sinai is practically a stone's throw away from America's capitalist shrine – the Mall. In this case, The Beverly Center, one of Los Angeles' largest shopping malls, would open its greedy arms to my friends on their breaks from visiting me. Invariably, they would return with the spoils and I would compliment them on their lovely purchases. Invariably, in turn, they would give me whatever they bought and then go back and replace them. Yes, I am very spoiled. I have been blessed with an incredible circle of friends and family.

Dad, Kathy, Wagi and I are having tea when Emma returns from her latest shopping excursion.

'I just bought my favourite perfume at an obscenely low price. I can't believe it.'

'Let's see.' I reach out. The bottle is unfamiliar. 'May I smell it?'

Emma sprays her wrist and holds it to my nose. Nothing. Not even a whiff of a scent. She sprays again. This time I can even see the liquid wetting her wrist. I still smell nothing.

Doctor Kalb enters the room. 'How's my star patient today?' he asks.

'I can't smell Emma's perfume', I puzzle.

He nods. Everyone looks to him for an answer. 'That was one of our concerns. It happens to many people who have suffered major head injuries. We should do some taste testing as well. That is probably gone as well.'

'What ...?' I laugh nervously. Probably gone *AS WELL*. What does that mean? My eyes are closed. I feel the textures of different things as they pass over my tongue and down my throat. I taste nothing. Doctor Kalb is right. My senses of smell and taste are a thing of the past.

It is hard to breathe through my left nostril; the swelling is so intense. The entire left side of my face is puffed almost to bursting. My left eye still refuses to open. The doctors tell me that I may have to resign myself to never opening it again. The eyelid may be permanently sealed due to muscle damage. I stare at the two doctors with my good eye.

'You're wrong. I will open this eye.'

Every day, I try to open my left eye. I try 100 times a day. I count the tries. I will make it open. I will.

My mouth is also very tight. I can open it only a couple of millimetres before it seizes up and refuses to budge. Dr Alessi puts his hands in my mouth and stretches. The sound is like a rotting door, locked and being pried off its rusty hinges. Every day he tries to loosen my jaw. It hurts. It's embarrassing. I will open my mouth. I will.

Emma and Wagi are going back to England. Emma sits on my bed and cries. Wagi hangs his head. What can they do? Their lives are there, across oceans, and I know that the bond between us will remain, will strengthen me in times of need. But it will be stretched so thin. Distance. The time difference ... so far away. I try not to cry. I remember that when they leave, Grandma and Abi will arrive. And then Ben, my ex, who is cutting short his tour around Australia to be with me. I am heartened by the abundance of people who care about me. Emma shifts on my bed and I look at her.

'Lou,' Emma starts. I can tell that she feels this is important. I brace myself. 'Do you remember the phone conversation we had a couple of days before your accident?'

I laugh. 'I can't remember much of this *year*, Emma. My brain's completely fried.'

'I called. It was very early in the morning in LA. Too early. You were still sleeping. As usual, I had the time change all wrong. I woke you up. You were really upset.' Emma waits for a light bulb to go off over my head. It's still dark here.

'What was I upset about ... you waking me up?'

'No, no.' She pauses. 'This is probably going to freak you out.'

'Go on. Tell me. What?' Now I must know.

'You had a dream. You dreamt that you were in a car accident and you lost all your hair.'

Heat floods through me. A rush of memories, of knowledge. *I knew.* I knew all along. The dream is still cloudy but I can remember the feeling of panic, of loss.

'So. Premonitions *do* happen.' There is comfort in this somehow. I suppose that it points to God, to meaning. Because the only way that the future could be known in the past, is if the plan is all laid out somewhere. And someone can see it. Too bad I didn't see it for what it was.

I'm quiet now, thinking these thoughts, and Emma holds my hand.
'I thought you would want to know,' she says softly.
'Thank you.'

★ ★ ★

Now that critical danger has receded to a safe distance, my body is catching up with all its aches and pains. The whiplash I suffered is severe. My entire body aches, my head is sore. Pain is ever present now and even the best available painkillers only manage to take the edge off for a little while. I am no longer using a catheter, which means that every time I have to urinate I must get up and go to the bathroom. My tummy screams in agony whenever I attempt to push. The doctors tell me that my body is still in tremendous shock.

My room finally feels familiar to me. The flowers, the gifts, my walls decorated with a huge Hollywood poster signed by all my fellow acting students make me feel somewhat at home here. The flow of visitors continues constantly, as do the phone calls. But sometimes I feel uncomfortable. Many of my friends, upon arriving and taking their first look at me, can no longer look me in the eye. Some of them make excuses to get out of here as soon as possible. I watch them blurting and stammering lies about meetings they have to run to, appointments just moments away. I watch their eyes focus on the flowers or the phone or anything but my face. I know I am a monster now. It must hurt to look upon such an ugly thing. I am sorry. My dad begins to set limitations on all the traffic in and out of my space.

One afternoon, two tall bald men in long white gowns walk into my room. I shoot a quick glance at Wagi who immediately looks away, afraid he's going to laugh.

'Hello?' I say, sure that they have taken a wrong turn down the corridor. 'Can I help you?'

'Hello,' they smile sweetly, 'I hope we've not come at an inconvenient time. Sally and Judy asked if we would come and say a prayer for you.'

I look at Dad – Sally and Judy are his friends – but far from seeing the humour in it, he seems very grateful and serious.

Oh no. I can feel it coming on. The giggles. Oh dear ... I can't stop myself. This happens to me at the most inopportune moments.

'If we've come at a bad time, please let us know.' They address my father since the patient is obviously a bit nutty. Except for my giggling, the room is absolutely silent.

'That is very kind of you.' Dad nods at them. 'Please go ahead. We'd be very happy for you to do this. Louise needs all the prayers she can get right now.'

'Dad!' I burst out, unable to stop myself. 'Don't say that like I'm some freak who's about to drop dead!'

This last remark is too much for Wagi who turns beetroot red and tries desperately to stifle his guffaws. This, in turn, sets Emma off. They both try to hold their respective breaths, which has the effect of making the laughter explode out of them.

The two priests look at each other, confused, not knowing what to make of the situation, or of me.

'I'm sorry,' I take control. 'Please, go ahead. I would be very grateful.' I try to focus my attention on them in a serious way. They step closer to the bed, one to my left, the other to my right. They raise their arms over me and close their eyes. Suddenly, a very peculiar sound begins to come from their mouths. 'Ohmmmmmmm. Ohhhhhh. Ahhh.' Oh Christ, I'm going to lose it ... Oh no ... Think of something else, don't be rude. I feel the giggles bubbling up again until they fill my cheeks where I trap them with sheer force. I hope they finish chanting soon or I'm definitely going to burst.

'Ohhhmmm ...' they finally die out. Thank God. Their eyes pop open. Their arms drop to their sides. They look at me, expectantly. 'How do you feel?' one of them asks hopefully.

'OH DEAR *GOD*!!' I roar from out of nowhere. '*WHAT HAVE YOU DONE?*!' These were words I had been thinking, not words I was intending to say. They just came out. I don't know what happened. It was only a joke. Please don't take me seriously. Immediately, everyone's faces completely pale in shock. Oh shit. I've really done it now.

'I'm sorry. I'm very sorry. I'm just joking,' I gush, already contrite. But, unfortunately, the damage is done. I cannot believe what I have done. I hadn't meant to. It just happened. I hadn't meant to offend these two men who had come to help me. To pray for me. To give me courage and strength. The priests leave offended. My father is baffled by my behaviour. I am quiet.

For good or ill, my sense of humour refuses to express itself more conventionally. When Dr Grode, my very sexy neurologist, comes to check up on me, I tease him mercilessly.

'Louise,' he says seriously, as I look at his handsome unscarred, unbruised, perfectly proportioned face, feeling weaker by the minute, 'are you having a problem hearing?'

Silence. Long silence.

'*Louise.* Can you hear me OK?'

I scrunch up my face and stare at him. 'I'm sorry, Dr Grode, did you say something?'

Dr Alessi has the most incredible blue eyes. Staring into them as he does his daily tests, I feel transported into a calm, blue eye planet where nothing can go wrong. I am finding myself studying the faces of my visitors, looking for signs from their past. Dr Kalb asks me the same question every day.

'On a scale from one to ten, ten being the worst, what is your headache?'

'Two.' I always give the same answer.

His overgrown features light up every time he hears it. Maybe that's why I keep saying the same thing. 'Amazing girl. You never complain. Miracle.'

I sense a very strong bond between us. He is definitely emotionally involved. He even comes to see me on his day off. Today, he's brought his fiancée and she tells me that I am all he talks about. It makes me feel special. I am flattered. I like being different from all his other patients. It makes it seem worthwhile.

It's true. I have fallen in love with all my doctors. It's not that odd, really. They saved my life. When they're around, I feel safe. I think many patients feel that way. I also love my nurses. I love to horrify them with the stories and songs I make up about my misfortune. They can't believe the things I make fun of. I have taken to calling myself Little Red Riding Turban. Kathy thought that one up. I call her my PPSM (Pseudo-Psycho-Surrogate-Mummy). And that she is, no doubt about it.

Emma and Wagi are gone now. Grandma and Abi are on their way to LA. Charlie, an ex-boyfriend who I've known since I was 11, is on his way in to see me. I must admit that I'm quite nervous about Charlie's visit. If only it wasn't my *face* that was all messed up. It's kind of hard to disguise something that's in the front of your head. Ugh. Why don't I just put a burlap sack over my watermelon head and cut out a little peephole. That would solve the problem, wouldn't it? I decide to wrap my whole face loosely with white gauze strips, leaving only an opening for my right eye. I spend what seems to take for ever, to balance the sterile fabric in the necessary positions, careful not to breathe heavily throwing them to the side of my bed. I try to believe that it looks somewhat fashionable or, at least, medically necessary.

When Charlie comes in, he pulls a chair over to the bed. As he talks, I notice him leaning strangely in the chair. He almost looks like he's going to tip over.

'What?'

'What what?' Charlie replies, confused.

'What are you looking at in that ... odd way?' I insist.

'Nothing.'

'You're trying to look under the bandages.'

'All right,' he admits, caught. 'Can I?'

I tell him that the doctors insist that I remain fully covered. I think he buys it. But for how long? How long before I will have to expose myself to the entire world, ex-boyfriends included? I can't think about it. Don't make me think about it. I look at Charlie take a deep breath and let the moment pass. The visit is uncomfortable. I want to be alone now.

I get a phone call. Abi and Grandma are on their way to the hospital, straight from the airport. They will be exhausted. I don't think that I can get away with having my whole face covered like I did with Charlie but I compromise by draping a bunch of cloth over the left side of my face. I hope it doesn't scare them.

They enter the room; Grandma's brow lined with worry and love, Abigail trying to cover her emotions by pretending that everything is perfectly normal. I realise by their faces that my attempts to prettify myself have failed miserably. I obviously still look like a fright mask. They both look tired. They need to sleep. I see their pained exhaustion in the frowns that appear.

Grandma, her short white hair freshly combed against her small head, peers at us both from the chair where she sits, resting her painful feet. Grandma, whose mission in life is to take care of people. Grandma gets up wanting to smooth troubled waters.

'Louise, can I get you something to eat? You look a bit peckish.' I smile, feeling such love for this woman, her constant need to feed everyone.

'Thank you, Grandma, but I'm fine. I had a big lunch.'

Not sure that she believes this, Grandma nonetheless leaves the room, elegant as always, despite the slight shuffle that gives away her pain in walking.

Abigail immediately launches into a litany of her woes; her father, school, London, her friends ... I interrupt her gently. 'Abi, calm down.'

'I know, but ...' Abi is like a pit-bull with a bone.

'It's OK. It's going to be OK.'

And just like that, her mood changes and her face softens. 'I love you, Lou Lou.'

'I love you too, Abi. Would you please go find Grandma?'

My grandmother has had to go through very difficult times in the last few years. My mum was her eldest daughter and her long terminal illness put immense strain on her. I refuse to give her more worry than I already have.

'Are you all right, Grandma?' I ask gently when she comes back in. 'Are you tired? How was the trip?'

'It was fine, darling, just fine.'

Dad takes them back to my apartment where my little brother, Oli, has already left messages, too young to understand the full story, but old enough to sense that something serious is in the air. Thankfully, he is still in school, so not bringing him along makes sense to him. I wouldn't want him to see me like this.

It is quiet. I am alone. My thoughts drift away from me as I begin to fall into that twilight between consciousness and sleep. Suddenly, I hear a rustle of laughter and before I can pull myself out of the heavy depths, there is a loud crash. My eyes fly open. There is Ben. Am I dreaming this? Typically, he has given me no warning, no inkling that he was even on the continent, let alone coming to see me today. His hair is sun-bleached white, his face tanned and shiny and he wears a hat with wine corks hanging off of it (this is a peculiar Australian style that goes with their love affair with alcohol). He has dropped his suitcases on the floor.

'Hello, my little Louie! Now what have you done?' he booms in that familiar voice, all warm and deep.

'I'm sorry,' I laugh. I am so happy to see him. I can tell that the nurses are, too; they are already surrounding him. Can't say I blame them. Ben was my first love. We started our affair at the tender age of 16 and it has continued, in some fashion, on and off until I left London to come here.

'You sure have a lot of people that care for you, Miss Louise,' says one of the nurses. I can't help but blush – it's true.

When the nurses have left, Ben gives me a big hug, careful to avoid the sensitive areas. I know that he is finding it hard to look at me but he is very strong and determined not to make me feel self-conscious. He is really a good man and now, after all the years of drama between us, I realise that he will always be my friend. We will always love each other.

They tell me that I am leaving the hospital. I can use the bathroom alone now, through cries of pain. I am eating a bit more. It is safe for me to go.

It isn't safe. It isn't safe at all. Please. Please don't throw me out there yet.

They tell me they will see me every day. I must come in for daily checks with doctors. As the nurse continues calmly reassuring me, I break down. My words garbled through tears.

I will die if I leave. No one will be there to save me. I am scared. I am too fucking scared. Please let me stay just a little bit longer.

'You can call us whenever you want, Louise. We're here for you 24 hours a day. Don't worry. You are going to be just fine.'

No. I'm not going to be just fine. There is nothing 'just fine' about any of this. Don't make me go. Please. It's dangerous out there.

There is something about being in a hospital that calms the sick. A wide net of people, attentive, ready to spring into action if rescue is necessary. There is also room for denial. Not having to face the fact that this period in time is just the beginning. The road to recovery is long and strewn with unknown pitfalls. I don't want to face that. I want it to be over now. I want to walk out of the hospital with my life back. Completely. 100 per cent. I want to leave the hospital as I had left the airport when I arrived only a few weeks ago – whole and complete. But I can't. Nothing I say will change their minds. It's time for me to go. Time for the new Louise – the deformed Louise – to meet the real world again. I will confront this challenge head on.

Home Sweet Home

'Opportunities are usually disguised by hard work,
so most people don't recognise them.'
Ann Landers

I sit in the wheelchair by the entrance to the patient pick-up point. My father's rental car is parked by the kerb.

'Louise, are you ready to get in the car?' he asks as he rushes to reorganise the back seat.

'Kathy, will you sit in the back with me?' I request, wanting to get in and hide as soon as I can.

'Louise, do you want Kathy to drive and I'll sit in the back with you?' My father asks, complicating things.

'I don't care, I just want someone in the back with me.'

I am being fussed over. I know I am causing them to do so. This is my first trip in a car. I am apprehensive. I have never been a good passenger, not in a plane, on a boat and now not in a car. Even the trip down in the wheelchair was nerve-racking. I sense that I'm being stared at. I bow my head as much as I can without my neck sending a sudden spasm to my head. The stares are obvious and I feel that I may as well have put a head on my lap for a more direct view.

'John, you drive and I'll sit in the back with Louise,' Kathy says finally.

'Bye, Louise, and remember we'll call you this evening to see how you are. Kathy has all your medications and sleeping pills and gauze pads.' The nurse smiles reassuringly. 'You are going to be just fine.'

There was that 'just fine' again.

As we drive away, I turn stiffly to see her waving goodbye. The hospital has been my safety and now I feel naked and alone. I feel susceptible to everything around me. I don't know who I am with this new disfigurement and these disabilities. I know I have lost my smell and taste and that other losses will be apparent with time. I am claustrophobic, not sure if I will fit in with the outside world and the strangers' gazes.

Dad drives slowly. Kathy holds my hand. I sit in the back remorseful. My life is different now. I am different now. We pull up outside the apartment building on Doheny. My life had almost been taken away from me, only blocks away. One split-second had changed everything. Fate was in control. I had to stay still. My dreams, my desires shattered along with my head. The turban is in place. The scar is itching and uncomfortable, like me. The swelling in my face has gone down a little bit. Not enough. I am irritated. I feel like the scar on my head, to the rest of the world. I don't want to go home. I am doleful. I am miserable about my life and what is to become of me. I am unable to walk well and now a sideshow freak. I can't think like this. I place an imaginary stop sign in front of my eye to try and stop the thoughts. Be strong. Be an example. Be positive.

Ben, Abi and Grandma are staying in my apartment. They come down to greet me. I don't want this made into a scene. I fear that passers-by will stop to look. They will see my face, my wounds, my itching to leave this body. My legs are weak and skinny as is the rest of me. My melon-sized deformity is too heavy to carry. I can feel the fluid inside it, heavy and hot.

'I am fine,' I keep repeating as I hobble slowly to the entrance with Ben and my father on either side steadying me. It's strange to be back in my apartment. It looks different from how I remember. All along one of the walls are tinted mirrors with ugly brown blotchy stains at the tops. Now my reflection will be the ugly tint. There will be no way of getting away from me.

Grandma suggests we have some tea. Dad suggests I have a bath and change into some new bedclothes, and Abi and Ben suggest I sit with them and watch TV. Kathy suggests I lie down. My head is swimming. I need to breathe. I need to be alone. I suggest some alleviation, some time alone to collect myself. All are in agreement.

The bedroom is dark and feels cold. Above the bed there is a tiny window to let in light; it also allows the noise of traffic from the busy street to stream through, making my headache worse. I need to be left alone and allowed to adjust to my surroundings, so I quietly shut the door. I limp awkwardly over to the bed where I perch, directing my gaze ahead into the mirror. There she is. No hair. My mother stares back at me, and for the first time I understand her pain of losing her hair and femininity. Tears flow out of the open eye. Not only tears of sadness, but tears of being able to feel what my mother had felt. I understand now, Mum. I am sorry I couldn't before when you used to sob your frustrations to me. The understanding comforts me. I can feel she is with me. She's holding my hand in our common experience. I feel her warmth around me, surrounding me with comfort. 'You're OK,' she whispers.

I pick up a glossy magazine from the side table. I cover the left side of my face so only the right uninjured half will be seen. I stare at it for a while. It, too, is swollen and doesn't look like Louise. I hold the magazine in front of the right side so I can still just peer out of the gap on the left. Only a month ago, I complained about a red blemish. Now this. Again I hear the whisper, 'You're OK.'

I don't know how long I sat for. I can't tell you exactly the emotions I felt, as there were so many trapped into one ball of confusion. I am still Louise. The exterior may have changed, but the interior is only strengthening. I had to keep telling myself this as I had overheard someone talking about me earlier, saying, 'Well, when she was normal ...'

Dad reluctantly leaves with Kathy. It is my first night at home and already I miss the hospital. Dr Alessi calls to see how I am. 'Don't forget not to sneeze. Your head can't take the pressure,' he says.

Unsure of how I can control sneezing, I simply agree with him. 'No, don't worry, I won't sneeze.'

His voice comforts me. I feel the safety of my life in his knowledge of how to take care of me. My saviour hangs up the phone and I go back to my first night at home. My brave face reappears to my family. I have a shallow bath, with Grandma watching over my skinny body and melon-sized head as it sits naked and weak. Ben and Abi have all their sleeping equipment laid out and are deciding which movie channel to watch next. They are bickering as if brother and sister. This is soon quietened as a large tub of ice cream is skilfully placed in front of them. Their bickering turns to a pleasant calm. Grandma comes and gets into bed with me, looking so dear in her nightdress and slippers. The pillows are adjusted and raised to the orders of the doctors to help with the swelling, pressure build-up and assiduous neck pain.

'Night, Lou. Is there anything else you need?' she says in her most gentle voice.

'Oh, no thank you, Grandma. Maybe a new head, but I don't think we can arrange that right now. Thank you for your help.'

'Don't be silly. I love you. Wake me if you need me,' she says as she touches her head to the pillow.

I can't remember falling asleep. I can't remember sneezing. I cannot remember the words that came out of my mouth as the fluid poured from my nose. I saw the stains on my pillow when I awoke in the morning. I am prescribed a set of pills to add to my eminently large collection.

Building the Mask

While my original mission was to become a Hollywood star, my new mission is to find a way to hide my offensive face. Abi and Ben are in front of the television set. They have moved on from breakfast cereal to cookies and toast and hardly notice me leaving. I find myself becoming curt, fidgeting for them to notice me. I'm unable to control myself and snap, 'Don't worry, I'll get the door.' Two faces slowly look up with one eye still on the television in fear of missing the first showing of Madonna's new music video.

Once inside Dr Grode's office, he begins his examination, first testing reflexes, then hearing, sticking cold metal equipment up my nose to look for unsavoury and unwanted fluids, and then he begins feeling my misshapen head. I feel so ashamed when he touches me. I am embarrassed at my deformity. It is not just the feeling of being self-conscious at having other people see me; it is also my own feelings about seeing myself. I am discovering new pieces to my face that I never knew about. New sensations, pains and blockages. Once the turban comes off, there I am, bald and scarred, and still in the process of finding out what else has been destroyed. Dr Grode explains that I have to have tests done with a specialist who will now deduce the extent of my brain and memory damage. It is as if I am in a dream. I don't allow myself to listen to the words 'damage', 'disability' or 'deformity'. Brain damage. It is thanks to my memory damage that this conversation and fear soon fade into the darkness from which they first came.

In contrast, my appointment with Dr Kalb is relaxed and I feel relieved to see him in new surroundings. His nurses seem to know about me and tell me stories of how the doctor talks of his star patient. Not much can yet be done with regards to sight tests, as my eye hasn't opened. My mind is filled with confusion. I cannot remember instances from only five minutes ago. How can these people who love me so much bear to look at me? How can they eat around this figure of deformity? I need to get a mask and hide my hideous scars.

I wish I had thought to keep some of Mum's wigs as now I'm sitting, sweating, in the depths of the valley, in a wig store. All around are mannequins' heads, covered in hair, long and short, thick and thin. Blonde, dark, red and the odd punk style, too. My hair loss is a sensitive topic. It magnifies all my injuries. Kathy and Dad sit patiently as I have an eruption. I have been a volcano waiting to happen. Embarrassed by myself and my words of self-pity, I try to make a joke out of the situation. Kathy is uncomfortable. Dad isn't happy. I get the feeling it has all become a little too much. He is getting impatient and short-tempered. I know it's because he cares so deeply. He has never been one to watch emotional pain as it upsets him too much.

'Come on, Dad, try not to be so serious,' I say, attempting to cut through some of the tension. I feel it is my responsibility to do this.

'Louise, I don't know how you do it,' he answers, shaking his head from side to side. 'Come on, let's get this wig and get out of here.'

I sit on the narrow stool that moves freely when I do. The assistant is sympathetic to my baldness and shares that she had to wear a wig from an accident, too. As I scan the room, searching for the hair that would build the new Louise, I settle on a brown piece. It is similar to my old hair. Not the same but similar. I am gently positioned for the application so as not to knock any of my bruised and delicate parts. My most sensitive part is already crushed – my ego. The wig is itchy on my scar, but when I look ahead at my reflection, the itching vanishes as I see that the hair eases the pain. The fleshy scar from ear to ear, the unwanted bumps and the holes miraculously disappear. I feel able to breathe a little easier than I could five minutes ago. My mask is being built. Only I would have to see my offensive wounds. Kathy, who is quick to make up songs about my appearance, expresses that I am no longer Little Red Riding Turban but 'Princess Lou Lou, Hair of Many Colours'. Now I have a long, brown, thick wig and protective dark glasses.

That night, even though tired from our busy day, I am restless. I decide that I'll try staying with Steve and Kathy for a few nights. I am in desperate need to have my own bed and rest. I notice others changing as to how they treat me. Should they say this? Maybe I should do that. I won't treat her any differently. I will! I'm very sensitive to this and start to take care of their feelings. Not something new to me. As a child, I always thought this to be my responsibility. I became aware that when someone has been damaged physically, however many times you say, 'I'm OK', no one believes you, as you don't *look* OK. The most annoying remark I heard was, 'Well, when you're *normal* again ...' Was I the only person who knew that I was still the same me? Only my mind was more conscious of the world's imperfections and how these can make us more wise and perfect then we actually were before. Even though I could only see out of one open eye at the moment, I felt at times I could see more than some people with two. My logic and thinking had become broadened because of the circumstances I found myself in. I had to figure out my own views and ideas as to why this would have happened to me. I believe that we come into this world with a pre-ordained destiny but then destiny is what we make it. The most important thing to me at this juncture is to get through each day with a smile on my face and as little pain as possible. There is nothing as important to me as making my father proud and feeling the beam of warmth from his gaze. I knew then that I was special. Now his gaze is shattered and forced.

We were in the car driving back to Steve's house in the valley. We were heading over Coldwater Canyon, the radio played quietly and I sat humbly in the back seat dreaming of the sleep-filled night I would soon have. Steve turns to my father and ignorant of the consequence, says, 'And to think that the man who hit Louise lives off this canyon.'

My father's body shifts quickly. 'How do you know that?' my father responds, irked by this piece of information.

'Well it's on the legal papers that you showed me today. The ones that George Stanbury gave you to read over', Steven continues.

Silence in the car. A silence that fills me with dread.

'Where abouts in the canyon?' my father asks.

As Steve tells him, I beg for him to discontinue. The mood in the car shifts from pleasant calm to repellent anger. We wind through hills and sharp turns, until we are situated outside the house of the man who hit me. My father becomes a wolf excited to kill his prey, saliva dripping from the sides of his mouth as he imagines the torture he would inflict upon this old man. I sit swollen and bruised and watch in terror, while my father's curses fill the thick tense air. He storms out of the car heading for the old man's front door. Panicking at what his anger might lead to, I, in turn, limp after him, shouting back at Steve, 'Make him stop, Steve, please help me make him stop.' I beg my father to get back in the car and 'let it go'. He looks at me desperately and I see his eyes fill with tears. The frustration he is feeling is shared and I wish I could relieve him of it and make it all better. He throws his arms up in a helpless manner and turns once again to the old man's door and then back at me. With the only eye that I have open, I try to persuade him to change his mind, to really think about what he is doing and then after a few large sighs and 'but ... but ...' we solemnly get back in the car. I sit back, filled with relief.

I understand his need to protect me. His anger from this wreck is building and he needs someone to blame. My arms and legs are shaking and my head is throbbing more than before. I have a strange sensation under the surface of my skin around my mouth, nose and cheekbone on the left. It feels like I have a thousand insects underneath my skin, scratching and crawling to get out. I begin to itch and this only sends more strange sensations and tickles into my left eye. I close my open eye and try to ignore this new annoyance and get some sleep while Steve calms my father down.

Kathy is as attentive and as concerned for me as if I were her own daughter. My moods are volatile. I keep snapping. I have a thought and then, without any control, only an impulse, I say the thought. Sometimes it's funny and sometimes it would have been better left unsaid. It is noticeable and so is my frustration to it.

One morning, after finishing my eye-wash and treatment, Kathy speaks to Dr Grode about it and he tells her this is an effect of my losing that piece of my brain. 'Unfortunately – well, in some cases fortunately – Louise has no control over her emotions. Anything she feels just comes straight to the surface. She has lost her inhibitions,' he explains.

Top: Me as a baby in Sydney, where I was born.

Below: Pictured with my beautiful mother, Linda King, who was an actress and model in the 60s.

I started my acting career early. Here I am in my first role in a Vegemite advertisement.

Top: Young Louise Ashby.

Below: Getting ready for an early TV appearance in the dressing room of *Crackerjack*.

On the stage, doing what I know and love best!

Top: The house in Wimbledon, where I grew up.

Below: My beloved Grandma, pictured here with me and my brothers and sisters. Abi is on the far right.

Top: From show business to snow business. With my Dad, John Ashby,
entertainment agent.

Below: My courageous Mum, who tragically lost her fight against Leukaemia in 1991.

Top: My friend Charlotte, who was in the car accident with me.

Below: My best friend, Wagi. Wagi was one of the friends who rushed out to the States as soon as he heard of my accident.

Top: Out enjoying myself with Alex and my little brother Oli. Oli is showing a bit of brotherly love!

Below: My dear friends, whose support has meant so much to me. (*From left to right*) Emma, Tom, Belinda and Wagi.

'Well, it's driving her crazy,' she tells him.

'I have to tell you that Louise's body is suffering from a lot of shock at the moment. She just had 12 hours of brain surgery and then a further 22 hours of reconstructive surgery, so her brain is going to be in shock, too. When she next comes in, I'll explain all of the damages to her and, of course, she'll be doing many more tests.'

After two days, as nurturing as it is to be near Kathy and my father, I am frustrated at not having my things around me. I want to get back to normality and adjust to the changes in me in my own surroundings.

It is arranged for Grandma and Abi to stay in a hotel and Ben to stay with me in the apartment so I won't be alone. I want him to be there. As uplifting as it is, I'm exhausted having a constant flow of people around.

The swelling in my ankle now looks like I'm suffering from a bad case of elephantiasis and is painful to walk on. Thankfully, I have Ben to take care of my every need.

This particular afternoon, we're sitting in the sitting room having tea and relaxing. I'm wearing the turban; the scar is painful and itchy. Because of the heat, I can feel the pus weeping from my wound. The metal plates that are in my head are being rejected and so pushing forward, sending my forehead into a rage of bumps and spots. I keep pushing my hands under the turban to itch. It is apparent that my thin cotton headpiece bothers me.

'Louie, why don't you take the turban off?' Ben suggests as he watches my misery.

'No, don't worry, I'm fine,' I reply hesitantly, still scratching, scanning the dips.

'Come on, darling, it's me, you have nothing to hide. I love you and I'm here for you. Now take it off and air your little head,' he persists.

I look at him nervously, 'Are you sure?'

'Yes I'm sure,' he says softly.

I slowly remove the turban from my head to reveal my true naked self. As I turn my head delicately to catch a glimpse in the mirror, Ben turns white and stutters, 'Oh my God, you have a hole in the back of your head.' I quickly grab the turban and throw it back on, embarrassed at what he's seen.

'I'm sorry,' I say, 'I'm so sorry ... it's just awful to look at, isn't it?' I bow my head into my lap to hide the rest of my face.

Ben rushes over and holds my hands. 'No, no, it's not. It's fine. I'm sorry. It was just a shock, darling,' he assures. I'm filled with shame. I am so ugly. That was the last time anyone, apart from doctors, saw under my camouflage.

New information, new prescriptions, tests and doctors are approved each day. I am still being aggressive with my eyelid exercises. As I try to lift it with my face muscles, up and down, up and down, it stands firm. Then, one morning, the whole of Beverly Hills hears the shriek as the eyelid opens a millimetre. My first step in proving my determination to be fixed has been accomplished. My morale has been boosted, as is that of those close to me. Dr Kalb, excited by the news, says he wants to see how much it has opened so he can determine whether I have vision left in that eye or not.

'Vision?' I question. I hadn't been aware that this was a doubt. Because of all my other damages, this question is not as shocking to me as it would have been before. My mind is so scattered from the trauma that difficulties and possibilities find it hard to sink in to a thought before they are thrown back on the whirlwind of incomprehensibility.

Adjusting to the loss of smell and taste is more difficult than I'd imagined it would be. I go out on to my balcony and take a deep breath, trying to get at least something, to no avail. This makes me anxious and claustrophobic. I watch someone smoking a cigarette in front of me and find it alien that I can't smell the fumes.

My loss of taste is easier because other things make up for it. I now choose by texture. I can tell if something is salty or sweet but not the full flavour. I insist on being told what things taste like. Once I was given a cup of what I think is tea and when I taste it I can tell that it's very bitter and laugh to my friend, 'How long did you leave this tea bag in? This is so bitter.'

She looks at me sympathetically. 'It's coffee!'

I am trying to form my new image so that my appearance will be easier to deal with. So far it is a wig and dark glasses, or a wig and eye-patch. I know that the courageous thing to do is to accept change and to embrace the situation. I had come to terms with the facts pretty early on. I had to. No one else was going to get through these things for me so it was up to me to get on with it and feel blessed that I was experiencing life through new eyes – or eye, I should say. The wigs are uncomfortable and the scar across my head from ear to ear is very sensitive and sore. The sunglasses they had given me in the hospital were too big and that's when I decided to go for an alternative. I didn't have the money to spend on accessories like this but I justified the sunglasses were an important part of my recovery, therefore worth it. I wore my look with attitude. I wanted to be confident about myself, especially as I was being stared at all the time. I felt that if I were confident, then it would be easier for those around. If I squirmed, so would they. My mask is prepared and now I had to prepare my mind for the new life which I had never imagined.

New Discoveries

Understanding comes in the form of George's girlfriend, Matilda. The first time we meet, I bring pictures of myself before the accident. I want her to know this face is an accident. I am self-conscious at meeting someone new, looking the way I do. Her face and mouth gasp, 'Please don't feel that you have to do that, Lou.' Her long elegant fingers pick the glossy pictures up and place them face down on the glass surface.

'I just thought ...' I start to say.

'Georgie has told me everything,' she prompts. She is kind and warm and I am immediately drawn to her. She seems to understand.

One morning, Tilda and I take a trip to K-Mart, a cheap store for buying household goods. We shop around for a while, knowing it won't be long before I am hit with fatigue. I see a candle. A candle in a glass. Belinda's favourite. I know this as she has mentioned it on the phone to me, while freezing in London. It is Christmas. I pick up as many as I can manage in my hands and stand in a short line at the check-out. I'm wearing the black, thick, itchy eye-patch. I place the candles gently on the till by the cashier and stand behind a Mexican woman who is throwing her arms around like an angry ape, while talking. I turn to her and ask her politely, indicating my candles, to be careful. She stares at me, looks me up and down and then abruptly turns away. This makes me uncomfortable. This soon disappears when I hear, 'Hey', as Tilda shuffles into the queue, next to me. 'Look at these ...'

Decorations. Christmas decorations. All of a sudden, I feel a sharp, heavy pain on my right foot. I turn to the Mexican woman with the ape arms. She stares at me. All four candles are smashed around me, splintered glass covering my shoes. I look back at the woman, then to the glass and then back at the woman.

'Excuse me,' I begin calmly, 'but ...'

The Mexican woman squints her eyes, like a cowboy preparing to pull his gun from his holster. Then her heavily accented voice interrupts me.

'Just because you only have one eye, don't expect others to see out of the other.' She laughs as if she were the wicked witch of the west, 'HA HA HA HA HA HA HA.' Maybe that was in my imagination.

I stand still, in shock and disbelief that someone could be so cruel. Tilda smiles and holds on to my shaking arms. 'Take a deep breath and let it go; this woman is too shallow to know any better. Just feel sorry for her,' she says, her words and serenity already easing my laceration. I let the woman leave without hurting her as she had me. Once out of the shop, I break down in tears. I am now being discriminated against for my disabilities and deformity. I lean against the brick wall of the store and realise this is only the beginning. I will have to learn to accept this.

We are having lunch at the Beverly Hills Cheesecake Factory one afternoon when I notice people at other tables are staring over at me. Kathy whispers, 'Louise, you have to stop doing that with your head. You're not at home alone now.'

'What?' I question, uncertain of what I'm doing wrong.

Then I see myself in the mirror by the table. I'm itching my head underneath my wig so that my entire hand is under the wig exposing my bloody scar. I laugh at my carelessness and put everything back in place.

My top lip is numb; similar in feeling to when the dentist gives you too many injections, so I chew on it causing blisters to form. As I have no sensation in the left side of my mouth when I eat, the food stores itself under the lip and then embarrassingly drops out on to the plate later on in the meal. All at the table that day saw what I had been trying to hide. This happened a lot at mealtimes and sometimes the food would store itself until later on in the day at an even more embarrassing moment and it wouldn't be the plate it landed on.

I was having horribly vivid dreams. One night, I dream I am in the bath shaving my legs. I start to chop up my legs with the razor. The blood that pours out of my legs is bright red, filling the bathtub where I sit screaming. The dreams are persisting and my sleep is disturbed because of it.

At my next appointment with Dr Kalb, I tell him and we discover it to be from the sleeping pills I had been given, Halcyon, which in most places had been made illegal for this exact reason. When I stop taking the pills, the dreams end and I return to my blissful escape each night.

Dr Alessi is making progress with my jaw being opened a little further every visit. I have always prided myself in being able to fit my whole fist in my mouth (strange, I know) and now I can fit two whole fingers. This doesn't stop me from talking, though, much to everyone's dismay. Unfortunately, there is nothing that can be done regarding the loss of use of my left nostril, which I can no longer breathe through.

My memory loss is proving to be problematic for my friends who are calling me, as I tell them the same stories four or five times over throughout a conversation. Thankfully, I am told when to stop and that the same stories over and over again can become boring. But then, this leads me to being confused as to what I am saying and if I have already said it. I have absolutely no memory of the accident or the few weeks leading to it. I misplace things all the time, which proves an added frustration.

In retrospect, all things became livable and part of my new life. I don't ask questions and I don't panic about things, either. Maybe I was too tired for that emotion. One morning, I'm alone in the apartment on the phone to a friend in London. As he is talking, I am bringing my hand, with a spoonful of cereal in it, up to my mouth when my whole body jerks forward and starts rocking causing the bowl to fly across the room. I make a funny noise, a little like a squeak.

'Lou, are you all right? What's going on?' Phillip asks worried.

Flabbergasted and unsure myself, 'Oh, I'm fine, nothing happened,' I reply, too nervous to acknowledge it for myself.

My birthday arrives and some people have gathered at my apartment to celebrate with me. I don't want to celebrate. It doesn't seem right. It feels false to me. I want to be alone. Friends bring gifts and cake and sit and talk. George has a huge grin across his face as I unwrap his gift.

'Medical Monopoly! Thanks, George,' I smile. My guests are trying to be as merry as they can given the circumstances. Grandma rushes around making drinks and offering food. I feel I am being stared at or maybe it is my paranoia. I don't want to talk, I am tired and feel uncomfortable. I catch Craig's eye and he's busy reading my mind. He gestures to the door and we disappear with my sister to the local store. I can't walk; Craig has to carry me, I want to be alone or just to watch TV. The party ends early and my birthday wish is granted. Kathy has a birthday lunch for me at her house for family the following day, it is more intimate and easier to deal with. Having too many people around is overwhelming to me right now.

A few days later, my dad leaves to go back to England, followed by Grandma, Abi and then Ben. Kathy, George and Tilda take over. We do everything together; if Kathy couldn't take me to an appointment, then Tilda would.

In the daytime, I spend the morning in the gym with the trainer who I had been training with before the accident, as I'm very conscious about keeping fit. I am told that if I hadn't trained as much as I did before the accident, then my heart would not have been strong enough to pull me through. We had to take everything very slowly and I usually complained of exhaustion after 15 minutes and then the trainer would drop me home. Because of my self-consciousness over my appearance, we were working in a gym which no one else visited. I was told by the doctors that I wasn't Wonderwoman and to slow down. Money is tight, though, and I know it's a luxury that I won't be able to afford for long.

I have appointments with my lawyer, George Stanbury, to get things in order for the case that we're fighting. I become overwhelmed with some of the things I am told. It seems complicated. I haven't seen Charlotte since she had been to the hospital the day I was moved out of Intensive Care. I am hurt. I am told that she must be suffering some sort of survivor's guilt even though I couldn't see why she should be. Things become clearer with time.

About two weeks after everyone has left to return to England, George and Tilda inform me of a party that is being held at a friend's house. They ask me if I am up to going. I can't read or watch TV as both make my one open eye sore. Socialising seems a good option. I'm walking better and know that if I didn't feel good, George would bring me back home without a fuss. He is so patient with me. It takes me a while to decide what to wear as I am trying to disguise my new appearance. I feel pointless as I try on clothes. Nothing will hide the ugliness of Louise. The patch and the wig are my identity. The clothes will go unnoticed, but still I spend endless hours trying on and throwing to the ground. Then I am ready.

When we arrive at the party I search for someone I know. The house is a stunning bungalow, in an oriental design. Outside, a small water fountain suggests tranquillity. The glass table with a lonely orchid is surrounded by party favours. I feel my eye-patch has moved and reach to reposition the concave covering. I have been spotted and am suddenly surrounded by a group at the door to the kitchen. I am smiling and sighing trying to keep up with all the questions and comments. The only person in the group I know is a girlfriend, Rebecca. A tall, blonde girl stands next to her. I fail to recognise her but she knows all about me.

'This is Lou, remember I told you about her', Rebecca says to her, 'she had that terrible car accident I told you about', she continues, catching George's attention to refill her drink.

'Oh, you're the girl that had her face peeled off and rebuilt!' Susan blurts out without thinking that this information may be foreign to me.

I feel sick and turn white. Was that about me? My face peeled off? There must be some mistake. My face is damaged but it hasn't been peeled. Has it? I listen in horror as those around me describe the surgery I had had. My head had been opened from ear to ear and then my face had been peeled like an orange to expose my flesh and then the doctor had gone in through my mouth and gums hence the soreness and numbness. I am upset at being told this at a party by a bunch of people I hardly know, some complete strangers.

'What can I get you to drink?' the host interrupts.

As I think about it, I remember. 'Well, I guess it doesn't matter any more, seeing as I can't taste anything', I joke. This information becomes intriguing to all. 'You can't taste?' 'Oh my God.' 'Do you still get hungry?'

A dangerous game begins. 'Let's see if Lou can guess what this drink is?'

The more I play, the more I drink, the drunker I get, and the more I want to play. Suddenly, my pains are gone and a light giddy feeling replaces any traces of discomfort. By midnight, I am Cinderella whisked away by her carriage, only there is no handsome prince. Only George and Matilda, who had become more to me than royalty. I am sliding along the wall, for support. I look to George for help. He and Tilda fetch the car keys and say goodbyes.

Tilda helps me up the stairs between my stops to throw up, and then once in the apartment I throw up some more. When Tilda and I feel it is safe for her to leave, she nestles me into bed with a cold glass of water. I am alone. My head is pounding more violently than if a brass band were in bed with me, a drummer on top. It has come. My time to leave the planet. This is it. This is what is going to kill me. I search for the bright light tunnel that will appear for me to travel through. I hope I will be escorted, as walking is an unsteady option. The room is spinning and I am crying like a newborn baby through pain. I can't stand up. I am retching again. Bile pours out of the small stretched opening in my mouth. I pass out.

A decision has to be made with regard to my getting around, so George Stanbury suggests I hire a driver. All the receipts from parking at doctors' appointments and medications are all kept in a file for the court case and I am told if I get a driver then that, too, will be claimable. I tell him I'll think about it. Being offered a driver feels like a Hollywood moment, except not in the way I'd originally thought. My father is due back again in a week, and for now I have Kathy, George and Tilda.

I have an appointment with a new doctor who is going to test my memory and the extent of my brain damage. I am told to prepare to be in his office for around four hours. I am quite looking forward to the appointment, as the idea of seeing someone for logic questions sounds interesting and fun. Had I known how frustrated and upset I was going to get, it would have been a different story.

The first thing the doctor does is to get a bag of objects and lay them across the table. He then gave me a couple of minutes to look over them before he took them away again. I am then asked which of the objects I can remember.

'Apple, pen, lighter ... erm ... erm', I struggle.

'Take your time', he encourages.

'Erm ... erm ... Fuck, I don't know. Can't you give me a break? This isn't fun you know', I plead. This game is played unwillingly three or four times. Each time, I'm only able to remember the first three items. Then I have a maths quiz, spelling, name cards and more frustration. I become upset and confused. The more frustrated I become, the harder it is for me to stay focused and answer the questions. I freely snap at the doctor.

When we realise how bad my short-term memory is, I become scared.

'What is wrong with me?' I cry. 'Am I never going to get better?' A self-pitying cry. He tells me that the piece of my brain I have lost governs my inhibitions. It amazes me that the doctors can pinpoint what each piece of the brain does.

'What does this mean?' I panic, as I think about things I might start doing. 'Does this mean I'll be hit with impulses to run across the street naked?' I squirm as the vision appears before me.

'No, no ...' he quickly interrupts, holding back a laugh. 'What it means is that you have no control over any emotions, which is *not* always a good thing. Anything that you feel is acted upon or said out loud.'

I listen intently as he continues, remembering this happening in the last few weeks. The puzzle is coming together.

'Just be aware of it,' he finishes. He thanks me for my patience, which in itself is a lie, and tells me I have to return the following week for more testing. Rather than four hours I have been there for seven.

The loss of inhibitions has been one of the more difficult aspects of my injury for me to handle. For others, it can be highly amusing or embarrassing. The two major changes are that I have become openly sexual and impatient. Interesting combination. I can hear myself saying things that I know I shouldn't be saying and yet I am unable to control them. I say exactly what is on my mind to whoever is in front of me whether they are annoying me or flirting with me. There are times when I've tried to blame alcohol consumption, only to be reminded I hadn't had anything to drink.

As time progresses, more things are discovered. I begin physiotherapy for the severe whiplash that I suffered. I am going three times a week to have my neck, shoulders and ankle attended to. I have been persuaded to take the driver option, but I felt embarrassed having one. I just want to be able to get in a car myself and get on with my once-mapped-out life. I know things have changed. I may never have the career that I have always dreamed of and worked toward because my face is so badly damaged, yet I am still determined and will not quit. Whenever I tell the doctors this, they look at me unsure of what to say.

'Well, Louise, I really think you should be realistic. You're never going to look the same,' they say sympathetically.

'I'm not going to stop until I do, and I'll find the person to do it. I'm in a city which is based on appearance. If you think I'm going to let this accident beat me, you're wrong!' I argued. There was no way I was going to live the rest of my life looking like a monster.

All of the 200 metal bolts and plates now in my head were temporary and I had been forewarned that I would need more surgery, including brain surgery. As all the nerve endings and cells and metal were moving and adjusting around my head, I was feeling awkward and niggling itching sensations as if a thousand little bugs were running under the top layer of my skin and digging to get out. I was constantly itching and scratching and didn't realise just how hard I was rubbing. I had no warning sensation that I had reached the itch. My eyebrow was trying desperately to grow back, only to be scratched away. This caused my skin to break out into hundreds of little red spots. Now, along with everything else, I had to see a dermatologist.

By Thanksgiving, my friends Michael Strutt, Charlie Gardener and Julian Stevenson have decided to stay in LA. This news makes me happy as it makes me feel more at home. Mike and Julian had been travelling and Charlie was an aspiring musician. They were having a dinner and I thought I'd make an appearance.

When dinner is finished and coffee is being consumed, others arrive for drinks. I am sitting by a girl around my age who, upon looking at me, asks the usual question, 'Why do you wear an eye-patch?'

'Oh, I had a car accident', I reply in my usual, matter-of-fact way.

'Really? How long ago?' she probes.

I tell her the story and her facial expression is that of 'Oh my God'. Then she, in turn, shocks me.

'You're Louise Ashby-King, aren't you?'

How did she know my name?

'You were at Cedars Sinai and your doctors were Dr Kalb and Dr Alessi, right?' she gushes.

I look at her strangely and rather taken aback. 'How do you know that?'

Her name is Rowan and she goes on to tell me that she, too, had been in a car accident. She had also been at Cedars Sinai and had had the same doctors. Rowan tells me of the occasions when Dr Kalb asked her, 'On a scale from one to ten, ten being the worst, what is your headache?' When she answered him, he would reply, 'Louise Ashby-King always said a two and she was almost dead!' She had grown to despise me when she was in the hospital, as she would permanently hear 'Louise Ashby-King this' and 'Louise Ashby-King that'. I am touched by this news and tell her that I had paid the doctors to say that. It is amazing that when you have been through a tragedy and it is visible, how you become touched by other people's lives and pain. Everywhere I went, I was asked, 'What happened to your face?' I would always explain. My close friends got annoyed with the questions constantly thrown at me. They were protective.

One evening I am driving home with James, a friend of mine. He is driving and we are chatting about the evening's events. I am looking forward to getting into bed. A red and blue light catches our attention and we realise we are being pulled over. The officer comes over to the window, shining his flash light into the mirror and explains, 'Just a random test.' James is asked to get out of the car and answer some questions. I sit in the passenger seat dealing with an uncommon variation of the itch under the big black patch. The attending officer approaches my window, which I kindly wind down. I had never spoken to a Beverly Hills cop, and am keen to. Then I notice him staring at my face. I cover my embarrassment with a stupid question. Then he too responds with a question, one I didn't want to hear. 'What happened to your face? Why the patch?' He fiddles with his belt, as all policemen in the US tend to do.

'I had a car accident,' I say, almost casually.

'I'm sorry. Was it in London?'

'No, here. Not long ago.'

His face scrunches up, and I can see that he's thinking. I use the time to fight another itch.

'You weren't the passenger in the Ford Mustang convertible on Doheny?' he suddenly blurts.

I feel the blood and excitement rush to my head, almost too fast. 'No. I was the driver,' I stammer. Suddenly we have bonded.

'The driver! Oh my God, we thought you were dead!'

I move forward in my chair, leaning closer towards him, desperate to hear the gory details. 'How do you know this? Were you there?'

'No, I wasn't, but everyone knows about this accident. It was the worst in the area in thirty years.'

I lean back in the chair and am filled with a realisation that I really was in a serious car accident. When it is you that is going through things, sometimes it feels like it is someone else and as many times as you are reminded that it is you, it still doesn't make sense.

I had really down days, and I'm aware that if I hadn't, then there would have been something wrong with me. When I had those days of depression, they were the days that I felt most alive. I thought about all the pain and wondered what it would be like without it. I thought about darkness and felt myself sink lower into myself. I became insecure and self-obsessed and thought that I was the only one that had ever felt like this. It is on days like this that I appreciate beauty and wish that I wouldn't always be so up to the degree that I often skim over the surface of things rather than tunnel in deep. When Mum died, all I did was tunnel deep and, in some ways, those are the days I felt happiest, as I knew myself the best. I was surrounded by the truth of life. The reminder that this moment is all we have. The fact that nothing is permanent, be it good or bad. With so much to do and think about, I sometimes need to close my eyes and be still. This takes time, which I sometimes feel there is not enough of.

I'm sick of all the pains in my head and the anxiety and the shakes and wish they would all go away. How does one describe the journey it takes to the realisation that you are now different and, until you accept that, you will not be happy enough to fulfil your life as it is. I am not saying that you can't do what you have always wanted to do, as that is not true. It is taking me a while to understand what it is my body has been through and what it can take. Some people feel uncomfortable around me, as they don't know how they would have handled my situation or if they were meant to treat me in a different way. Relationships do change and, to begin with, that was very difficult to come to terms with. This is something I had to accept. I don't like being asked all the time if I am all right, and I especially don't like being told what to do. But, sometimes, it's OK and it's necessary to ask for help. I always thought of it as a weakness but now I know that it's not.

My father was arriving the following day and I awaited more doctors' visits and reports on the extent of my damages and whether or not my eye would now fully open and see. A new surgeon has to be found and we have a meeting with Steve Hofflin, Michael Jackson's plastic surgeon, lined up. I am looking forward to my father coming back out, but most of all I am looking forward to seeing Dr Hofflin. I had met him when I was 16 at a function for Matt Monroe, whom my father managed. I had been sitting next to Steve Hofflin at the dinner and he had pulled out a pen and, on a napkin, started to draw me.

'What are you doing?' I asked inquisitively.

'I am showing you how I would make you look like Brooke Shields', he answered, holding up his napkin proudly.

'Actually, I like the way I look as I am', I shyly explained. Now, ironically, I was going to see him about having my face put back together. I hope he still has that napkin. If he can change Michael Jackson's face, then he can change mine. I am positive about this. No doubt in my mind. It is only going to be a matter of when and how much. How much ... I hadn't thought about that. Something to ask George Stanbury.

My father is staying at the Beverly Hilton Hotel and Kathy picks me up to take me to him as soon as he arrives. Because it is so hot outside, my head is particularly sweaty and irritated. My scar is very sensitive and still bleeds occasionally. I suppose my picking at it doesn't help. I am glad my father is here for support as I have many important appointments lined up and I'm tired. My eyelid has opened a little more and Dr Kalb is to see me in a few days. When I see my father, I can tell he is anxious and very angry about what has happened. I would feel the same if someone had caused him to have this much pain and change to adapt to. I am aware of the pain my life is having on others, and I feel guilty. The good news is that Jason called me today.

At dinner that night, Dad asks how I am but brushes the surface lightly. This hurts my feelings but I'm growing more accustomed to it. I make myself look at it from his eyes and feel what he must have been feeling. *Why did I feel I had to do this? I don't know.* I seem so concerned with how everyone else is dealing with the situation and so forgot that I am the one going through it.

Steve Hofflin is also staying at the Beverly Hilton, as he is there to attend a business convention. We meet with him in his room where he and his wife greet us with smiles and warm hugs. The luxurious room is calming, with the pastel quilts and matching blinds. A bottle of champagne is being iced and four glasses are set next to a small bowl of cashew nuts. This will be for our celebration after the booking of the surgery. I am desperate to get on with the matter at hand but have to be patient as he and my father catch up. Steve's wife is very gentle and talks softly to me about how I am feeling. I tell her of my hope to be better and how difficult it is to live in this way. She nods sympathetically and touches my hand. The room is quiet and Steve looks over to me.

'Why don't you and I go into the bathroom where we can have some privacy and I can look at your face in a bright light?'

I feel apprehensive and anxious about showing him; the embarrassment as I show a new person never seems to get easier. I shoot my father a look of 'wish me luck' and manage a forced smile. I follow Steve, like a dog following its master waiting to be fed. We disappear into the bathroom and he closes the door behind me. I sit on the edge of the bath and look up at him, tears flowing out of my eyes and down my cheeks. The bathroom is offensively bright and the large mirror glares at me, ready to remind me of my ugliness.

'You're a very brave young lady, Louise.' He pauses. 'Now, let me see under the wig and patch.'

As I remove the patch, I free the tears that have been caught underneath it. I remove the wig and put both items by the sink. Dr Hofflin leans forward and rests both hands on my head. It feels like he is touching the depths of my soul as he feels around the nakedness. He pushes the dents and the bumps with his fingertips and feels around the once-broken bones. He lets out a sigh and stands back looking me in the eye. I can feel the tension and tightness of my skin around my eye. I look to him for his opinion.

'I can't do anything with this severe an injury, Louise.'

He raises his hands in a gesture as if to say 'I'm sorry.' I stop breathing, unable to really take in what he's just said.

'What? What do you mean? But you're a plastic surgeon and I know I will be fixed ... You must do it.' I am pleading with him.

'That's exactly it, Louise. I'm a plastic surgeon and I don't do rebuilding.' He takes a moment to think. I am waiting on the edge of the bath for him to change his mind. Please don't make this happen. This can't be real. I can't breathe. I can't breathe. God help me breathe. 'YOU HAVE TO FIX ME,' I want to scream at him.

Then he continues, 'There is one doctor I can suggest. He's the best in his field and, if anyone can help you, it would be him. His name is Dr Kawamoto, and I'll call him and tell him he has to see you as a favour to me. Try not to worry, I'll do the best I can.'

He comforts but unfortunately I don't feel it. I sit in the horror at the possibility of having to live the rest of my life like this. My fingers stroke the hair on the wig nervously, waiting for him to say, 'Just kidding. It's easy. I'll do it tomorrow.' Instead, he looks at me helplessly.

'I'm sorry, Louise. I'm truly sorry. What can I do?' he tries.

'Well, apparently nothing,' I say as I replace my hair, 'but, oh well, life goes on.' I try to brush it off as if what had happened hadn't really happened. I don't want to stand up. I don't want to repeat this news to my father. Then I hear the magical whisper from beside me.

'It's OK.' I stand up.

We come out of the bathroom. I am angry that I can feel my face stinging with the tears that are building up. I will not cry. God, I will not cry. Smile, smile, smile. Daddy's here. My father jumps up from his seat.

'So? What can be done?'

Steve explains the prognosis to him and gets straight on the phone to leave a message for Dr Kawamoto. My father becomes so upset that he can't look at me. He, too, is trying to hide his tears. I still hadn't realised how serious an accident I had had; this helped.

It was a never-ending journey to appointments. The day of my father's departure, we had an appointment with Dr Kalb. I repeated what had happened with Steve Hofflin. He reassures my father and I that he will make sure I'm taken care of. He says I have a strong spirit that has touched him very deeply. I sit in the chair in the examining room and remove the patch and wig. It feels good to get air to my head. Dad sits in the chair on the left and Dr Kalb switches the lights off and approaches me with a tiny torch in his hand. The eye testing begins, starting with my right eye, the seeing and open one. Everything responds, as it should. He stands up from the bent-over position and wanders to the counter where he puts ointment on to a cotton wool pad. Then he returns to me and cleans some of the gunk that has seeped out of the wound on the left eye. The lid opens a little bit more and now the sight test can be done. It is hard to keep what has opened open, as the lid is so tired and heavy.

'OK, Louise, now take your time. I want you to close your right eye and tell me how many fingers I'm holding up,' Dr Kalb instructs. I take a deep breath and continue to follow through with his request. On shutting the right eye, I see a glimmer of blurry light out of the left-hand corner of the eye, the rest is dark. The eye is burning as I am trying to focus. Was that the shadow of a thumb?

'Is that your thumb?' I ask.

'Yes, yes it is,' he cries joyously. My father starts to cry. He cries desperate tears of joy. 'Thank God.' He claps his hands. 'Good girl. Oh, that's great.' He is ecstatic. I feel bad to be the one to deflate their joy but, as the testing continues it becomes apparent that I have lost the vision in that eye, despite my being able to see a tiny bit of light and shadow out of the far top left corner. My father's joy turns to sorrow as Dr Kalb explains what this means and how the optic nerve had been severed. What we could see of the eyeball was mostly white. The eyelid hid the pupil and colouring. Because I am blind, the eye doesn't know to look anywhere and so stayed upward, not moving at all. My initial reaction was, 'OK, so I still have the other eye to see out of, it can't be that bad.'

The day became dark as my vision became only a memory. I was quick to let it go, the loss to me didn't seem as painful as to others. I am still able to see. I have the other eye. I repeat this over and over again. I am in so much shock when I look at the big picture that the loss of vision seems only a small piece.

I think my father was more devastated than I was at this point. My automatic motor inside told me that I was to keep strong as there was a lot more to go through and I couldn't afford to feel down. I try to console my father.

'Dad, it's fine. Please don't be upset. Come on, I have the other one.'

He wasn't satisfied and felt very depressed. I was feeling guilty that my tragedy was making his life more painful. I wanted to resolve the plans he had originally had for me in my life. Dr Kalb explained that, hopefully, with surgery the eye would be able to be brought down. It was another challenge to add to the list.

Dr Kawamoto

'Reach high, for stars lie hidden in your soul.
Dream deep, for every dream precedes the goal.'
Pamela Vaull Starr

I am sitting in the waiting room to Dr Kawamoto's office and peering around the clean and crisp oriental designs. There is another waiting room, which has an oval fish tank as the partition. There are tropically-coloured fish of all shapes and sizes swimming around, stopping every now and then to stare out at the patients staring in. A young girl is on the other side of the glass. She is watching the fish. Her face is disturbing to look at and I wonder if the oval tank is making this so. Her forehead is the size of an entire head, her eyes are popping out it seems, and her mouth is squashed into her chin. It is as though her features are flattened into her delicate head. I wonder if she was born this way. She can't be more than five years old. I think about how I am here and for what reason. I think about how strong I have been and then how I have no one to really talk to about this. I can think about it myself and I can share my pain, but I can't sit down with someone who will make it go away and who truly understands what it is like. My father finds it difficult to look at me and my mother is no longer visible. Kathy is supportive and my friends are there to listen, but who really knows what it is like? I look back to the fish tank at the brave little girl. She knows what it is like.

Kathy rearranges the X-rays we have just picked up from the hospital – all 80 of them. They were a shock to see. Only half my skull is visible, the other half apparently on the road. How unbelievable to consider that this has happened. The sensations in my face are becoming more annoying than before. The little bug-like feelings are spreading and the discomfort is becoming more unbearable. But I can't complain, as it isn't going to go away. And if I complain, then I am going to feel sorry for myself. I have chosen to be strong and to make fun of my situation. This is only easy to do if a mirror is not close by. Only if the pains are not too intense at that moment. Only if my ankle doesn't give way and if my lack of inhibitions aren't getting me into trouble. Only if I haven't walked into a wall or misplaced something and cannot remember ever having it.

I set the kitchen on fire the other day. I was making something in the microwave and didn't see the sparks flying as it was happening to the left of me. My blind-side. Next thing I know, there are smoke and flames, my eye is watering and burning and I feel a strong burning sensation in my nostril. Then I turn to see the appliance in flames. Tired and frustrated, I put it out and then had to sleep for a few hours.

'Louise Ashby?' Terri's voice rings out clearly. She has a head of brilliant red hair and a broad smile, which makes this easier. She stands in the doorway with a vanilla file in her hands and tilts her head to the side. 'Are you ready to come through?' she asks gently. I stand slowly and prepare myself quietly in my head for what may or may not be revealed in the next few minutes. Kathy follows.

After being taken along a narrow corridor, lined with pictures of oriental flowers, we are shown into a bright office. A large brown desk stands alone by the door and a couple of chairs are placed nearby. Kathy and I exchange an apprehensive smile and try to break the tension that has grown between us in the last 30 seconds. 'Are you OK? How is your headache?' she asks.

'Fine. Are you OK?' I say, smiling again. I can feel my humour mechanism trying to surface to make light of the situation and replace the overwhelming feeling of anxiety. Before I have a chance to make a joke or sing a song, two men sweep in and stand in front of us. The smaller oriental man with grey hair and large glasses must be Dr Kawamoto. The other man – Dr Buchman – is twice his size, has a large moustache and looks like he is on leave from the Army.

'You must be Louise,' Dr Kawamoto says, looking at me.

'No, this is Louise,' I say, pointing at Kathy. No laugh. No games. This obviously isn't the time and not the person to be doing it with.

Kathy quickly interrupts my helpless gaze and introduces herself and the large packet of X-rays. Immediately, they are strewn across the desk and both men start talking a language I can't comprehend.

'So, the orbital concave of the ... zygomatic bone fracture ... titanium mesh ...'

I try to add some points to their conversation but, after being ignored, realise it would be best for me to stop. I suddenly feel a tingling sensation in my right leg and, as I try to wiggle my toes, the sensation becomes more stiff. It grows more and more difficult for me to wiggle at all. I turn to Kathy and whisper (so as not to get into trouble with the sergeant), 'I can't move my right leg ... ow ... ow ... OW.'

'Well, stand up and try to walk', Kathy suggests while holding her arm out as support. I stand up and the heavy pain is too much to endure, so my leg causes my body to collapse. I land with a loud thud, hitting my head on the side of Dr Buchman's leg. I lie there embarrassed at my fall and new position. I hear a grunt from Kathy as she is trying to contain the laughter that is desperately trying to explode from her mouth. Nobody moves. The doctors don't flinch. They continue with their prognosis of the X-rays as if I were not in the room. I am being completely ignored and not asked if I am in any pain. I slide across the floor and climb back into my chair, searching for an explanation from Kathy. She leans over, whispering, 'That just shows you how focused they are on the work they have to do. This is a good sign. They didn't even notice ...'

'That is some injury you have, young lady', Dr Kawamoto states, his hand rubbing around his mouth and chin. 'Well', he starts, as he sits down, 'there is a lot of damage and I want you to understand that there is no magic. We can do an operation but I cannot promise you anything. This is not fixable, only improveable'.

Not fixable ... not fixable ... *not fixable*. The words echo through my head. The head I no longer wanted to be a part of. Take me out of this head. I can't contain myself and burst into tears. I am shattered and now the doctors are aware. I can't live a monster for the rest of my life.

Overcharged with the adrenalin of panic. 'But ... But you do this all the time ...' I stutter, sick of bad news.

'Louise, there is a lot of damage here and I'm telling you I'll do my best. We will have to go into your brain again and there is some danger with that. Also there will be more than one surgery.' He pauses and passes me a tissue taken from the strategically placed Kleenex box. 'In the first one we can undo some of the things that have already been done and repair them, take out the metal and put a different kind in and so on. It will take time and patience.'

'I've been patient and I am patient,' I interrupt, 'but I'm an actress and I have to be fixed. This is Hollywood. Monsters are not accepted here. Please, Dr Kawamoto, I don't meant to cry but ...'

Kathy rushes across to comfort me and the doctors sit in uneasy silence. Dr Buchman writes something on a piece of paper and slides it across to Dr Kawamoto who hastily reads it.

'Look at me,' I continue through sobs, 'look at my face.' I tear off the wig and the eye patch and show off my naked head. Kathy sits back down and Dr Kawamoto stands up and signals me to the door.

'Come with me please, Louise,' he says almost sternly. His eyes are sharp and intense. I am made nervous as I stand and walk over to where the door is held open, my mind open and running to what he is going to do or say. I feel like the child who is about to be taken out for a beating. This was my own mind, I know. Growing up, my stepfather told me I was a drama queen. What would he say now? A child who should not be seen and never be heard. I shooed these feelings from my head. This was Dr Kawamoto. What truth was going to come out now? My shoulders grow heavy as I feel the weight of my worries settling in. Suddenly, my mind wanders to sex. I don't know why or where it comes from. I kick myself back to the moment, following the small doctor along the corridor and into a small room. An inspection room. A stool sits waiting for me to place myself on it and Dr Kawamoto picks up a camera and stands directly in front of me.

'What are you doing with the camera?' I ask between sniffles.

'I have to have pictures of your damages before, and then after the operation we will be able to see how much more work needs to be done,' he answers.

'So you mean you can fix me?' I say, gasping for air at the excitement. Again I begin to cry. He looks uncomfortable and fidgety. I find myself in the arms of Dr Kawamoto, being comforted. His arms feel protecting and his words soothing as he explains gently, 'By law, I have to tell you everything, good and bad. You have been through hell,

Louise, and I will do my best. I can't promise perfection but I can promise a try. Now don't tell anyone I hugged you, it will ruin my reputation.'

As I laugh at his joke, I feel all the muscles in my body relax with relief. My neck is suddenly not so stiff and my headache is easier to bear. I feel temporary, not ruined. I would have a chance at my life. An opportunity at a new start.

Now back in the sterile office, with Kathy and Dr Buchman, it is explained that I will have to wait until six months have passed from my previous surgery, which is now already three months ago. The nerve endings and bone work have to settle first and it takes six months for a general anaesthetic to come through your system. It is felt that my body has suffered enough trauma and needs a little rest. Resting has never been my strongest point; sometimes lazy, but never resting.

On the way home, I stare out of the window watching the movement of others in their lives. I wonder what problems they are facing today and if they are using their natural faces to mask their own misery. I can't hide. My misery is the mask.

Legalities

'In a dark time, the eye begins to see.'
Theodore Roethke

George Stanbury is a man of integrity. He is small, he is direct and he is factual. So factual that I find myself drifting. I drift to earlier this morning, opening another bill from the hospital, which I can't afford to pay. I am assured that the doctors will wait. George says we will win the case. The case against who is being determined. To me, it is straightforward. The old man hit me and I bear no grudges but please pay my bills and get me fixed. I haven't looked around for another lawyer. Steve brought George to me so I trust I am in the right hands.

'Cup of tea?' Joanne questions from the shaded doorway.

'Mmmn, yes, that would be lovely.'

'Strawberry OK?'

'Great. Thanks, Joanne.' She turns to leave, shifting her pregnant belly around. I look back to George who is studying documents. There are no blinds on the floor-to-ceiling windows, making the room full with the light and warmth from the sun. Too warm. I wipe away drips of sweat creeping from beneath my wig and raise the hideous black eye patch so as to release some of the pressure. My knuckle knocks on some of the rebuilt sharp bone around my eye, probably causing a new bruise to form.

'So ... oh, hold on one second,' he starts, holding up his skinny index finger. 'OK, there we are.' The papers are pushed to the side as he rests both his arms on to the table and leans in toward me. 'How are you?' His eyes meet mine. They are soft, which makes it easier for me to trust him and be honest in my response. Joanne reappears and places down the strawberry tea with, ugh, milk in it. I smile falsely.

'Ooooh, milky tea. Great!'

It is hard to believe what I am suddenly involved in. My life is now very serious and I realise how much it means to me. George has found the previous owner of the Ford Mustang I was driving and they have done an interview. The information she had provided was crucial to my case against Midway Ford and also explained why I was so badly damaged but Charlotte wasn't.

'Before I tell you what we've discovered, I need you to tell me whatever you can remember about the day you and your father purchased the Mustang. Now take your time and if you need to stop, just let me know', he soothes.

I twist my neck to the right and as far to the left as I can to relieve some of the knots and stiffness. My memory of the weeks before the accident is vague, so I close my eyes and take myself back as far as I can.

'Well', I begin, taking a sip of my milky tea, 'it was early September and my father was in town on business. He told me he wanted to help me buy a car. I had it set in my mind that I wanted a convertible and, even though he fought the idea, I was adamant. We were having lunch with a friend of his from Australia and explained our plans for that afternoon. We asked him if he knew where the dealerships were located. He offered that a very good friend of his worked at a dealership in Hollywood called Midway Ford. He told us her name was Judy, made a phone call and later that day my father and I were sitting in front of a very large, bubbly and freckly-faced Judy making enquiries. I was fidgety and kept looking out of the window into the lot where all the cars were. One in particular. It was the black Ford Mustang convertible.

'"How much is that one?" I interrupted pointing to the car. The sales person laughed and looked at my father. "It looks like your daughter already knows what she wants." He sighed and turned his head to look at the car. I had $10,000 to spend on a car and, when she told me it was $9,500, I was already outside standing by my choice. It was perfect.

'The top was down and it had a light grey interior. I asked if I could sit in it and, only moments later, I was handed a key and told I could take it for a test drive. I had been driving a rental until then and so knew the way Californians drove and which side of the road to be on. When I sat in the driver's seat, it felt a little strange as the seat didn't feel straight. It was a little tilted to the right. What I mean is that the left side was more forward. When I put the belt on it would not pull tight and hung loosely in front!

'Did you say anything to whoever gave you the key?' George asked while taking notes.

'Well, no, not at that point. I wanted to enjoy my drive and chose to ignore my discoveries. It felt great driving with the top down and my excitement at finding this affordable car was hard to hide. When I pulled into the lot on my return, my father was standing by a red, regular-looking car with a hard-top roof and asking questions about it to the sales person. I waltzed over and announced that I wanted the car I'd been driving. The woman laughed again and looked at my father saying, "As I said, she knows what she wants." He was bemused but knew I wasn't going to be talked out of it. Once inside, we started asking questions about the car and its history. I didn't want to let on about the seat flaw and belt and so asked a question that would give me the answer if there was anything to worry about.

'"Has the car been in any previous accidents?"

'"No it hasn't," she replied. "The previous owner was moving to another state as far as I remember." There was my answer. No problem and nothing to worry about, but I thought I would tell the person who gets the car ready before I leave to see what he could do about sorting out those minor problems, and also the car alarm didn't work, so that needed to be sorted out, too. We asked about insurance and methods of payment, etc. and were taken to another desk where another salesman sat; this was his area of discussion. I filled out lots of paperwork and was given temporary insurance, which lasted for thirty days until the other one came through. We stated that we wanted fully comprehensive insurance, in England this means that if there is an accident, all medical expenses and car damage to your vehicle and any other is covered. It doesn't mean the same in the US and he corrected me by saying, "You mean liability?"

'"Does that cover everything?" I asked.

'"Yes, as I said, for 30 days," was the reply. I trusted all the information I'd been given, and it was arranged that the car would be fixed up and ready for collection in the morning. When I went back the next morning to pick up the car, the seat and the belt and the alarm had not been fixed but I was told to bring it back in the next week and it would be done. That never happened.'

George looked at me with a satisfied smirk. 'Well, Louise, we *have* contacted the previous owner of the car and she didn't move out of state.'

I sit up, eager for him to continue.

'The previous owner and her husband had had two very bad accidents in your car. When they took the Mustang to Midway Ford, the driver's side of the car was crushed and the front bumper needed replacing. The previous owner said it was in really bad shape and was in no way driveable. We have had our expert go and look at your car. The car was severely crushed, primarily in the front and on the front portion of the car. One of the things that our expert has found is that the front lower portion of the bumper of the Mustang has red paint underneath the black paint and that suggests that the bumper has been replaced. Due to this evidence, we feel that we may have what is called a product liability or fraudulent misrepresentation claim.'

I wasn't really clear on what was being said at the time, so I uttered one of California's most frequently asked questions: 'Does this mean we can sue?'

George nodded, 'Yes, and I think we have a strong case against Midway.'

I didn't feel bitter against the man who'd hit me, as I knew he hadn't done so on purpose, but Midway Ford had unashamedly lied to me. I felt cheated of my life and I wanted them to pay for their lie.

'I have spoken to Charlotte about the accident and she has told me what she remembers. I have sent her a two-page statement to sign but she hasn't signed it as her lawyer has told her not to sign a declaration,' George told me.

I can't understand exactly what is being said. Too much information in a short space of time is hard to absorb for me in my present condition. My mind is filling with fog and needs a rest. On observing my despair and confusion, George urges that it isn't a problem and he trusts what she had told him to be true and, if it becomes ultimately necessary for him to act as a witness to testify that

that is what she told him, he would.

George's office is at the top of Doheny and I only live a few blocks away. I walk past the point where my accident occurred. I stare at the palm tree I had apparently hit. I survey the skid marks on the road. No triggers are felt. No memories come rushing back to haunt me. Why can't I remember anything? Would I ever know what really happened and how?

December 1992

Waiting rooms are boring me. I've read all the magazines and studied the paintings surrounding me.

'Louise Ashby? You can come through now.'

We make our way to the examination room. Kathy is making me laugh as she makes up more songs to disguise my pain.

'And then we'll add a drum roll at the beginning to Princess Lou Lou, hair of many colours – look, we'll see what Dr Alessi thinks. He might prefer it without the roll', she babbles.

'I'll prefer what?' Dr Alessi overhears. I don't know how he hears anything with that large helmet contraption clamped to his head. He is following us.

'Nothing – Kathy is being as *mad* as ever', I laugh.

It is a time when I can't do anything on my own. I need help to get to and from places. I need permission to travel and now that my trip to London is planned, I need medication to get me through the flight. I need emergency numbers in case something happens in London. I need sleep to keep my mind from diverting from its mission. I need my doctors around to make me feel safe. I don't want to leave Kathy and certainly not the medical team who are at the end of the phone to quieten any of my concerns. Without all this, I'll feel like a bird thrown from the nest unable to fly. When my mother drove away and left me at boarding school, I felt such a deep panic and aloneness which was riddled with fear, knowing that I couldn't let any of the other girls sense my insecurity. I had to fit in and be popular. This felt the same. I didn't want to lose the place I had in society. A society where everyone had to be perfect and beautiful. Now that I thought about it, I ridiculed it. This is me. I am still who I am and my awareness of the petty expectations forced upon us can lead to misery. If I can accept that, underneath my painful mask, I am still the same person, then it will be easier to be seen.

I have dreamed and dreaded many experiences, but never losing my face. This was one scenario that even my wild imagination didn't touch on. It is the unimaginable, something you read about or see in the movies, not something that is suddenly your life. And now here I am, perched again on a doctor's stool, about to have my jaw stretched. To once again feel his magical hands covered with sticky rubber gloves, pull my mouth open. Then I will have the freezing-cold metal rod shoved up my nostrils to look for some unseeming fluids.

The door clicks shut. My jokes begin. Once again, I am trying to find a way to make my life humorous. Dr Alessi is laughing and Kathy is singing. I am finding ways to make my misery amusing. It works. It stings. It is getting me through the day.

'So you leave on Friday? Day after tomorrow?' Dr Alessi's eyes are electric blue and send me searching for a wedding ring on his finger. I can't see one. How romantic it would be to have an affair with the man who saved my life. No. No. No. I fling myself back to the cold stick in my nose.

'Yes, but I don't arrive in London until Saturday,' I reply with my head uncomfortably forced back.

'And are you travelling alone or with a friend?'

'Actually, I found out that a friend of mine is on the same flight, so I think we're both going to try and get upgraded.' I was able to move my head again now, so quickly twisted away the forming knots.

'Well ... how is your head? OK?' He seems concerned. 'I'll write a letter and give you these prescriptions for the flight. Various types of pills and sprays to be taken at three-hour intervals to help with the pressure build-up in your head. Your friend will help you hopefully. OK?' He searches for an understanding nod.

'Oh, I can't wait, pills and sprays,' I say with sarcasm dripping from each syllable.

'Right ... Right.' He is only half-listening. Dr Alessi stands up firmly, hands Kathy the prescriptions and embraces me quickly. 'Now, take care, have fun and call me if you need to – you're a strong woman and will be just fine.'

A Different Louise in London

'What doesn't kill me makes me stronger.'
Albert Camus

The most beautiful time of day in Los Angeles is just before the sun sets. This is what time it is when George and Tilda drop me at the airport. I stand for one last time and glare at the magical pink brush strokes painted across the electric sky. Beautiful blends of blues and pinks that take my mind away from the apprehension I feel about going home for Christmas.

Joe is easy to find. The 6ft 3in, dark-haired, big-nosed, skinny, aspiring rock star stands with his cases.

'Hey, Joe! Have you been waiting long?' I say as I approach with my dysfunctional airport trolley whose wheels have a mind of their own. The large, over-packed case begins to topple off the edge.

'I'll get it, Lou. Don't worry. Chill, babe.' He bends over awkwardly and retrieves the case from the ground. There is an excited buzz as the crowds check in and prepare for their journeys.

'So, we have been upgraded into first class,' I inform him while spreading my bottles across the table in the departure lounge. 'Now, these are all the pills and sprays you have to help me with.'

'Cool, yeah, cool,' he responds. OK, so his conversation skills seem a little rusty at present. I hope he is going to help me through the flight with more than 'Yeah, yeah.'

'Cool, Lou, cool. I've never flown first class before. Yeah, cool,' Joe declares. His eyes are sharp and he is searching the room. For what I am not sure and I am feeling a little uncomfortable. My wig is irritating me and I'm also now feeling very tired. How am I going to get through the flight without giving my head some breathing space?

The first-class seats are welcoming to my tired, aching body.

'So, what did you get up to last night?' I ask.

'Oh we went to this really cool ...' His head falls forward and he's asleep. As I try to make conversation with Joe and calm my nerves, he drifts away to a far-off place. I lean in gently to peer up at his eyes, through his long greasy hair, to confirm that, yes, Joe is asleep. Passed out and not waking up. I shoot a quick, panicked look down to my medical kit and then back to Joe. 'But, but you promised to help me ...' I want to shake him and bring him back from wherever it is he's just gone. How could he have just fallen asleep in mid-sentence? Was I boring? Does he not like me any more or has he taken something? Oh my God! How have I inconveniently forgotten that Joe is a drug addict? Heroin, smack, whatever it is that makes you fall asleep like he just has. I feel sick and dirty sitting next to him in his state. I want to be taken care of and not to worry about my pills and sprays. Dr Alessi? Dr Kalb? Can't you come with me? Then I'll be safe and won't have to worry about being taken care of. If you are with me, then I won't die.

I signal to the stewardess and explain my emergency. The generous smile is given and the pills are taken away, only to be brought back at the necessary times. Three hours before landing in London, having just settled back into my seat after a stretch, Joe stirs.

'... club with Charlie and then went home,' he mutters, finishing the sentence he had started telling me over six hours ago. I look at him in amazement and unsure whether to tell him that he is 'a fucking junkie' or to smile agreeably and say, 'Oh, that sounds nice,' I choose to close my eyes and ignore him altogether, only speaking again at Heathrow when my bags needed carrying.

The news that greets me when I arrive with my father at his home in Guildford should have warned me that I was still vulnerable and sensitive. My aunt Ruth helps me to collapse into a cushioned kitchen chair. She has once again repainted the narrow room under my father's strict supervision. The mahogany walls match the kitchen tiles, which match the tablecloth, which match the candles and the fruit bowl filled with mahogany-coloured fruit. Unable to talk, and drowning through the waves of exhaustion, I want desperately to remove myself and disappear for a sleep. My head feels heavy. The wig needs to come off and the eye patch is digging into my eye socket. I need to think. I am unable to smell the delightful aroma of roast lamb in the oven. My favourite. The roast onions, roast potatoes and dessert. I can feel the exhaustion turning to emotion. Ruth is watching me, desperate to have a peek under the mask. I don't feel like showing her now and, without her saying anything, I manage a smile.

'Do you mind if we do that part later?' I lift myself slowly out of my seat and as I reach the door, Ruth says, 'I can't wait for you to meet your dad's new girlfriend.' Quick sip of tea. 'You'll get on so well, especially as you're the same age.'

'I am 22,' I say, stunned, unaware that Dad has a girlfriend.

'I know, and she's an actress, too,' Ruth continues, unaware of the damage being done.

'Except she's a working actress,' my father finishes.

My heart sinks. My face stings. The knife lands deeper than any wound so far. *'Except she's a working actress'* kept going round and round in my head. How unthought-out that statement was. I wanted my mother and I wanted her now. I needed her comforting arms around my pained head, around my shoulders. I needed her whispers that I was being strong. No voices were heard, just those in my head that I was different now and maybe I would never work as an actress again. Maybe I would never look the same. I didn't plan this face, this traumatic experience, and this deformity. It happened one day and now it was my life and, unfortunately for them, theirs too.

I was unable to reconcile my self-consciousness with comfortable reactions. My friends found it hard. My brother Oli tried to be strong but I saw him grimace. My friend Edward said he needed time. Time to accept what had been life-altering for me. My courage appeared as patience and tolerance. Patience with myself and the time it took to prepare myself to see a relative or a friend. Tolerance for the reactions and comments. The love around me is felt deeply and fills me with tremendous gratitude at my choice of companions. Strangers are mostly rude and one night at a bar in Soho, an entire group gathered inside stop talking and stare upon my entrance.

I'm humiliated. I'm hurt. 'WHAT? HAVE YOU NEVER SEEN AN EYE PATCH?' I yell, while my two girlfriends pull me back out on to the street. I knew it wasn't just the eye patch attracting attention. It was the whole façade.

My sister Abi is having a difficult time with her own life. One afternoon, I am visiting her at the house where she lives with my stepfather and his girlfriend. I am not expecting to see him. I was sitting in her spacious bedroom in the basement when I heard the front door shut upstairs. I feel a rush of nerves shiver through me as he shouts out, 'Hello. Is anyone home?'

'I'm down here with Lou,' Abigail shouts back. 'She's back from America.' I haven't seen him since the funeral. There is no acknowledgement her words have been heard. I don't want to see him; it upsets me too much, considering he played such a large role in my upbringing and now we don't talk. I don't want him to see the deformity of my face. I thought if he did he would laugh and say something like, 'Oh good God, look at the state of you!' in his teasing tone. I glare at Abigail and plead, 'I don't want to see him. Please don't let him come down here.' I don't want to be around it again. I notice a door that opens on to the street from her bedroom and I shuffle towards it.

'Louise,' I hear from behind me.

I turn nervously and force a smile. 'Hi, how are you?' I manage.

'Fine.' He turns back to Abigail. 'What are you doing?'

There have been other pains, to be sure. The pain of being tortured by him when things weren't done his way. But this pain somehow seems simple now. In fact, for much of my childhood, I assumed that it was the natural state of things. I'm sure that my stepfather himself, coming from a large Irish family, was brought up with equal severity. I made allowances for that pain. It seemed a proper trade-off for the beautiful house in Wimbledon, the glorious holidays, the gratitude I felt to him up until the divorce treating me as if I were his own. Yet when his face darkened with rage, a pulsing, violent red, and his teeth were clenched like a vice, I was upset. His eyes narrowing, bright with fury.

My real father was a God who swept in for one weekend a month and when he did, the clouds parted and there was light. There was nothing as important to me as making my father proud and feeling the beam of warmth from his gaze. I knew then I was special. Now, his beautiful little girl a frightening apparition, I have lost that soul-sustaining gaze. I am damaged. My image in his mind is shattered like the mirror, whose sheet has slipped to reveal my image beneath, that I dash to pieces on the bathroom floor.

At 14, I witnessed the subsequent separation and divorce that were the first course of my mother's bitter meal. Six years later she died of leukaemia and I lost my best and only true friend.

I've found that change in life comes quickly; the past is too easily taken for granted in the present. My brother and sister are sent to live with my stepfather. Our two homes, in Lymington and London, are sold. Even my possessions are thrown into a vortex of change, transported to my father's home in Guildford. I embraced the change all around me and moved to LA. Only the dreams remain.

The only person who would understand my situation would be someone who had themselves been subjected to a similar fate. My grandmother, my father's mother, while eight months pregnant, had been this person. Grandma Marjorie had been hit by a drunk driver and was thrown through the windscreen, tearing her arm from her body and scarring her face and head. Bitter and unable to talk about her experience, shy of her missing limb, I want to see her. If there were any good to come of my experience, it would be to show her that I knew how she felt facially.

My dad and I drive down to Portsmouth where my grandparents live. 'Your grandmother is thrilled that you're going to see her. If anyone knows how you feel, Louise, it's her. I can't tell you what this means to her. She didn't have the kind of help that you're able to get today,' Dad says.

'I know, Dad. It means a lot to me, too,' I assure.

The house is situated at the end of a cul-de-sac. Grandad is in the lot, doing his gardening. Ruth is helping Grandma make tea when we interrupt. Grandma approaches me with her awkward waddle, not helped by her high shoes. Her dress is silky long and the left sleeve hangs loosely, knowing no other way.

'Hello, Louise, come in, come in,' she greets while studying my face. I feel a little uneasy and reassure myself that this is a person who is allowed to study obtrusively.

'Hello, John,' she continues, 'sit down. Make yourself comfortable. How was the drive? I have made some tea. How's Louise feeling?'

'I'm fine,' I answer for myself.

'Good. Good. You look well. I mean, I can tell you ... well ... let's have some tea and then I'd like to have a look if I can,' she says.

The house feels chilly and I try to stay close to the fireplace. The metal in my head is reacting to the cold weather and therefore becoming cold, causing headaches and dull pains. My right eye is flickering from being tired and irritating me. I feel like the room is jumping up and down. It isn't. Grandma nudges me with her hip. 'Come with me into the bedroom,' she says.

The bed is low down and soft. I feel myself sink into the mattress and I look at the antique dresser with its large mirror. Wedding pictures decorate the shiny surface. Grandma perches on the edge of the mattress like a chicken shaking its behind, readying to sit on its eggs. I feel her anticipation and gently remove my mask. She is not someone to keep waiting. There I am, my head naked and now even colder. She lifts her hand and approaches my wounds. Carefully brushing my bumps and lumps with her fingers. I feel a strange sentiment as I know how spooky it is that we have both got this in common.

'It's remarkable,' she says, wiping an escaping tear from her eye. 'We have the same lumps.' I then raise my hands and ask if I can touch her head. Grandma leans forward and tilts her head. I hesitate a little before approaching. Even though I don't mind having mine touched by her, I feel awkward about touching someone else's. I then remove my eye patch. Grandma doesn't gasp like others do. In fact, she does the opposite which makes me feel that I'm being fussed over and there is nothing wrong with me. This would have been good if it were true. Again she studies.

'Do people stare at you?' she enquires while fingering my rebuilt face.

'All the time,' I answer. 'They stare, they ask questions, they vomit. It's quite shocking to me that some people are so up front.'

She understands. She really knows how I feel. I really knew how she feels. Grandma tells me about her pain and misery over the years. She tells me how she couldn't talk about it and how this has helped. I feel stronger. I feel that my accident has made someone feel better and able to express themselves. I feel that if this was the reason that it happened, then it was OK. I bond with my grandmother that day and every time someone stares or says something rude, I think about her. This was the highlight of my trip to London. It eases my uncomfortable journey. My trying to be normal when I no longer was. It helps with my determination to reach my goal to be fixed.

Glad To Be Me

'Life shrinks or expands in proportion to one's courage.'
Anais Nin

Alone. My itchy couch welcomes my jet-lagged body. The discoloured beige carpet and stained windows speak of innumerable ghostly tenants. The fireplace threatens to throw open its wire netting with its excruciating shriek that never fails to set my teeth on edge. And yet I'm happy. This is my place, my space – all mine. I can be who I am, feel what I feel. Nothing else matters.

England was a headache. Literally. Whether it was the cold, dank weather, the metal that now sculpts my head like internal armour or perhaps the arthritis that has crept up uninvited, I felt awful. Thoughts, half-formulated, crackled like static on an old transistor radio through my tender, throbbing brain. Most of these thoughts were of Mum. Conflicting snatches of memories, aching longings and frustrated resentments.

I lift my hand to scratch cruelly at the thick scar across my head. At least the hair seems to be growing back. Perhaps it will be green or fuschia this time. The alien turn of events in my life leaves open any possibility. Mum's hair had grown back three times during the chemical warfare known as chemotherapy.

During her illness, Mum had insisted that I put my acting career on hold. Money was an issue and during these discussions my dreams bubbled and boiled on the back burner. These thoughts bring tears of self-pity to my eyes, which I quickly and mercilessly flick away. No time for self-pity. Turn on the TV instead ... it works like Valium on my fevered mind. The static evaporates. I wonder if Mum would be proud.

When the phone rings, I gratefully allow technology to take control. The answerphone bridges the gap between wanting to know and choosing to avoid.

'Louise ... it's Dad. Just wanted to know how you're doing and how the flight was. Give me a call. The kids miss you and send their love.' Click.

'Hey, Lou, it's Tilda. What are you doing? Do you want to come and have dinner with Georgie and I? Let us know, we'd love to see you.' Click.

'Lou. Hi. It's Jason.' A flood of relief and something else – excitement? I interrupt him leaving a message. This I had to hear. I now had dinner plans that I was interested in.

When Jason comes to collect me, I'm concerned that my heart, beating frantically as it is, will leap out of my chest and into his arms. He can sense it but has the courtesy to pretend to believe my charade of nonchalance. His choice for dinner, the Cat and Fiddle, is one of Los Angeles' few attempts at a British pub, but of course the perennial sunshine here renders it as false as a movie set.

Jason is downright sexy in that laddish, English public schoolboy way. Messy, mousy brown hair, sleepy chocolate eyes with a cigarette invariably dangling from his lips. A British Mickey Rourke. I am determined that my head, which is pulsating painfully, will not interfere with this ... date. That is what it is, isn't it? A thread of uncertainty crackles through my synapses. Maybe he just wants to be friends. No. Absolutely not. The chemistry between us is unmistakable.

At a back table, a couple of lagers and some fish and chips in front of us, I listen and giggle at all the right times. Rambling on about my trip to London, I trail off, staring at his lips, willing him to lean over and kiss me ...

'Lou, are you OK?' he breaks the spell, worry creasing his brow.

'Yes,' I stutter, caught. 'Why?'

'You just suddenly stopped talking – you looked upset about something,' he misinterprets. The concern on his face is like acid flung on my fragile ego. I manage to laugh it off somehow.

The next thing I know, four hours have vanished into the past. But when I remark, gaily, on the time, Jason panics.

'I've got to get home.'

The bill arrives and, after the briefest of hesitations, I offer to pay my share. He accepts and takes me home. Outside his car, in front of my home, he brushes his lips lightly against mine and fades away. Alone. I trudge up the stairs and try to convince myself that our time together has made me feel better. And it has.

All the silk in China couldn't cover the mirrors that face me at every turn. My little apartment appears shrouded as I have draped every single mirror with sheets and towels. And I tell you now, from the depths of my heart, that all of my considerable strength and will, that intangible quality that overwhelms my loved ones with awe, is nothing in the face of that shiny, polished silver glass. One unsuspecting glance can send my emotions tumbling into the abyss. I am a monster. I say it now with the incredulity of a child that finds their favourite toy shattered and cannot believe that, like Humpty Dumpty, it will not be put together again. No amount of money will act as salve on my wounds. No amount of courage will erase the scars. And even as I paint my brave face on, hide the jagged flesh and affix my lion's badge of courage, I am undone. Because even alone, I remain monstrous to myself.

Sitting now in my apartment on Doheny Drive, my resolve stiffens. I have embraced the unknown before and will do it again. It is my nature. And nothing – not pain, nor death, nor even mirrors – will take my dream away from me. I can feel my mother near me. It was she, I am certain, who whispered survival into my ear during my hours of unconsciousness. I feel her all around me, signs and sighs easily missed but no less real. I plod through this time. I cannot tell you that I busy myself with the work I love because all I can handle is surviving. Moment to moment, trying to find the strength to make it through this. I read every book I can find on healing and self-help. I write to my many distant friends and receive their letters; gifts of support that keep my spirit above water. My phone bills skyrocket and my bank account plummets. But I never hit bottom. Something always comes to me in the darkest hour.

My first day to give blood is here. Needles. Big sharp needles will be stuck into my arm and there will be nowhere for me to go. I will have to sit there. Sit through my terror of the obtrusive metal object stuck into my arm, and think of something else. Craig is the victim I choose to accompany me. The 6ft, blue-eyed creature is as terrified as me. He tries as I do, to make jokes. His hair is growing back at a faster pace than mine. My saviour at the time of my accident who had shaved his head to heal my pain. We sit watching daytime soaps, waiting for my name to be called. I fill out more paperwork and pay another cheque. A cheque, which I am sure, will bounce.

'How are you going to pay for the surgery?' Craig asks, seeing the one eyebrow frown appear.

'Well ... I ... I don't know. I haven't thought about it.' I hesitate, quickly pulling my notebook from my bag to scribble down the new questions for George. The question was added to the bottom of a long list: 'Will taste come back?' 'Do you have to shave my head again?'

My name is called. The sweat appears. I see the door, which leads out of the hospital, and think about how fast I can escape. My entire body trembles as I stand, knowing I cannot run.

'Don't worry, Lou, I'm with you. Just make sure they don't stick any needles into me. OK, Lou?'

The blood-giving room is offensively bright. Blood-filled bottles run across the mantles and shelves, making me nauseous. Could this not be easier or a little fun? My head begins to talk to me. This is silly. I had blood taken four times a morning when I had the accident. Why is this getting to me? Think of something else. Visualise your face as perfect.

'Excuse me.' I clear my throat. 'But ... exactly how long will the ... erm ... needle be in my arm for?'

'About 15 to 20 minutes,' the nurse replies, 'depending on how good the vein is.'

Oh, the *vein*. Of course. How could I forget a word as descriptive of the procedure as the word 'vein'? I begin to clench my fist to make the vein appear quickly so that it will be ready sooner and maybe the blood would run faster. Craig looks at me and starts laughing,

'Lou, what are you doing? She's not ready yet.'

An awkward pause. 'I know. I was just kidding,' I say, embarrassed. Another clipboard is handed to me, with more questions. It wasn't like in the past, when I had nothing to fill out on my medical history. Now I have so many problems that I have to ask for extra paper.

The same questions re-appear in my mind: 'How will you pay for the surgery?' 'How will you pay for the doctors?' I have no money. Not even enough to pay for the parking, I don't think. I want to find a phone and call George and hear that it's going to be OK. No need to worry. I'll be taken care of. No phones. No time. I feel like a train stopping at stations to pick up or drop off until I reach my destination. Each station being an obstacle to overcome. Depending on what decisions I make and what I leave behind will provide another opportunity for me to gain strength from the lesson. I will discard what I no longer need. The damages that are no longer part of me.

While the needle pierces my vein, I worry and dictate questions for Craig to write in my notebook. I know I have to be brave. I have to take charge of my life and understand as many of the circumstances that have happened to me as possible.

As Craig writes, he interrupts my thoughts.

'Whatever happened to Charlotte?' he asks.

'I don't know and it upsets me too much to talk about it. Some say she finds it too hard to see me,' I reply.

Unable to rely on anyone for the strength to get me through, I must be aware of everything happening and come out of the horrible isolation of being sheltered from the facts. And then, in one flash, I'm overwhelmed and my brave thoughts disappear into thin air. I begin to cry. I can't take it all in. My feelings of being overwhelmed are coming from my mouth in spits and hisses. My mind fills with fear and, without my control, is spoken.

'This is fucking bullshit. How long is this needle going to be in my arm?' I squeal. The nurse ignores my cries and leaves the room, shooting Craig a look of 'Control her'. I want to be still. To be silent. But I'm unable to control myself.

'I can't help it!' I look to Craig, pleading for his understanding. 'I really can't fucking help it. It just comes out.'

He sighs and raises his silver eyebrows at me, leaning back into the uncomfortable, red, plastic, cushioned, hospital chair. He clicks the biro, and scribbles more questions into the notebook. These are his questions now. I feel as if I'm drunk and yelling profanities and secrets that I had been sworn to keep hidden. I have no filter and yet I know I am no longer in control. It makes me nervous. I don't want to offend and at the same time it is an honesty to be admired. I find myself amused when I offend as I am in shock at myself. My face tells of my pain and my mouth tells the rest.

My anger and frustration carries the black cloud that rests above my head to George Stanbury's office for our meeting.

'I'm finding it difficult George,' I say.

'Talk to me.'

'This lack of inhibitions thing is making me nervous. I just say things. I can't control myself.'

'OK. Well, let's write this down and ...' and then he is taken away on a whim. A new discovery. Some helpful news to the case. I don't care. I'm tired and angry today. My strawberry tea is placed on the table. Joanne stands waiting for me to make her laugh. It's not in me today. She leaves disappointed.

'Is Charlotte going to sue me?' I blurt. 'I was speaking to a friend of mine and he said that he was sued by someone who was in the car with him when he had a crash.'

I know the answer is 'No'. Charlotte had been a friend for too long. I feel saddened that we haven't had contact. Others reassure me that she is finding it too painful. I have to try and understand it from her side. One day, I hope she knows that she hasn't anything to feel guilty for.

'We have now filed a claim against Midway Ford and Dr Rubin, the driver of the other car.' George hesitates. 'Louise?'

I start to weep. Tears of disappointment. This was not in my plans. I moved here for different reasons, not this. Please would someone take this away? The joke is getting really tiring and very painful. What has my life become, but doctors and lawyers and a hidden face? I am unsure of who I am. I am updating my family and friends on my progress and yet every day I am discovering the difficulties of living disfigured. The accident has made me think that maybe I'm to rethink my life. Are my dreams to be swept away like pebbles in the tide? I know I have to learn from my experiences, otherwise the experience has gone to waste. But I am trying to stay positive for everyone around me and feel that I need someone to tell me that one day I will have my dream.

'I could do horror movies,' I say, 'or *Star Trek*?'

'Louise, are you all right? We could continue this another day.'

The room is silent as George beckons for me to answer. I try to pull myself together, embarrassed that my pillar of strength failed me this time.

'I'm OK.' I wipe away the tears and breathe out my moment of doubt. 'Honestly, I'm fine. It just gets a little tiring staying positive, but I'm OK.'

The seat offers me comfort and heals my painful shoulders for the seconds that I can sit back. I spurt all my dreams out to George, along with all my frustrations and then, before long, he, too, has a tear rolling down his cheek. I am touched.

'I think you should see a therapist. It would be good for you to talk to a professional, someone who can help you collect your thoughts.'

'Maybe you're right.' I reach for my strawberry tea, which gives me relief as it loosens the lump in my dry throat. 'I don't have any money, though, George. I don't even know how I'm going to pay my rent this month. How am I going to pay for the surgery? Does Dr Kawamoto do the same thing the other doctors did?'

The questions pour from my mouth. George gathers all the information, and hands me the number for a psychiatrist. 'I'll find out what I can and, in the meantime, why don't you give Wendy a call? She'll bill the office and we'll pay her when we settle.' He slides around his big oak desk and squeezes my shoulder reassuringly. 'Please get some rest. You've been through a lot.'

Wendy's eyes are magnified to the size of two pieces of kiwi fruit. To my horror, I am seated on a couch. A box of Kleenex close by. Pictures of wild roses. A large wooden dolphin sits on the glass table by Wendy's comfortable chair. Self-help books line the shelves of her bookcase and then a picture of herself smiling sweetly. Sickly sweet. The small, Jewish woman smiles broadly, and asks the correct spelling of my name as she scribbles it into her lined note pad.

'Don't worry. I only write notes in the first session. Just so I have some reference notes,' she says. 'Are you comfortable sitting, or would you like to lie down?'

'Oh no ... no, I'm fine sitting,' I reply. My God, if I lie down there are problems.

'Explain the problem areas to me,' she begins, softening her gaze.

'Well, as you can see, they're in my face,' I say, smiling back at her. She shrieks with laughter, ending with a loud snort.

'I see you're a girl with a sense of humour.'

'Oh good,' I say with a trace of sarcasm.

'And if you can't think of anything funny to say, then don't say anything at all. Do you understand? Only speak when you have a pun.' His face peered down at me, waiting for my whimper.

'What's a pun?' I manage, through fear of not knowing but not wanting to get it wrong.

'It's when you say something funny, dummy.'

'Come on, leave her alone, darling. Let her eat her dinner,' my mother's gentle voice pleads. I was still and sulked. I didn't want my dinner any more.

'Get your ...' WHACK '... elbows off of the table. How many times do I have to tell you?'

'Sorry,' I whimper to my step-father who is teaching me to be funny.

'Are your mother and father still alive, Louise?'

'Em, my father is but my mother died last year,' I reply, suddenly aware of why the box of Kleenex was placed nearby.

'How did she die?' she says while scribbling away. I don't want to talk to someone who scribbles while I remember my mother. I wait for her to bring her head and eyes back to me.

'Leukaemia.'

I was cold and felt very strange that day. Something wasn't right. I sat at my desk and opened the mail as normal, turned on my computer and the switchboard. It was 9.30am and the phones were already going crazy. 'Morning, Louise,' as all were walking into the office. I was very quiet and had an uneasy stomach.

'Ketley, Hayles and Holmes,' I answered into the receiver.

'Hello, darling. How ...' The voice was very faint.

'Mum?'

'I love you.'

'I love you too. Are you OK? Mum?'

The phone went dead. I called someone to cover for me while I went to get permission to leave. Something was wrong, I had to go to the hospital. I got back to the desk to get my bag. Someone said, 'Lou, your mum called but I couldn't hear her very well. I told her you'd call back.'

I called Grandma and told her to get Oli ready to come to the hospital, as he hadn't seen her yet.

'Something is wrong today. He has to come,' I added.

The train took for ever. It was stopping for too long or people were being too slow and had no consideration that I had an emergency, to get out of my way. I was not going to be too late for what I was afraid of and it wasn't going to happen. No way! She was the only person who understood me and loved me more than anyone else. I wasn't an outsider to her and we had been through too much together. No way. I was wrong. It was a false alarm. It doesn't happen just like that with no warning. What was I getting myself wound up about? As usual, I was being over-dramatic. Still, I run up the hill to the hospital and run through the corridors and to her room. I swing open the doors and Grandma and Oli are there, sitting down looking at my mother in the bed. She is ALIVE. Brom, one of Mum's boyfriends, was leaving and I walked out of the room with him.

'Bye Min,' he said throatily, with tears welling up in his eyes. Why was he crying?

I took him aside in the corridor,

'Stop it. It's OK, she's OK, now pull yourself together. Whatever will happen is for the best and she will be out of pain.'

This strength had suddenly entered me and I felt I understood. I put my arms around him and he cried a little and then I told him to get a tissue and be strong for her.

Then I went in. The sky was clear blue and the room was bright from the sun. I sat at the end of her bed and started massaging her feet, and today I didn't mind. It was the one thing I hated doing but not today.

'He came to bury me,' she whispered. 'He came dressed as a caretaker in a big black coat.'

I exchanged looks with Grandma. I knew who she was talking about.

'He came, Louise, he finally came.'

Now that he had seen her, I wondered if he had remorse. Oli seemed detached from what was going on. He was 12. He was in his school uniform and looked so young and delicate. The phone rang. It was my father saying for us to go and meet him in the lobby and then we would get some lunch and then all come up. As Grandma and Oli stood up, Mum mouthed to me, 'I love you.' I squeezed her foot; 'I love you, too.'

When we came back from lunch, she had a doctor and

physiotherapist in with her. Her door was ajar and I could see in. They had her sitting up with her head forward and one of them was holding a tube down her throat. Then she choked. The door shut and an alarm went off. There was chaos everywhere. Everyone who had been doing something somewhere else was running to her room with trays and machines. The alarm was piercing my eardrums. I saw them pushing down on her body with the heart massage machine. The room was going round and round and I started screaming at the top of my voice. This had to stop now. Make it stop now. Don't let her die. I was really, really hot and clinging on to my grandmother screaming. Someone grabbed me and pushed me into a room and locked the door. I screamed louder through crying and was banging on the door. LET ME OUT. GIVE ME MY MUMMY. I panicked. I couldn't breathe fast enough. What was happening? I was in a film. That's right, this is a film and now they are going to come in and say, 'I'm so sorry, but we've lost her.' Well, come on then. Come and say it. I waited but no one came. Now I was tired from crying and still alone. Then the door was opened and my father was standing before me. I heard the door lock behind him.

'She's dead, isn't she?'

'No, but it's not good, Louise.'

I started screaming again in my head. Alone. Alone. Alone.

Oh my God, what am I going to do without her? She's the only one who loves me. Despite the last five years, and those evil medications that had turned her into someone else, she was home to me.

'Louise, I love you and I will take care of you.'

'But you have a new family now and I was only special to her. No one else finds me special like she does.'

'You're wrong, Louise, you are special to me.'

It was all too much. I didn't know what was going on and was struggling to breath through the thick air.

'Come here.' He took me into a big bear hug, his voice was strong but I could tell the pain he was in, too. After a while, a nurse came in and explained that Mum was in Intensive Care which was upstairs and could we go with her as the doctor wanted to see us and explain what was happening. Grandma was there and Oli had been picked up by the mother of a friend, as he didn't need to see all of this and was too young for it. It wasn't fair for him to be around. She wouldn't want him to see her like this. He was her baby.

The doctor explained to us privately that Mum was being kept alive by a machine. All her organs were unusable, her lungs were like leather and there was no way she would pull through as nothing in her body could keep her alive unless operated by machinery. He said the next minutes, hours or days should be used for goodbyes.

At the end of the corridor were the doors to Intensive Care, big, cold and closed. This was the end of what we had all gone through as a team. It felt like now we were all separate beings and off-balance, like one body that needs to be aligned in order to go on.

What followed is a blur of memories. Lots of people came to the hospital and lots of hearts were broken on leaving. Mine feeling like the biggest of all. My grandmother was so incredibly brave while her little girl slept through the end of her life. I went into the ICU a few times but it didn't feel like being with my mother at all. The steroids had made her body swell up and there was no movement. I sang to her once as she has always joked about what a terrible voice I have, and when I did her ears twitched. I took it as a sign that she knew what was going on. Nurses were there 24 hours so there was no privacy to say what you wanted out loud, but she knew what I was thinking.

She died on Wednesday, 31 July and took a large part of my heart with her. She left me her strength but took my heart. I will always thank her for the lessons she taught me, however hard they seemed at the time.

It had been the first time I'd talked about my mother's death. I feel relieved and tired from crying. Soaked tissues are clenched in my hands. I don't care that my eye-patch is flung to the side through the wiping of my tears. I don't care if Wendy can see my damages. This is her job, I suppose. But when I look up at her, she can't see. She can't see because she is asleep. The woman had her head tilted and her large kiwi eyes closed as she sleeps through my breakthrough. I don't wake her up. I get up and leave. I take it as a sign that I should keep my pains to myself. I don't go back to Wendy again. I start writing a journal instead.

Sexual Interaction

February 1993

I am realising that my journey isn't only to get from A to B. My journey is inwards. Inside my heart. Inside my soul. I am discovering my faults and what I have hidden from the world with my face. I have woken up to the reality that I am determined to overcome the problems inflicted by my head injury but was I accepting the reality of the permanent damage I'd received? My aches and pains are now suffered throughout each day and sometimes keep me awake at night. My friends offer distractions in the form of parties and dinners out. If I'm tired, I leave in a cab.

I am missing the physical touch of a man. It has been months and I'm wrapped in my cloth of loneliness. When I think about the intimacy I crave, I wonder if I am ready. Could I and should I remove my mask to open my heart? The prospect of the repellent reaction to my appearance gave me the simple 'no', I wasn't ready.

The night I bumped into Matthew was different. My lack of inhibitions was enough without the effect of alcohol, which only intensified my verbal gymnastics.

This night at a party, I stand watching the crowds. The ice soothes my raw lip when I press the glass filled with vodka and cranberry. My nerves are becoming calmed by the liquid, which flows freely down my throat. I can feel myself loosening up and not being so affected by the surrounding view. I have surveyed the party. Beautiful men and beautiful woman. This is Hollywood and my visions confirm that. Platinum hair. Firm, stationary breasts. Men's wandering eyes and then guilty smiles to their girlfriends. I am unique in that no one else there wears an eye-patch. No wigs are spotted. I am in a room of perfection and I stand alone. The questions are still yelled at me through the loud music and high-pitched chatter: 'Why the patch?' 'Is that a wig?' 'What happened to your face?'

The effects of these are not as they used to be. I have, over time, become accustomed to the questions, and to the effect my answers have on the nosey parker. I have their attention as I tell the story and sometimes fabricate the truth to add some humour for my own entertainment. To see if they believe the far-fetched drama. And they do. I tell one helplessly drunken individual that my eye was somewhere at the party and I needed it back. Hours later, I find him searching through closets in a panic. His taste for cocaine has added to his worried frenzy to rescue my vision.

Outside by the pool, the air is refreshing but cold. I place my shawl around my bare shoulders to give me some warmth and comfort. It's a clear night and the Hollywood sign is visible. The smog is held back from the earlier rain. Hollyweird, it had become to me.

'Is that Louise Ashby?' I hear from behind me and, as I turn, see the familiar face of Matthew, a friend from London, for years and years.

'Oh my God, Matthew. What are you doing here?'

'It *is* you!' His face turns to shock as he takes in my new appearance. He falls silent and approaches to hug me, unsure of whether to ask. 'You look ... great', he says.

'Oh, thanks. What do you mean ... considering what I've been through or considering what's been through me?' I laugh trying to make him comfortable.

'Actually, I heard what happened, Lou. I'm sorry.'

His arms hold me tightly and I feel my body relax through his comfort. I could have sunk all the way into his clinch and never woken up.

'I really mean you look great. I always thought you looked great anyway, so ...' I believe him. He seems sincere.

As I sit with him, drinking more than I'm aware of, I speak about

London and my dreams. He listens. We're telling stories and laughing. It is so good to see him. He gets me another drink, and another and another. My words come out faster and then my admissions and profanities. And then to my horror, with no control, I say, 'I find you really attractive.' My stomach tightens as I realise what I've said. It has just come out. No holding back. And now that it is out, I continue. Matthew laughs which only encourages me. I wasn't prepared for his words.

'I'm attracted to you, too.'

I shriek with laughter, 'Yeah right, Quasimodo's sister is damned sexy.'

His face fills with concern. 'Lou, don't put yourself down like that. You're still beautiful. You have more on the inside, don't you see that?'

'Well, I don't see much these days. Just one eye for that.' I laugh again. It is painful how I make the jokes about myself in all their transparency, not faintly amusing to Matthew.

'I'm taking you home,' he says, standing and grabbing my arm to help me up.

I flop down on my large couch and rest my head back against the pillows. Matthew disappears into the kitchen and comes back with water. He sits down and I reach for the remote control to switch on the television to add some background noise. I suddenly feel nervous about being alone with him. I feel worried that he might approach me and want to touch my head. I shoo the thoughts away and take a large gulp of water.

'Aaah, that's better,' I shrug.

'Can I see?'

My body suddenly goes stiff. Why has he asked? Why couldn't he be content just the way it was? The uncomfortable feeling flies around my stomach. I feel nauseous and self-conscious and unsure of how to say 'No' without being rude. I don't want him to feel any discomfort. Maybe he would feel more if he saw me, than if he didn't. Should I tell him the truth? Should I let him know that I'm not as confident about it as it may appear?

'Well ...' I hesitate, rubbing my palms together, the sweat warm and sticky. 'Really? I mean it isn't very nice,' I discourage, but it doesn't prompt him to stop pressing his desire. He moves forward until he is so close that I can feel his breath on my face. I swallow and try to pull back. I feel the butterflies in my stomach. His soft hand strokes my uninjured cheek. As he moves to stroke my hair, I stop him with my free hand.

'No. You can't do that. It'll come off, it's a wig,' I whisper, feeling the tension stiffen in my shoulders. He bends his head into mine. I keep panicking that my wig will slip. I can't enjoy his touch as then I might not notice the eye-patch moving. I writhe and squirm, taking different positions to distract his attention from my face. His breath is getting longer and slower as he moves towards my mouth with his. I feel his lips brush mine and then firmly kiss me. My heart beats fast and I feel dizzy as his warmth presses into me. I am taken away by his kiss, but my insecurities about my deformity have surfaced. His hand moves to the elastic of my eye-patch and slowly removes it. I take a risk. I shut my eyes tightly. I don't want to see his reaction.

'Look at me,' he whispers. I open my eyes and he is smiling. We move to the bedroom and I open my heart and I trust him. Despite my monstrosity, he makes me feel beautiful. He is gentle and kind. Our moments of intimacy take away my pains. I forget what has happened. I feel loved and needed. He doesn't seem to care about the lumps and the bumps, the scars and the bruises. The only part of me that matters to him is me. This is enough.

Pained Relationships

'If you knew Louise, she could be falling off a cliff backwards and she wouldn't lose hope; she'd think she was going to grow wings and fly away.'
John Ashby

April 1993

The door clicks shut. Matthew is gone. The few months that we've been seeing each other have offered comfort and given me confidence. The most important man in my life is in Los Angeles to help me get through the next surgery, which is now only days away.

Moments before my father honks the horn of the rental car, I sit down to collect my thoughts. My complacency at the surgery is dissipating and being replaced by fear and anxiety. This week has offered more tension and worry than I would have liked before taking this next step. Dr Kawamoto had wanted to be paid up front. The opposition said 'No', as it would be an admission of guilt. The trustees of my mother's estate came through and advanced me my share. It wasn't a lot. But it was enough to pay for an attempt at giving me my face. I wasn't prepared to hear that I needed more brain surgery. I wasn't prepared for the anaesthetic and more recovery. For the hospital room to resemble my mother's deathbed. All of my energy and determination to take me to the next step seeped out of me now. The time is here and I had failed to think about nerves and pain.

Today, I am going to see the neurologist to talk about my brain surgery and the risks. Dad will be with me. He will hold my hand. A hug will heal me. A bear hug from Dad. Depression is showing its face. This is the first time I can admit to myself that I am not superhuman and I'm scared. I feel that I have to tell someone and I need strength. The walls in my apartment move in towards me, making it hard for me to breathe. I want to scream. Scream for someone to save me. To help me. To take me away from this exhausting ordeal. This inevitable fate. I am learning. I have learnt. That was enough. Now can I please have my life back and wake up and be all right? I am a burden to my friends, to my family. I cry and cry. The tears finally come through. The ones that I have been blocking deep down in my chest. I want to leave now and hide away where I cannot be found. Like I did when I was little. I would pack up my case and run from my mother, even if only to the next street. But I would sit there alone and cry. Cry myself into an exhausted sleep. I wanted them to worry about me. To come looking and prove that they cared. I felt out of place. Like I didn't fit.

And now I'm in my apartment wanting to run again. There is nowhere to go. Nowhere to hide. The tears that I cry aren't just from my accident; they are from past old pains. I can't do this any more. I am tired. I am in a self-piteous funk. I am destroyed. Fuck this pain. This journey. I can't stop crying. What is wrong with me? I want someone to do this for me. Someone to be strong for me.

Doubt had crept into my mind, without knocking first to prepare me to fight. I hadn't the energy to yell abuse and force it away. Instead, I let it stay awhile. I let it whisper stories of 'what ifs'. The depression is slowing me down. I need to rest. I need to sleep. My head is throbbing. The painkillers on my mantlepiece dance in front of my swollen eyes. I stumble to the kitchen and fill a glass with water. Then back to the mantlepiece to open the tinted orange bottle. The large pill is swallowed. My head lightens as the opiate desensitises. I am swimming freely again, no longer sinking. I have been lifted.

My face is still red and swollen from crying when my father honks the horn to take me to see the neurologist. I open the car door and, as I slip into the seat and breathe out a long sigh, my father says, 'What's wrong with you?'

Gratified that he has asked and, in need of his attention, I tell him, 'I really need a hug.' Unbeknownst to me, my father was finding my situation, along with his own life, difficult to put into perspective. Had I been aware, I wouldn't have asked for his arms to comfort me. His tone is angry and his words unfriendly.

'You need a hug? I'm the one that needs a hug. You're strong, Louise.'

'What?'

'I need you to be strong for me.'

'Dad, this is the first time I've reached out. I'm having surgery tomorrow and I'm going to see a brain surgeon to talk about what risks are involved.' I am shaking with rage. My tolerance has run out. 'Stop the car.'

'Louise ...'

'Stop the car,' I scream, my head filling with blood-curdling anger. He doesn't stop the car. He drives without looking over at me. I feel my body trembling with the fury I have been trying to tame. The silence between us is filled with the anxiety and nerves we both feel for the following day.

'I'm scared,' I whisper. He doesn't respond.

It is no surprise that I went into the doctor's office alone. My father sits in the waiting room, silently. Still no words have been exchanged, just grunts. Dr Segal and I meet for the first time. His room feels cold. The older man, with thick, white hair and large spectacles, sits straight down. His lab coat is fastened and 'Dr Segal' is embroidered in blue. The grey walls are bare, only a bright, white strip light across the white ceiling. His manner is cold. He is indifferent to me and only wants the facts. He sticks pins in my head, which I am unable to feel. I glance in the mirror to see that I resemble the *Hellraiser* character with sharp silver pins piercing his face. The numbness in my forehead makes it impossible to feel. I think about my father sitting in the waiting room. I want him to come in and hold my hand. If Mum were here, she would be with me. I can't compare, that isn't fair. The tension comes through the walls like sound waves. I knew I'd lists of questions to ask, only I had left them at home, in my hazy mood this morning.

'Are there any risks tomorrow?' I ask, making sure to say it quietly so as not to disturb him.

'Of course,' he replies, not looking up, continuing to fill out his papers and flick through his book. My entire being shudders. What am I doing here? Help is not offered to me generously today. I have asked twice now and I have been brushed away. My mood is faltering and my patience wearing thin.

'Well, do you think you could tell me what the risks are, please?' My tone gives away my mood.

Still without looking up, 'You could die, be paralysed, or become a vegetable. We are going to be working on your brain so it's not risk free.'

I can't contain myself. I hate today. My body rocks as I cry helplessly. The busy doctor hands me a tissue and stands up. 'Right, if you could come over here, please.'

'*Right, if you could come over here, please.*' I have become a part of their routine. I am someone not to have any emotional contact with. God forbid they say something to make me feel better or to calm my nerves. I am only having BRAIN SURGERY tomorrow and then having my FACE RE-SMASHED. Then I will be in Intensive Care for a day or two to be monitored. The sarcasm is dripping from the words that flick through my mind. Am I being a baby? Is it my fear of death or my fear of being paralysed? Which one is worse for me? The latter to be sure. My fear of death has subsided since the accident. I am now confident that the pains of death are not remembered. My pains from the accident have already gone. The accident was never there. I had left my body for that adventure, that's for sure. I look back at the doctor. He is doing his job. Why would he need to get emotionally involved with every patient? He is there to aid us on our journey of recovery. To rebuild our machinery. To give us another chance of life. I am alone. Only I can find my answers and strength, somewhere inside me. They are there, it has worked before, but I need to be quiet and find them.

A part of me dreaded having to bring my father out of his mood. Was this my job to do when he said he had flown here to support me? I had asked for a hug and had not got one. As with the visit to Wendy, it was another sign for me not to ask for help. I had to go through this alone. My father wasn't interested in hearing my fears and pains. He wanted the strong Louise, the Louise that could help him feel better. It is moments like this that, although making me feel more alone, made me stronger. They made me sit up and realise that if I got depressed, only I would suffer. It wasn't worth it.

'All right, Louise, that's it for today. I'll see you tomorrow. Well, you'll be asleep actually,' Dr Segal said.

'Well, let's *hope* I'm asleep.' Another one of my attempts to lighten the mood is ignored.

'Yes, well, thank you, Louise.' He finishes and closes the door behind me.

Dad is reading a magazine when I walk in. He doesn't look up at me, closes the pages, stands up and walks towards the door. His ignoring me sends me to tears. I follow him out. He says nothing.

'He said I might die tomorrow, or be paralysed or a vegetable.' I attempt to get some acknowledgement. Still absolutely nothing. I am hurting. Why is he doing this to me? What is his problem? Didn't he realise he wasn't the only one who felt pain on this whole planet. 'I'm behind you,' I want to scream. At least look at me. Still nothing. I want to be alone. I can't deal with this the night before my surgery. I am scared.

'What is wrong with you?' I scream. 'I'm the one who's actually having surgery tomorrow, Dad.'

'Come on, Louise, get in the car. I have to get back to the hotel and make some business calls.' He speaks. He didn't know what to say. I am cut inside my heart. The wound bleeds freely as I feel the pain from my father. And now I feel I am being dramatic. The drama queen has surfaced and wants some attention. He couldn't face me or my injuries. It gave him too much pain. Nothing I could do or say would change that. I had hurt him deeper than I could ever have imagined. He couldn't bear to see me go through this.

Later, much later, Dad tried to express his feelings to a friend. 'Well, obviously the situation doesn't go away with Louise; it's still there, she still gets the depressions, she's recently had trauma and it's not something that goes away. I mean, she rings me up in a state of depression from time to time and it upsets me to hear her like that, it's an ongoing situation; it hasn't gone away.

'She has never looked for self-pity, never. I mean, you sometimes think ... well, it's a hard situation to handle for a grown girl. She's handled it admirably.'

At dinner that evening, my father is a different man. He offers his words of support and encouragement for the following day. I am apprehensive and unsure of how I will sleep through the night, knowing that when the alarm clock rings at 4.00am, I will be three hours away from surgery. I get on my knees before crawling into bed and pray to God to have my mother watch over me, to make sure nothing goes wrong. I drift into a sleep ...

I am crying when Abigail finds me in the park. I am sitting in a pool of mud, surrounded by long grass and a playground.

'What's wrong?' she asks.

'I'm scared,' I reply.

She comes over to me and wraps her arms around me. 'Why don't you go and see Mum? She'll help you,' she says.

I look at her with my sad eyes. 'Abi ... Mum's dead.'

'No she's not,' she says, looking at me, baffled. 'I'll take you to her.'

We walk through the park until we get to a long path, which disappears into a hill. At the top of the hill is a building with a deck surrounding it.

'She's up there,' she points.

I follow the path, which then turns into steps. I climb each step feeling exhaustion flood through me. Excitement builds – what if she really is alive? As I reach the top, I turn on to the deck and there, sitting on a bench, smiling at me with a glowing light around her, is Mum. I run over to her and throw myself into her arms.

'I thought you were dead,' I cry, 'I was told you were dead.' I keep crying.

She strokes my head and whispers in my ear, 'No, darling, I never died. I've always been here. You just never looked for me.'

'I'm scared,' I cry, feeling her comfort.

'You're uncomfortable and tired. You've chosen this journey and you shall grow. Take it on with strength and an open heart.'

I close my eyes. I can smell her smell. Feel her warmth. I am safe.

Baby Steps

'Be really whole and all things will come to you.'
Lao-Tzu

The early morning crisp air has thrown me to an alert state, so that when I walk into the hospital, I am wide awake. It's 5.30 in the morning. My nerves are tight, as are my fingers. I will probably never be ready for surgery. Last night's dream has soothed my spinning head a little and I am shocked when I enter my hospital room to find Dr Kalb sitting in a chair, waiting for me. Dr Kalb had suffered a stroke only two months earlier, yet he still felt it necessary to keep his promise and accompany me into my surgery with Dr Kawamoto and the brain surgeon. The room is sterile, and I must remember, temporary. The clothing I am to wear for my operation has been laid on a chair. A cotton, backless gown from which my bare behind will peek out. Surgical fabric booties and the betadine scrub. This bright yellow solution is to be scrubbed around my face, neck and head to disinfect. The nurse helps me with this. I ask for a Valium to calm my nerves and prepare me for the pre-med. Dr Kalb offers his words of wisdom and reassures that he will be watching over me and nothing will go wrong. His presence is not only comforting to me, but also my father. The anaesthesiologist appears in the doorway equipped with IVs and liquid Valium. He pokes my vein and inserts the fluid. I drift into a land of lull and wave goodbye to my father and the doctors.

Dr Kawamoto later offered his thoughts on my impending surgery. 'When I first saw Louise, I thought she had a really devastating injury.

The bones were badly out of position and I put down in my mental notes that she had profound enophthalmos, which is the sinking of the eyeball. It is very, very difficult to correct. On top of that the bones of the eye socket were all displaced.

'When I first saw the CAT scans of Louise, I noticed the damage to the forehead area and that it was displaced downward about 5–7mm. At that time, I realised that we would have to go back into the brain case because there is no way of getting to it and fixing the area. Also, having had the kind of injury Louise had sustained to the brain, we knew there was a lot of scar patchwork there. We knew it was going to be fairly difficult. But nonetheless, that's why I had a neurosurgeon, Dr Segal, come in. He could make the little hole for me so that we could return the pieces of the brain case back to their normal position.

'The operation was around 12 to 16 hours – I can't recall. It was just long enough to get things done. The first part of the operation is called "exploration". Louise had sustained severe trauma to the left forehead and eye socket region resulting in displaced fractures of the forehead, orbit, and cheekbone. The combination was very complex. She had had correction under emergency conditions in the past and the roof of the eye socket was pushed downwards and that, in turn, caused the cheekbone to be pushed downwards and off to the side. Also, there was a large opening present in the floor of the orbit as well as the depression of the orbital wall near the nose. That means that there was a big old hole underneath the eyeball that communicated with the sinus. The hole in the wall by the nose sometimes occurs and is often overlooked so, in essence, Louise had all four walls around the eye socket broken – the one that communicates with the brain, another with the nose, an inferior hole connecting to the sinus in the cheekbone and the temple. The eyeball had sunken down and back. There is a bone that goes from the side of the ear up to the cheekbone and this was crushed backwards and the cheekbone was also crushed backwards. The cheekbone wasn't forward enough. In addition, bones had buckled outward, making the face too wide as well as too far back. That is a bad combination. There were also complaints of feeling the plates and screws in the face from the previous construction.

'What we did was to prepare the entire face and scalp with an antiseptic solution. We sometimes use epinephrine, which is like adrenalin to keep the blood loss down. We used the old scar from the past operation. The scar ran from ear to ear. This allowed us essentially to peel the forehead skin downwards so that we could look at the whole forehead area down to the eye socket. It takes a while, but it is not difficult if you do it all the time. It is sort of like peeling a banana, not as easy but more like peeling an orange [giggle]. When we got to the eye socket rim, we went into the eye socket. Over the bone there is a layer called the periosteum and it is under this layer that we made the dissection in order to see the bone. We started at the top and worked down the side of the eye socket and on to the cheekbone. The skin that was peeled down isn't held back with anything, it just stays down once it is down.

The next thing we did was to make a cut in the inside of the lower eyelid. This was done so Louise wouldn't have any visible scars. Through this cut we are able to look at the floor of the eye socket and see the opening. Once we did that we continued further back until we found a part that was not involved. This stable area is used as our point of reference. It is a dangerous manoeuvre, too, because we go deep into the eye socket and, in this particular case, we went back 40mm. The eye socket itself is only about 45–50mm. This is what we had to do to get the right correction.

Then we made a cut underneath the gum in her mouth on the left side. From all the incisions, we are now able to expose all the bones on the entire left side of Louise's face. We took away all the plates and screws that were previously made and then we isolated the cheekbone out a little bit more. The next thing that happened was that Dr Segal came and made an opening into the brain case. It was a like a little square box at the top left of her forehead. The flesh was all turned down and so he was able to cut the square through the bone. That allowed us to go in and look at the exact position of the bone separating the brain from the eye socket. We saw that it was not in a good position. Louise had what is called a titanium mesh, an artificial material to separate the brain from the eye socket. She actually still has that in there. Now it was easy for me to move the bones back into the right position and rebuild the eye socket.

The next thing I did was to look at the cheekbone. We saw where it was fractured and essentially I recreated the fractures using little special saws. This allowed us to free up the cheekbone completely. We were then able to move the cheekbone back to where it should have been. This is all done from the incisions through the eye and the mouth. We used little plates and screws to hold it together. Then we affixed a little metal plate to connect the front part of the fracture to the eye socket to the back reference point. Then we took a thin shaving of bone from the skullcap to recreate the bones that were missing and we transplanted from the skullcap in to the eye socket to rebuild the eye socket. That bone is now resting on top of that little metal plate. What you end up with is an entirely rebuilt eye socket. We purposely push the eyeball too far upwards and too far forwards, because when the swelling goes down, and the bone heals, the eyeball will go back and settle a little bit.

'We took the bone plate in the forehead and made it more curved and brought it forward to give Louise a rounder forehead. While the neurosurgeon is drilling holes in the brain case, you get what we call sawdust – we save that. We use it as seams between the grafts so it looks smooth. Dr Segal then replaces the bone square in the head and we go ahead and close all the wounds. A dry sterile dressing is placed over the scalp.'

The room is out of focus. I feel nauseous. Oh my God, I'm going to throw up. Where is the nurse? I am pressing the button for the nurse. I'm going to be sick. Too late. Oh my God, it's red, it's blood. There's blood pouring from my mouth. I pass out.

I wake up to yelling in my room. It's Craig and a nurse.

'Why is she lying in a pool of blood?' He is angry.

'Look, sir, I'm doing the best I can. It's change-over time. She's OK.'

I don't feel OK.

'I'm not OK,' I murmur and then more blood spurts from my mouth. I am unsure of what time it is or how long I've been throwing up for. I have a morphine drip and it's making me sicker. My head has a powerful pain delving deep into the bone. I want to die. I can't stand this pain any longer. I'm angry with the nurse. Why can't she take this pain away?

I suddenly rush my hands to my head to check if my short hair has been granted its wish to remain upon my head. I feel bandages and my face has grown four times its normal size. As I press the surface, I hear a squelching sound from under my skin. Craig recoils suddenly.

'Oh, Lou, please don't do that. That's disgusting.'

'What? You mean this?' I say as I repeat the action, still trying through my pain to amuse myself.

When Dr Kawamoto and Dr Buchman come to check on me, I have been awake for a while. The hospital room is floating, as is the inside of my head. The pains are intense. My depression is heavy and bleak. The nurse is irritating me and I have thrown the phone beside my bed across the room to hush the insistent ringing. My body, in essence, is not having a positive reaction to the morphine. The news that my surgery has gone well doesn't please me, it only depresses me that I'd had surgery at all. I feel all my training to be a grateful child has departed and been replaced with a hormonal raging woman. When I move my head, I think it will come crashing to the floor as I can feel the weighted liquids moving around it. This intensifies the nausea, and my pressing on the morphine drip again intensifies it more.

'Oh my goodness. You look like a pumpkin,' Dr Kawamoto laughs, staring down at my swollen bloody head. 'I have never seen that much swelling before,' he says as he approaches me. Upon inspection of my bandaged flesh he states, 'Oh, you have a blood clot in your head. I'll be back in a minute.' He vanishes.

My mouth is dry and my tongue has the tangy fur coating you get after being sick. I see the jug of water by my bed, but the energy it will take to lift my arms to reach it is unthinkable.

I'm sure my face turned the same bleached white as Craig's when I see the size of the needle Dr Kawamoto holds in his hand.

'Craig ...' I stammer,

'I'm sorry, Lou. I just can't stay for this.' He leaves me.

Dr Kawamoto waltzes over to the bed with his foot-long, inch-thick needle. Suddenly, my BCG injection at age 13 seems a walk in the park. The excuses come quickly. The reasons as to why I don't need to be pierced. How I had to leave as I had left something at home. They all came out. Dr Kawamoto points to the morphine button.

'Just press on it, if it gets too much,' he says.

'But wait ...wait ...' I cry, 'where are you putting the needle?' Before I get my answer verbally, the needle is stabbed into my forehead. My left index finger shoots down on to the morphine button and click, click, click. This is unfair. This is not fun. OK, enough now. Dr Kawamoto's other hand pushes down on my forehead, forcing the squishy thick fluid to the area where the syringe is sucking the clot. I sing. I curse. I sweat.

'Oh God ... Oh God ... Oh God ...' I keep repeating.

Dr Kawamoto is finished. 'See you tomorrow,' he says gaily. 'It went well, Louise. You did great.'

'Oh terrific,' I say, exhausted from his visit and bemused by his needles.

To think that we take for granted the normality in our days. We are frivolous with our actions and moans of the trivialities of life and then we are struck down. Something has to wake us up, to give us a nudge and say, 'Haven't you been listening? When are you going to learn?'

Now I am learning and my thoughts wonder what it was I wasn't listening to. What have I been taking for granted? I dream of simplicity. I dream of feeling ice-cold water washing over my face. Cleaning through the pores. Wiping my eyes and smelling the soap that rubs off on the towel. I am different now. I have accepted that and in some sycophantic way I am pleased to have all the attention. To have people ask me what has happened so that I can be interesting to them. To be someone out of the ordinary and have a unique addition to my appearance. No longer just blue eyes and brown hair, but now blue eye, big black patch, scars and bumps, short brown hair and a visible scar from ear to ear where the hair no longer grows.

I want to see how I look now. My father has been to visit and promises me that before the swelling had started, when I was in the recovery room, he had cried as he saw I had been rebuilt to the next stage. I didn't believe him after the nurse held up a portable mirror. Once again, I see a freak. Not sure of how the swelling could ever disappear to reveal a face again, I search for a hole to drain more fluid from. The swelling and bruising hide my features. What is happening to me? I resemble a picture that a small child draws of a face with wiggly outlines and tiny dots for eyes, two black dots for nostrils and a blob for the mouth, the first time pen is put to paper. This is a nightmare. Please, please, please, wake me up.

My relief is my father's attempt to steal a hospital pillow in a bag he had brought in, for me to use when I was sent home. I have to listen for the nurse and when I hear footsteps he runs to the bathroom with a pillow beneath the bag, only to reappear moments later, empty-handed and smiling.

'I did it, Lou, don't you worry. You'll sleep in comfort when you get home.' A nudge and a wink.

I have visitors, which helps my morphine-induced depression. George brings my new friend Alicia, whose already pale complexion turns paler when she sees me and then to sadness as she hands me her gift, a bottle of perfume. I would have lied if George hadn't squealed, 'Alicia, Lou can't smell.' She steps back, embarrassed, as if she had done

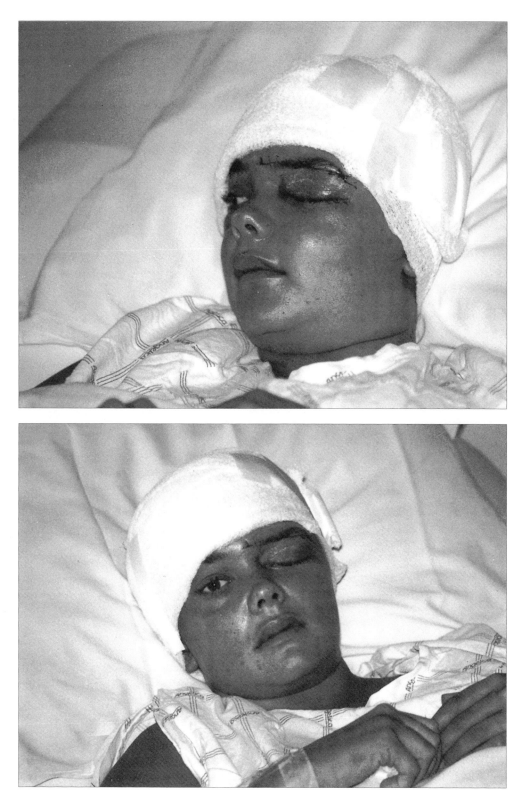

Pictures of me taken soon after the accident: you can see the extensive damage caused to the left side of my face.

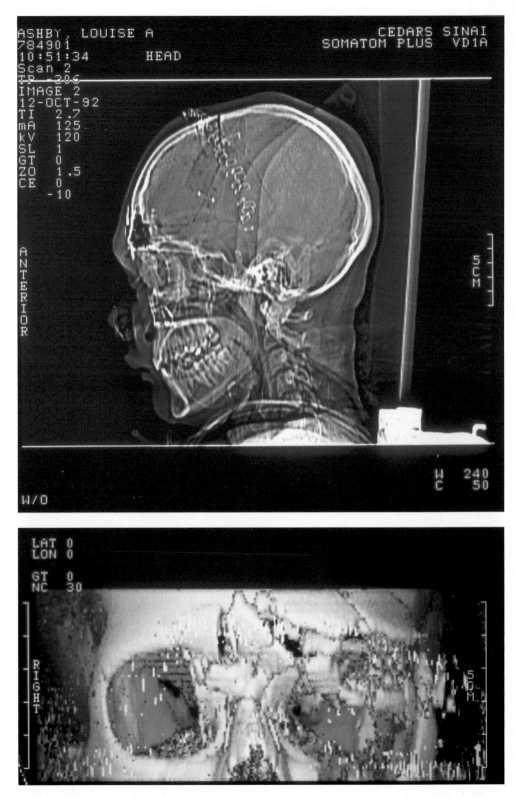

X-rays taken after the accident: notice both the metal in my head and the extensive bone damage to my skull.

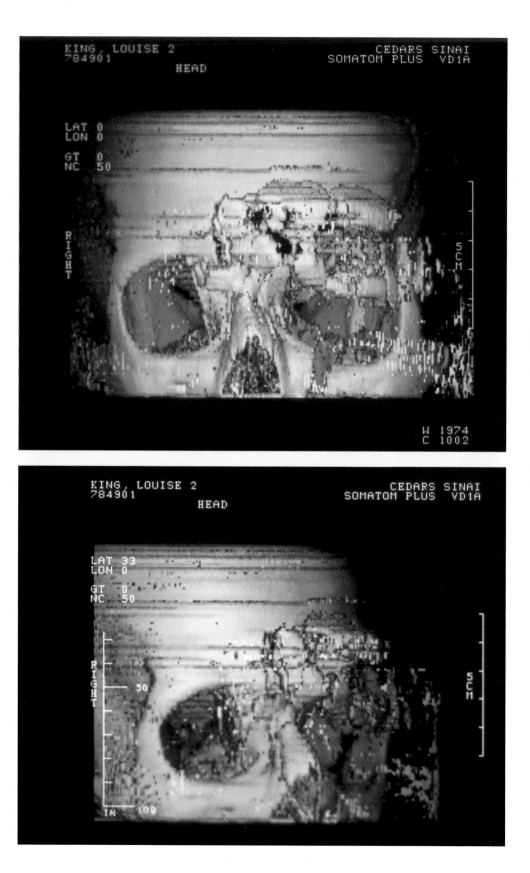

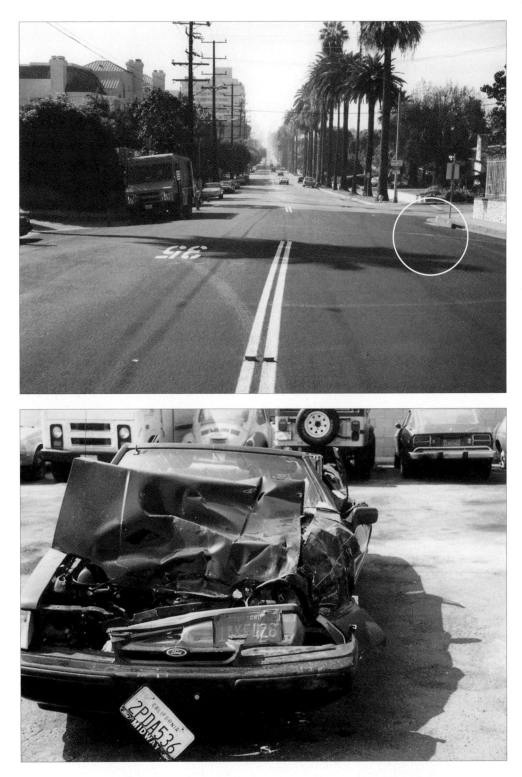

Top left: The stretch of road where the crash took place: I have marked the exact spot.

Below and right: These pictures show the amount of damage done to the car I was driving. City authorities said that it was the worst car accident in the area in thirty years.

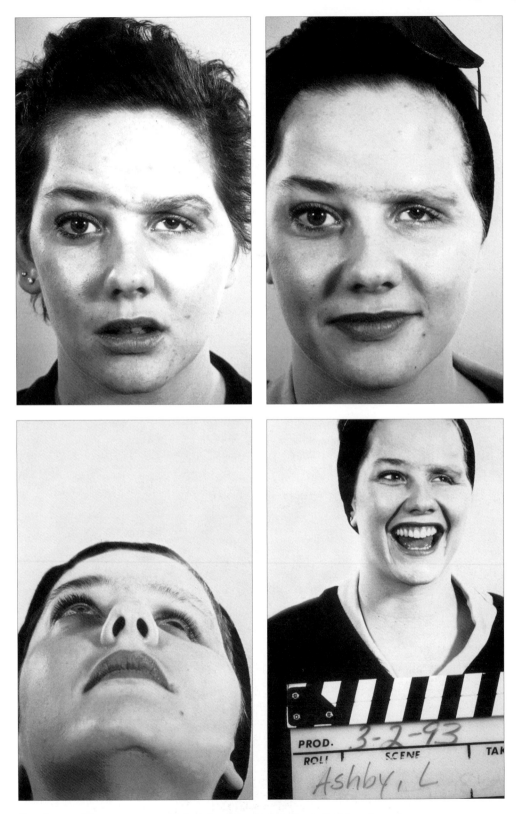

On the road to recovery – notice the scar across the left side of my face.

Top: My birthday in 1996 – there was plenty for me to wish for when I cut the cake that year.

Below: With Alex, my boyfriend throughout a large part of my recovery.

Top: My great friend Jason, who supported me for much of the time after my accident in L.A.

Below Left: Craig Lynn.

Below Right: With Judd, a recent ex-boyfriend.

Top: My home in L.A. from 1994 to 1996.

Below: A night out with friends, (*left to right*), Emma, actor Gabriel Byrne, me and Jimmy.

One of the pictures of me featured in a *Hello* magazine interview.

Top: Kathy Cooper, with her son, Daniel, on his 16th birthday.

Below: Good friends of mine from my life in Hollywood, (*from left to right*), Kate Driver, Minnie Driver and Debra Anderson.

something terrible.

'Oh my God, I'm so sorry. I had no idea.'

I am not good company. I sleep through my moods. On the third day when I look at my face in the mirror, the swelling has hidden itself so well that I am able to see what my new face represents. As subtle as it is, it is a huge relief. The left side no longer caves in. My eye has swollen up and the scar across my eyebrow is covered in dried blood from where Dr Kawamoto had tightened the scar. My eye looks very bruised and is seeping a yellow liquid, like a honeysuckle flower when gently squeezed, although my eye is far from resembling a flower in appearance. What was once referred to as beautiful, large and blue is now nothing but a bruised pustule. The covering of the swelling appears as a boil. Dr Kawamoto says that if the swelling hasn't gone down after I leave the hospital, then he would be forced to stitch the lids together as it would show that my eye was infected. The swelling *would* go down. Now that I had his threat looming over my pumpkin head, I would make sure the swelling disappeared. No doctor would be stitching my eyelids together. Especially having seen the size of the needles that he is prone to using.

The IV is taken out of my arm and my moods stabilise. Now that I can see my improved appearance, I feel positive about going home. I make sure to hide my eye under the bandage as the bruising is still visible and now the liquids from inside have grown into a jelly mould. It looks like something from a horror film. I cannot have Dr Kawamoto see that, and be after me with his monstrous needles. The gowns are taken off and regular clothes are carefully placed over my head to cover my skinny, weak body. As before, I don't want to be fussed over. My mind races to possibilities of finding an agent and working again. My father can see the mayhem inside my head as my lips begin to mutter for a book in which to write lists of things to do. He hushes the voices. The end of surgery number three and time to recoup once again in my small apartment on Doheny drive. I don't want to become depressed at the prospect of recovering and pains and more eye drops and painkillers. One step at a time is the motto that puts my mind at ease.

The day after my return home, to my alarm, I see that my eyelids have turned inside out and now resemble two blood-sucking ticks. Much to my horror and through my screams, a phone call is made to Dr Needle as I now nickname him. I am once again inside Dr Kawamoto's office being held down by my father and Dr Buchman. As fast as I try to run from my fear of the needle, I cannot escape. It is as if I were in a dream, however fast I run, my feet are stuck in thick, gunky glue to the ground. My eye has become infected. Dr Kawamoto is preparing the needle and thread with which he will skilfully stitch my eyelids together. No matter how loud I scream, no ears were willing to bend and offer sympathy and release me. I am trapped and the only words of comfort offered to my shocked nervous system and sweat-soaked paws are, 'Squeeze my hand'. I shake my legs like a spoiled child who can't get her own way. The dentist-like chair is electronically moved back into a satisfactory position for Dr Kawamoto's drudgery.

'Squeeze harder', Dr Buchman yells.

'I hope that's his hand you're squeezing, Louise', my dad jokes.

As numb as Dr Kawamoto tries to make the area around my eye, I feel the needle pierce the top lid and then the lower lid. Pierce, pull thread, pierce, pull thread. The sensation sends shivers through my screaming limbs. Enough. Enough.

'I CAN FEEL IT,' I keep screaming, but no knight in shining armour comes to the rescue. How I would have loved to have been rescued then, to have been thrown on to a beautiful white mare and taken into the life of a princess with no pain or misery. To have a handsome prince look into my two beautiful eyes and say, 'Don't worry, I'll take care of you for ever and ever. No harm will ever come to you.' What a fantasy that was – as if no other woman has had that same fantasy time and time again.

Back to my world of reality where I lie in a chair having pieces of my wounded jelly-like face stitched together. If my mother could see me now. If she could know how much she was needed by my side right now, then she would know how much I loved her. Nothing can replace the touch or words of comfort than a mother. The squeeze on the tips of my toes reminds me that my father is here. He is at the end of the bed doing his best to take away my pain. And then it is done. I am still. My eye is sealed. Another test accomplished. It feels as though my days are filled with medical tests of how much pain and uncomfortability I can and will endure. If God could only lighten up with the uncomfortable pain and provide more jokes for me to amuse myself with, then I might be able to make it through to the next round.

PART TWO
The Gift

Alice laughed. 'There's no use trying,' she
said. 'One can't believe impossible things.'
'I daresay you haven't had much practice,'
said the Queen. 'When I was your age, I always
did it for half-an-hour a day. Why, sometimes,
I've believed as many as six impossible things
before breakfast.'

Through the Looking Glass
Lewis Carroll

Daydream Believer

'Far away there in the sunshine are my highest aspirations.
I may never reach them but I can look up and
see their beauty, believe in them and try to follow them.'
Louisa May Alcott

Autumn 1993

Six months has passed and a new season is beginning. My new life is unfolding and my new face is healing. With that come more strange sensations around my face. The niggling creatures that provide itching and burnings are actually my nerves adjusting and relocating. I am scratching, desperate to get to the bottom of each itch and in doing so have removed my eyebrow twice. Now it is once again re-growing, as is my hair. The wigs are no longer necessary as my hair has grown to a length into which I'm able to weave hair extensions. The extensions have given me more confidence and helped me feel closer to my old appearance. It is a relief to be free from the hot irritations from the wigs. I feel more ready to approach my dreams.

The summer has been spent socialising, obsessing about Jason and when he would make a pass at me and dreaming of my acting career and new face. As time progresses, others are adjusting to my new looks. I am being told to be realistic and think of a career doing something else. These are mostly the words of my father who is trying to shield me from the pain of rejection – rejection being Hollywood's most used word.

I feel it is time to put myself back out there, to start dreaming about the bigger picture again. I am far from fixed but I feel that at this stage in my career, due to my disfigured face, I can do horror movies or perhaps be a series regular on *Star Trek*. I see the faces of my loved ones stifle a laugh when I share this with them. But then when they see that I'm absolutely serious and my determination is resolute, their words of protection ooze out.

I enrol in an acting class, as I feel this is the first step. I have found a teacher in the *Dramalogue*, an actors' newspaper. I circle his advertisement with a big red marker pen and swiftly dial the number. When I feel these whims, I make sure not to look in the unkind mirror and remind myself that my career seems a long way off – will it ever be near again? I have sent out my resumés and headshots to agents. They are my old headshots, the ones in which my face is unscarred. Hollywood is filled with beautiful men and women with dreams of fame and fortune. It is difficult to be noticed, even with your beauty. Here I am, trying to put myself back into the game of feast or famine. I choose to ignore the warnings and forge ahead in the pursuit of my dreams. It's not easy to tell someone who has had a goal from the age of four to put it away. Why should one's appearance hinder one's life? Unfortunately, in our shallow society, it can. But if you believe in yourself, then your belief will outshine the negatives. If I didn't give it a try then I would never know. The feeling of death inside my once creative body would only grow. I would feel cheated and it would be my fault for never having seen if I was realistic or not. Although I have accepted my accident, was I being realistic about my handicaps and disfigurements? I have never seen a leading lady with one eye, which was plain white and too far back. I could feel myself getting angry inside as I thought about how unfair a situation this was to someone whose career relies upon appearance. Still, I mail the submissions and wait to start my first day back in class.

About a week later, I'm called in to see one of the agents to whom I have sent my picture. I had failed to mention in my covering letter, that I didn't look exactly like the picture any more. In fact, I looked *nothing* like the picture. After washing my extensions, and carefully situating my obtrusive black patch across my damaged eye, I prepare myself for persuasion. My black suit is freshly chipper from the dry cleaner's and blends in well with the eye-patch. A crisp, baby-blue shirt is unbuttoned at the top leaving enough room for seduction. I don't need to make time for make-up, as I'm still unable to put anything on my face. Lip gloss. This is my make-up. I can feel the niggling doubt creeping into my mind. Why are you going? What do you think you're going to gain from going on this appointment? Shut up! I have to scream into my jaded head. There is no time for doubt. If there were, I would be dead.

The offices are situated in a cul-de-sac, surrounded by antique shops and fashionable hair salons. The long carpeted stairway leads to a plush marble surrounding. I am greeted by an energetic young man who I realise won't be concerned with my attempts at seduction. I hold out my hand and introduce myself. There is an awkward silence as he gapes at my appearance. Silence. Stare. Silence. Stare. *OK, you can shut your mouth now.*

'I have an appointment,' I say, breaking the quizzical tension. I knew what he was thinking and what he was too embarrassed to say. He ummed and aaahed and checked in his leather appointment book. After I have sat down, he picks up the phone and holding his freshly licked lips as close to the mouthpiece as he can, to try and hide what he is saying. I hear the words, 'You're not going to believe this,' come through his whisper. I feel my nerve failing and have to sit up straighter to try and give myself some courage and confidence. I only need five minutes to tell them my suggestions. I know I can act, my face will be fixed soon. I'd make them feel guilty if they passed judgement on my looks. I am hesitant and the left side of my face starts twitching. It is my nerves. *Please stop. Please stop.* I try to send secret messages to my brain. I moved to LA for a reason. I couldn't let some car accident come between me and my dreams. My fingers play with each other and fiddle and twirl. I glance down at the picture I have brought with me. Was I ridiculous for coming here? No. I had to do this. The assistant replaces the receiver and shoots me a sharp look, almost angry that I'm wasting his time.

'He won't be long,' he says caustically.

'Great. Thanks.' My voice crackles. I clear my throat. He doesn't like that.

The minutes that pass feel like hours. Hours of anxiety. What was I going to say? Please don't make me feel stupid. Don't laugh at my appearance or I'll hurt you. *Breathe, Louise.*

'Louise Ashby. Hi, I'm Jake. Come in, please,' he looks directly at my eye-patch. He can't take his eyes away from my black patch. I follow him into his high-ceilinged office, with thick wooden beams across the arch.

Before he can speak, I begin, 'Look. I know that you're thinking, "Oh my God, she's wearing a patch." The thing is that I had a bad car accident but I'm going to be fixed. I just need an agent to get me working.' I pause, as I notice the disbelief at my words across his face. Again I clear my throat. 'I feel that I would be great in horror movies and also things like *Star Trek.*' I take another pause, as his reaction isn't changing. He still has shock and disbelief written all over his tanned face. I wish I had a tan. I wish I had a face that would look good tanned. Don't go there, Louise. No self-pity today. Not here. Not now. I am feeling very uncomfortable. Sometimes no words are more difficult to deal with than many.

'Louise, when I saw your picture I wanted to bring you in. But ... I don't know how to say this, but ...' he picks up the picture, 'you don't look anything like this picture. I can't help you. Why don't you come back and see me when you're fixed?' Then he stands up and holds out his large, tanned, bony hand.

I am completely mortified. Embarrassed. Humiliated. My feelings of unworthiness and disfigurement, discrimination, everything all comes at me at once. I can't say, 'You'll regret this. One day you'll regret this.' I can't say it, because what if he's right and what if I'm never fixed?

This happens to me twice more, with more words to crush any confidence that I'd tried to conjure up. I feel desperate and my disappointments only make me more determined. I couldn't wait to start class, and then I'd prove myself through my talent.

Simple Minds

'I shut my eyes in order to see.'
Paul Gauguin

With money being an issue and having now moved into a new apartment with my girlfriend Louise Golley, I'd got a part-time job working with Steven. I had been best friends with Louise at Cheltenham Ladies College and, when I bumped into her in a cafeteria in Hollywood, it only seemed logical that we share an apartment. Louise was studying fashion at a college and had originally planned to stay for three months. Now, thanks to my persuasion, she is staying for a year. Apart from having the same names, we have the same sense of humour, which offers great solace when I'm going through my moments of doubt. Still suffering from memory loss, my job with Steven isn't going that well. On occasions he would ask for files, which I explain to him I've never seen, only to be shown them seconds later, where he has seen me set them down. My frustrations are building, my headaches remain heavy and the court case is still being assembled. My doctor's appointments are still frequent and now, to add to my diary, I am starting acting class.

The small theatre space sends shrills of excitement through me when I walk in. The stage has lights beaming down into the centre and props were spotted behind a panel. The other students sit in the carpeted flip seats, with pads of paper in their hands. I giggle to myself as I wonder if they think that my eye-patch is a costume I had brought with me to prepare for a scene. No one asks. No one stares. Why would they? This is Hollywood. Then the tall, grey-haired, thin, brown-eyed teacher enters. He strolls down to the stage like a pelican and then swings around to look at his class. We sit silent. Anticipating his words. Eager to learn and linger on his wisdom. If we had sat any further on the edge of our seats, they would have flipped back to their regular positions.

'This certainly isn't fuckin' New York,' he sighs in a thick Brooklyn accent. He surveys his students. Then he spots me, and my patch. He notices and he makes it apparent to the class that he has. Like a beady-eyed bird he stares and then shuffles his feet. Then he looks back up again. Then down again. The lecture begins. I am inspired and then I'm insulted.

'This is Los Angeles and in Los Angeles people don't have a fuckin' clue how to act. People come here to become stars, not actors. If you want to be actors then you should be in New York.' He is an angry man. My lack of inhibitions kicks in.

'So why are you here then?' I question. Heads turn. Eyes gaze.

'Because there's no fuckin' work in New York,' he says, sharpening his tone. The class are shocked that I have spoken to the teacher in such a way.

'Come down here,' he points to me. I become nervous but try to hide it with a false air of confidence. I have got used to doing that, having gone out in public with my patch, wigs and whatever else. I have had to, with all the comments thrown at me all of the time.

'Sit in the chair,' he says, pulling a wooden chair into the middle of the stage. All eyes are on me. On the ceiling are coloured flags hanging downwards, attached to metal poles. 'What's your name?' he asks.

'Louise,' I reply, now a little hesitant.

'Well, firstly, Louise, you're not going to get anywhere in Hollywood unless you lose weight.'

'Excuse me?'

'Now, you see those flags ... I want you to make them come down by talking to them. Do what you need to do – shout, plead, cry, whatever – just get them down,' he orders.

I'm still upset by the weight comment, as any normal woman would be. He hadn't picked on my face, but my body. I feel sick to my stomach and suddenly want to get as far away from this man as possible. But not wanting to be a baby, I glare at him with my unhidden eye instead.

'Don't glare at *me*, Louise, it's the *flags* you need to get down!' He points up to the ceiling.

Suddenly, flashes of my stepfather's words flew through my mind. My body stiffens and I can't move. My tongue is caught and I can't speak. I begin quivering and have no clue how I'm going to get the damned flags from the ceiling. I am suddenly conscious of every scar and dent on my face. I feel naked and feel that I am being criticised for my facial differences. I feel all my insecurities swimming around the outside of my skin for all to see. I feel the other students' thoughts of pity for me. I don't want their pity. I don't want his criticism. I scream at the ceiling and in my mind see the fucking flags crashing to the stage floor, only just missing my new-found misery.

He picks on me every class. Louise tries to explain to me every week when I return from class that it was because he liked me. I didn't care. It wasn't working and it didn't make me like him. I thought he was a prick. The final straw came when he made jokes about my eye-patch and disfigurements to the class.

'So Louise thinks she's special because she has no mum and now has to wear an eye-patch,' he says. I look at him with disgust. No longer was I affected by his games. I was bored with him and his manipulations. 'Louise thinks that she has been through all the pain that she's ever going to go through in her life. Wouldn't it be great if she put on some weight because, since I told her she was fat, she's now got too fuckin' thin!'

It was true, I had. I had listened to him and gone on a diet and now he said I was too thin.

'Louise, do you think you're a good actress?' he starts again and this time I'd had enough.

I stand up and look at him. 'You know what? I'm sick of you picking on me. I'm sick of hearing about your auditions and how much you hate Los Angeles. I'm sick of hearing you tell us that you know EVERYTHING and I'm sick of your class!'

As soon as I was finished, the class cheered. I couldn't believe it. I didn't leave the class alone that night. Everyone left with me. No one returned to him. In different circumstances I would have stayed and learnt some wonderful lessons, but in this case I was too exhausted from all the other activities in my life. I was drained and tired of the court case meetings. I was stressed out from working and I was being constantly told to slow down. The following day, he called me and said, 'I knew you wouldn't step up to the plate, Louise. I was just testing you because you were the most talented person in that class.'

I laughed at him, 'You know what. I am stepping up to the plate in my life and I don't need your bullshit attitude to teach me how to act. I think I'm doing pretty well.'

I hung up and I've never spoken to him again.

Things To Do

'Toleration is the greatest gift of the mind.'
Helen Keller

My resistance to depression is weakening. Steve and Kathy have decided to divorce and Kathy is moving to Florida. I don't want her to leave. It is true that she has become my surrogate mother, I suppose. I feel safer when she's around and I have become dependent on her. She stayed with me while I had my second surgery with Dr Kawamoto, but then she had to go. The surgery was successful but, as before, exhausting. My face is reshaped and mostly back in place. It wasn't necessary for me to have a brain surgeon present this time. Although I am becoming used to having surgery, my nerves the night before were as on edge as each previous occasion. I couldn't sleep until I had had a Valium to calm me down, and then felt sufficiently drowsy on arriving at the hospital for me not to dwell on the possibilities of death, brain damage, etc. The nausea was bearable, having been prepared from my last operation. My father stayed in London as my surgeries were no longer a novelty, just a part of my new life. My feelings to the new stages my appearance was taking were more matter-of-fact than excited. I felt that I would never be happy, the scars will always be visible, inside and out. I knew there was still a lot of work to be done.

Now, back at home, I can see remnants of the damage but the only physical scars were across my head, covered with hair and across my eyebrow, and the most visible of all was the eye that was too far back, unable to move and mostly white. My head pains are still severe and I know that they will be for most of my life. My memory loss isn't bad, only when I've had too much to drink, which, according to Craig and various others, is most of the time. I feel they are being over-protective and suddenly my life has become an open book for all to comment on. I am completely in love with Jason who is paying a lot of attention to me but not following through. He tells me how attracted he is to me, but then doesn't proceed with his promises. Everything is adding to my mood being flattened. I am finding it more difficult to stay positive. It is taking more energy than I have. I know what my purpose is but I'm forgetting how tiring it is along the way. I need to give myself time to heal, and I'm not good at being patient.

I write out a list of things to do for the week:

- See George to discuss court case
- Find a new Acting Coach
- Accident Reconstruction with exact replica of Ford Mustang (Tilda will come with me)
- Dr Kawamoto for post-op check up
- Physical therapy on back, neck and ankle
- Speak to Dr Kalb about an eye surgeon for operation
- Epilepsy tests for brain – What is going on? Enough please!!!
- Opposition's doctors' tests to affirm my damages; first one, eye doctor in the valley.
- Work for Steven
- Get into bed and never get up

Another exhausting and stressful week ahead. No time to bitch and moan. I have no time for doubt even though it creeps into my mind. I am beginning to feel more alone than ever. I need to write in my journal.

October 16th 1993
I am feeling miserable. I don't feel attractive in any way possible. I hate my hair and my face. I know that if I lose weight I'll feel better about myself and can't stop thinking

about why this has happened to me. I try and try to think of reasons. I know it has taught me a great deal about other people with disabilities but, selfishly, I have days when I can't think like that. I don't feel whole and am fed up with feeling so unhappy about things that have happened in my life. I miss Mum so much and just want to pick up the phone and call her. I want to hear her voice and talk to her. She was my best friend and losing her took away a large part of my heart. I have these days full of confusion when I don't know what I want any more. Why did this happen? Hadn't I been through enough pain in the last four years? Living is tough, and I know I want to succeed, but even that seems to be a doubt in my mind. Why I am thinking like this I don't know. I know I can be so strong and don't like to burden others with my sadness and I am grateful that I had the mother I did and that she gave me such a wonderful upbringing and filled me with love and gave me such a beautiful brother and sister. Mum, I wish you could hear me. I never thought you would die and I hope that I wasn't any added cause to your illness. I love you. Please give me some more strength and help me through this.

As I put the pen down, I hear the front door slam shut and know that Louise is home. This is enough reason not to stay miserable and my journal entry has helped. I open my bedroom door in our rabbit hutch-like apartment, and see her blonde bouncing curls disappearing into her room. I remember the hours she would spend at school with her hair in the heated grips of the curling tongs and then when questioned would say her hair had a natural bounce. As I pass the kitchen mantelpiece, I see a bag of marijuana and some rizlas. What a relief, my misery is solved. I'll have a joint and escape from the pain for a few hours. My heavy head is lightened, as I lie on Louise's bed and tell her of my worries, which I soon begin laughing at. The trauma suddenly feels softened as the tightness from my wretched head is eased with the inhalation of my herbal cigarette. There were so many reasons for me to be depressed that all I can do is laugh. Louise tells me about her day at college as she prepares herself to go out on a date. I watch her apply her make-up. Her face looks beautiful. Her eye make-up sits on her eyelids with ease. Her face is flawless. It has been over a year since

I had any powders or blush or mascara near me. I want to go out on a date. The phone rings and Tilda reminds me why I must stay home and rest.

'Lou, I'll pick you up at 9.30am and then we'll drive over to the valley to do the accident reconstruction,' Tilda's organised voice explains. 'Now, are you all right?'

'I'm fine,' I reassure, 'just a little tired and stoned.'

'Lou, come on, cheer up. I'll be with you tomorrow and then it'll be another thing out of the way.'

She is right. It will be out of the way. I am dreading doing the reconstruction. What if I remember something? What if it makes me too afraid to get into a car again? I can't let my mind take me to that dreaded place.

The accident reconstruction is done in a warehouse. We arrive at the same time as George. Inside the warehouse is a red Ford Mustang convertible. It sends shivers down my spine. I don't want to sit in it and I'm not sure what they're going to ask me to do. I am hoping it'll be painless.

'Your car is in the other warehouse,' George informs me. I wished he hadn't as now I'm obsessing about whether my blood is still covering the windshield. My head fills with images of what it looks like. Who has touched it? Is the Chinese take-away still there? Tilda, who can see my active mind racing, comes over to me and squeezes my hand. An older man approaches us.

'I know this must be very hard for you, Louise. When you're ready, would you please come and get into the car. And if your friend could get into the passenger side, that would really help.'

I feel nauseous. I visually search the car for imperfections. I slowly walk over to it, as if it were a rabid dog. Upon seeing the interior, I flashback to my old car. The radio cassette player. The grey upholstery. The gearstick, the steering wheel. It's all the same as the other. I tug on the driver's seat to see if it's in the correct position. It is. Mine hadn't been. I hesitantly step in and miraculously I am alone and leave the lawyers and mechanics behind. My mind dissolves to the day of my crash. The day my life changed for ever. The blue sky. Running out to my car in the morning to search for my modelling pictures to send to an agent. Only feelings of elation. The roof being down. The smell of the October day. The thoughts of my new life. The excitement for the appointments I am going on that week. And now, here I am in a warehouse, the beast in the next-door room. The reconstruction expert interrupts my thoughts.

'I need you to put the chair in exactly the same place you used to have yours, and if you could arrange the mirrors, too, and the height of your chair. Thanks, Louise, I understand this is hard', he says again.

Yes it is hard but, no, I can't remember anything. I can only guess the positions, but my thoughts are still with my car in the other warehouse.

'Can I go and see my car, George?'

'No'.

It is firm and final and not to be pushed. Tilda has to let me try and position her seating area. Why they thought I would remember the seat fittings when I couldn't remember much of those few weeks, I have no idea. The warehouse is airy and cold and these sensations are rubbing off on me. I can feel myself sinking into a mood of sadness. I want to go home now. I need to sleep. The scar on my head is seeping from the recent surgery and I want to clean it.

I snap, 'I need to leave now'.

George nods his thin head. 'Of course. No problem. Thank you for coming down. I know it was hard for you'.

We cannot leave immediately. There are papers to fill out and signatures to be scrawled. I am feeling the chill from the breeze outside. As I shiver, George nods to Tilda who then takes her cue and we leave.

The following day, I have to return to the valley – this time, alone. I'm given the address and the name of the doctor I'm going to see. The unlucky man is an eye doctor and the opposing lawyers have made the appointment. His job is to assess my damages and make sure they are as bad as my doctors have said. I'm in a filthy mood and can't understand why I have to see more doctors than I already do. I feel this is an open-and-shut case. I feel intruded upon and just want time to recover from my surgery. I feel I'm being called a liar. The taxi alone cost me more than I can afford. The drive gives me time to calm down.

The name of the clinic is posted above the building. I am here. I pay the driver and walk into the spacious waiting area. Brown chairs are dotted around the room, with tables of magazines along each side.

In the middle of the room is a large cubicle where the receptionists sit. They ignore me as I stand waiting to give my name.

'Excuse me. I'm here to see the doctor,' I inform the heavily made-up, voluptuous-looking blonde, possibly awaiting her acting break. She puts her hand up to my face and mouths, 'One minute, madam.' When she hangs up the receiver, she hands me a clipboard with papers of questions. 'If you could sit over there and fill out the forms, then the doctor will see you,' she curls in her thick, rounded accent.

'Actually, I'm here for a court case and I'm sure the doctor knows why he has to see me. I shouldn't have to fill out these forms as I've already done that with my doctors.'

She looks at me with a puzzled expression. 'Could you just fill out the forms?'

'Did you not understand what I just said?' I am irritated and aware I'm being rude, but thanks to my lack of inhibitions I can't control it. Slap. Bang. My attitude is on the table. I want to pull it back and be mysterious.

As I am about to apologise, she says, 'How will you be paying for your visit today?'

'Excuse me?' I pause. 'I'm not paying for my visit today. I just told you I'm here because of a court case.'

I am now agitated. She picks up the phone and tries to tell the person at the other end that I'm being problematic. I spot a pay phone attached to the wall in the far corner. I fumble through my crammed bag and find some change. When George comes to the phone, I scream all my frustrations.

'He doesn't know why I'm here. They've asked me to pay for the visit and I have a clipboard with another 50 sheets of questions to answer. George, I'm really fucking tired, I don't mean to swear but I don't need this right now.' The proto-Madonna in me has surfaced. 'You should be here,' I suggest forcefully. I felt that for 33 per cent of what they could make for this case, someone should be here with me to make sure that I am treated with a little compassion. I'd only had surgery a week ago. I feel like a spoilt brat making demands on her tired parent.

'Let me make some calls and I'll sort something out,' George gushes. I wander back to the front desk and am directed to sit down until the doctor is ready to see me. I wait for over two hours. Now my patience fails me. I am pacing. I am sighing. I want to go home and leave the clinic. Just as my tumultuous mood has got the better of me, my name is called out. A short woman stands in a doorway with a file and a pen in her hands.

'This way, please, Louise,' she says.

Another 45-minute wait of impending doom. I can feel my nerves wriggling around with agitation. The voice in my throat wants to scream out, 'GET A MOVE ON!' I have to kick myself to be quiet. This is an important visit and I have to be kind to the doctor because this is all for my case. Suddenly I feel guilty for something I haven't done. I wasn't lying about my injuries so I should be myself. No need to still the voice. It is hard to sit still. The seat isn't upright; it is tilted a little back for examinations. In front of my face is an eye-test board with the letters of the alphabet forming a triangle, and varying in size. The last two rows are impossible for me to read at all.

When the doctor comes in, I think he's an intern.

'Excuse me, but do you know when the doctor will be in to see me?' I say.

'I am the doctor,' he responds, pulling over a wheeling stool. 'Now. What seems to be the problem?' he asks, apparently unaware why I am here. I feel my blood boiling. If he's Bugs Bunny then I'm Elmer Fudd.

'The lawyers sent me. Don't you know why I'm here?' I add, unfortunately my tone showing, too.

'Yes, I know,' he says, 'But what seems to be the problem?'

'I don't believe this,' I sigh, on the verge of tears and rage.

'OK, look,' he looks down at the papers for confirmation of my name, 'Louise. Cover your right eye and read me the board. Hold on while I turn these lights down.' The little doctor leans over to the light switch and taps it off. He doesn't see the disbelief in my face.

'Read the board?' I repeat.

'Yes, Louise, read the board. Is there a problem?'

I turn to face the board and cover my right eye so that I am able to see absolutely nothing. 'Black. Black. Black,' I read.

Suddenly the lights come on and the doctor frowns. 'Look, I don't know why you're giving me this attitude, Louise, but I'm finding it really tiresome.'

'Because if you knew why I was here, doctor, then you would know that I am blind in my left eye. So I'm not giving you attitude, I'm just blind.'

Visions of him failing my tests and giving rude notes to the lawyers pour into my mind and I realise that I need to make amends and try and explain myself.

'I'm sorry,' I cry, 'this whole thing has just been so hard ...'

He hands me a tissue and scribbles notes in his papers. I explain my damages to him and he hadn't realised the extent of them. He is shocked that I have been sent to see him for an assessment seeing as he is an *optician*.

George accompanies me for my many other tests with the other doctors. New head doctors, brain doctors, eye doctors, ear, nose and throat doctors. I had to visit them all in preparation for the upcoming depositions. We are gathering information and evidence.

Depositions

December 1993

Joanne offers me an excuse to leave George's office and breathe. A cigarette. Today is day number one of my depositions. My father, Charlotte and Steve Cooper have already been deposed. They lasted between two and four hours. Mine, I have been warned, could go on for days. The lawyers have not yet arrived. Neither has the driver of the other car. I will be meeting him. I will be looking into the face of the man whose negligence has caused me so much pain. And yet he is not to blame and be cursed. It was a mistake, an accident, exactly that.

I am dressed casually. I had thought this morning that I might dress in rags for sympathy but then, upon looking in the mirror, realised the pointlessness of this exercise. There were pictures. The ones of me before the accident were enough. I'm a little apprehensive, not sure of what to expect from the day's proceedings. A cigarette, I hoped, would calm my nerves.

As we reach the door to the hallway, I turn to Joanne who is looking for her lighter frantically in her pocket. I turn the handle and pull the door open in preparation for our exit. There, in front of me, is a small old man. I don't need to be told who he is. We stand there. We stare at each other. His eyes are large, tired and brown, like a big sleepy dog. They fill with tears as he looks at my one open eye. A suited man stands beside him. A lawyer. He tries to prod the old man towards the open door. He doesn't move. He continues looking up at me. I feel uneasy and not sure of what to do. Then Joanne appears and she, too, is silent. The four of us are now silent and uncomfortable. I open the door a little wider and signal to the old man to come through. As he stands in front of me, he bows his head and then slowly looks up again and says, 'I'm sorry.' Before I can reply, the suited man has pushed him through and they are gone.

My body shudders as I realise who I have just met. I have no recollection of meeting him that fateful night. I don't remember his car or his old face.

'How about that cigarette?' Joanne says to break the awkward silence.

'Oh ... yes.'

Thankfully, the old man is not in the deposition with me. I sit at the long table surrounded by suited men. George and I are sitting together on one side of the table. To the left of me there is a certified short-hand reporter. Then there are the three lawyers. Today's proceedings, I am told, are going to be for Midway Ford.

'Good morning. Would you please give us your full name for the record,' suit one asks.

'Louise Frances Ashby,' I respond, feeling a wave of excitement at how serious everything is. I felt this same wave at my mother's funeral as they brought her casket down the aisle in the church. I had turned to look at it and I felt like I was in a film. I wasn't able to feel the reality of the situation.

'What is your present home address?'

Answer.

'How long have you lived there?'

These mundane questions grew tedious. They lasted, it seemed, for ever. They started with 'Where do you live?' And went on to, 'Tell us about the first few weeks spent in Los Angeles.'

I could hardly remember what I had done in my first few weeks because my memory damage had erased that period of time from my mind. The time was going quickly and when I look at my watch, I have already been sitting at the table for three hours.

'When had you first done any work in England?' is the question that takes me back to how my life was when I felt my dreams were reachable.

'Well, ever since I was a kid I did commercials. The first commercial I did was when I was 18 months old in Australia. I was the Vegimite kid.'

The images of my baby face, face down in the pot of salty spread, flash in my mind.

'Had you set any kind of parameters for yourself, in terms of you not going beyond a certain time frame if you didn't reach the goal within that time frame?' the suit asks.

'Not at all. Acting is what I've always wanted to do. And I've never seen anything else for me to do. So I wouldn't set myself a time frame, because I can't see anything else for me to do.'

As I say these words, I feel the realisation of what has become of my life. What was I going to do? Agents were rejecting me. My face was going to hinder me. I play with the tissues I had put in my jeans pockets this morning before leaving the house. Now they are wiping away the sorrow from my itchy, wet cheeks.

'Do you need to take a break?' George asks softly.

'No, I'm OK.'

'Louise, I'm sorry. If you wish, we can take a ten-minute break?' the suit says. I have to prove myself to these suits.

'No, really. I just want to get this done,' I say. I am feeling tired from the questions and I'm getting irritable.

I am ready to leave the room when the suit says, 'Have your goals, in terms of a career, changed since the accident?'

'I haven't wanted them to change, but they have been. I wouldn't say they've changed. They've just been taken away from me, is what I would say. Can we take a break now?'

'Of course.'

The break ends and, after a hot cup of tea, I feel rejuvenated. I am ready to return with my brave face and false smile. A smile that hides how I'm really feeling. A smile that leads the suits to believe that I cannot see through their transparency. We sit back down and the questions begin again. Thank goodness for some lawyer tension which had been brewing to add a little excitement.

'Do you have your driver's licence with you today?' the suit asks.

'Yes, I do.'

'I made as many copies as I thought there were going to be here. I didn't realise we were going to have a new participant. I would have made you a copy,' George says politely, handing the copies around the table.

'Then you shouldn't have sued so many people,' the suit says, sending an electric jolt of rage through my veins.

'I haven't sued everyone in this room,' George says, 'and there's an easy way to get out.'

To this, there is no response. I fiddle with my damp tissue. I hadn't thought this was going to be as exhausting as it is. It is depleting, too. Some of the questions are upsetting and bring up some memories that I haven't really wanted to reflect upon at that given moment and in so matter-of-fact a way. The deposition for day number one concludes at 4.55pm and I am shattered. I have been there since 8.30am.

When I get home, Louise is sitting watching a movie. She leaps out of the couch to hug me as I walk in through the door. I feel the agitation in my mind. I am foggy and drained. I can't speak in the order that I want the words to come out. I need to escape from my fraught mind and am not excited about having another day of questions tomorrow.

'I got you something to cheer you up and help you relax,' Louise says, holding up a brown paper bag with a bottle of red wine inside. The scary thing is that, for the first time in my life, I felt I needed the drink. I need to escape from the torment in my brain. With no hesitation, I stomp to the kitchen and reappear holding two large glasses and a corkscrew. Out of the bag comes the wine and a fresh packet of cigarettes. I sit at the kitchen table and lay my head down on the surface while Louise pours the drinks. A large groan comes from my open mouth. My hand flips the patch from my eye and then scratches my head with a strong force to try and awaken any cells that have died from the day.

'Here you are, babe,' she hands over the bloody liquid. I take a sip and feel the bitter solution pass through my throat. I take another and enjoy the sensations in my back as I begin to relax. My shoulders loosen. My frown disappears. A cigarette is lit and another glass poured. Now the day doesn't seem so bad.

'How did it go?' Louise asks.

'Would you mind if I didn't answer any more questions right now?'

I suggest, not wanting to hurt her feelings. Her understanding is so great. I love her even more. I can't answer the phone. I can't speak. We drink. We smoke. We watch movies and I sleep so that I will feel ready for the next day.

Day Two

'Miss Ashby, do you understand that you are still under oath?' begins the following morning. I am well aware and have nothing to lie about. I understand. My understanding is that I am the only one telling the truth. It has been brought to my attention that the dealership is saying that the individual who sold me the car doesn't exist. This news fills me with terror as I think about the prospect of losing the case through this shock news. My bills are around $300,000 so far and I have a mere $10 in my purse. George reassures me that this is to be expected and I shouldn't worry. But I do. The questions resume their intrusive probing into my life and my mistakes.

A lunch break is had. I sit with George and discuss my fears and my life. I see a tear trickle softly down his cheek. I like George. He understands how to fight for one's life. He has overcome cancer. He is healthy again. He is determined to fulfil his dreams. I subsequently learned how George felt about what I was going through.

'Louise was emotional but, in my opinion, not all the time. It was only when she really thought about it and in her deposition when she was asked to remember certain things. Certain pieces of evidence were disclosed to her and that would make her deeply emotional. She might cry, she might just space out or not be able to deal with it. It was hard for her. The uncertainty of how far she would progress, how her face would look, how her eye would look, how that would affect her career, how she was going to pay for all this. How her relationships with family, friends and strangers were going to be given to the brain injury. All of these were issues, which were hard for her. It would be hard for anyone, whether you had a court case or not. The court case made it even more difficult. Their doctors examined Louise quite a lot, which they have an absolute right by our law to do. They sent her to psychologists and one doctor spent two days in his office taking a series of tests designed to identify and quantify the significance of her brain injury. Louise was trying to maintain her acting classes, work a job and go through the uncertainty. It was a hard period.'

★ ★ ★

Once back in the sticky, hot office, I am once again examined.

'Did you activate or turn on the headlights of the Mustang when you got into the car at the Chin Chin restaurant parking lot?'

'I can't remember.'

'Can you actually remember driving out of the parking lot?'

'I can, just ... everything is just patches. I can remember sitting in the car by the second exit. That's all I can remember. I can't remember actually driving.'

'When you reached the area of Sunset Boulevard, were the street lights on?'

'I can't remember,' I say, feeling unhelpful.

'Have you come to a conclusion of where your memory then picks up in terms of you remember being at the exit and then there is a blank spot?'

'Uh huh.'

'Could you please answer with a "yes" or a "no", not a "Uh huh" as the court reporter cannot understand that?'

'Uh huh, I mean yes.'

Pause.

'Once you come to the conclusion, what is the next thing you remember?' He taps his pen on the glossy oak table, the tip of the biro, disappearing and then reappearing. I feel like a child who is about to get a beating if she can't remember. I am trying. My head is static. Remember, Louise. Come on, remember. How can I remember a time in my life that has been eradicated from my mind? I could be here for months. Suddenly, a thought. A remembrance.

'The next thing I remember is waking up in Intensive Care, with my father, and one of my best friends was there from England. Maybe one of the doctors, too. I remember waking up and noticing all of the machines attached to me and all the injuries. I think it was about three days after the accident. Two or three days.'

Day number two proves to be more pressure and more in-depth questions than day one. This doesn't lead me to believe that day number three is going to get any better. The questions are getting more personal and more difficult to answer. My head is irritated as my memory is being tested. I feel stupid, unable to answer simple questions. I study the opposing lawyers and know what they must be thinking. 'What a stupid girl. Poor thing. I mean, she looks funny and, to add to it, she can't string a sentence together.' Either that or 'Liar.'

Day Three

'Do you keep a diary?'

'Yes, I do.'

'Could you describe it for me?'

'It's a small, little grey, blank-page book with a black elastic strap around the outside,' I reply, feeling edgy as to why he wants to know about my diary.

'Do you have any other diaries?'

'Yes, I have a total of four.'

'We will likely ask for them. I want you to retain those. Don't throw them out.'

'But you can't read them,' I say quickly, protectively.

'The court may decide that.'

I hate him. How dare he tell me what to do with my private belongings. I haven't done anything wrong except pick up a friend who had the 'flu and needed some attention. Now my life has changed because some old man possibly hadn't resat his driving test, perhaps failed to realise he had night blindness and has taken away my face. Now they felt they had every right to read my private diaries. I was opening my mouth to yell and scream when I feel a sharp nudge at my ankle. I close my mouth and whisper my anger into my head where no one else can hear.

'How frequently have you made entries in this lined-page book diary that you have written your feelings in this year?'

'When I have been really, really down,' I sigh, feeling the heavy mood showing its face to me once again. I feel tired and sad. Sad that my feelings are being questioned along with my life's goals and decisions. They wanted to know about Mum and how she had died. How long was she sick for? Did I take good care of her? I question the relevance of this.

'And can you elaborate on what sorts of things you would write in there? I know you mentioned your feelings,' he continues.

'How I have come to terms with what is going on.'

I can feel my patience failing. I am getting anxious that at any moment my lack of inhibitions are going to lead me to tell this scrawny, ugly man exactly what I think of him.

'Do you want to take a break?' George asks kindly. My saviour has spoken. But I don't want to take a break. I want to answer their questions and go home to my bottle of red wine and packet of cigarettes.

'No. I'm all right,' I nod gently.

The afternoon continues with more confusion. The questions are coming faster and harder. The intent, it seems, is to make me struggle and then say something I don't mean to say. It begins working as I am being questioned about the day I bought the car. Some of the people they are describing at the dealership, I have never heard of and had no recollection of ever meeting.

'I object to the question as argumentative and instruct her not to answer. She responded to your question as best she could by telling you what she told you,' George steps in to ease the pressure.

My answers have started coming out as 'But ... what? Sorry.' I can feel the recently opened scar seeping, and I search for a tissue to wipe away the hot, sticky pus that is making its way across my scalp and into my hair.

'I want to go over with you, and I know this is going to be difficult for you, but with some specificity your injuries from this accident. And I will ask you to start at your toes and work up your body.'

My ankle alone took 40 minutes to discuss. My foot is elevated on a chair and the table of suits discuss it. The texture. The scars on it and at which point in my life, those scars had arrived. The movement.

I tell them about the stomach cramps, the bruises on my ribs, the tubes that have left scars from being in my chest.

'When you talk about the shooting pains, starting in the neck, do they tend to be on one side or the other or right in the middle?' he asks, with his pen poised at his notebook. Notes are being taken. I answer. I tell them of the numbness and tingling in my arms. The cramps in my neck, starting at the base of my skull, the spasms, and the inability to move my head and neck at times because of the pain. I tell them of the pains in my kidneys, my increased menstrual cramps, the haemorrhoids because of all the medication, the foot cramps, my ankle giving way when I run, and many more. As I continue on to the head, I find myself unable to control the tears that are now running down my cheeks.

'Would you like some tissues?' the suit asks, and it seems he is sincere. I hold up my hand with a tear-sodden tissue already torn apart and scrunched up. I am handed a fresh one.

We continue with the loss of smell and taste, and then the loss of inhibitions, which becomes the most interesting of all for the prying lawyers as they cross question things I tell them I have done because of this. I describe every cramp, bump and lump in my face and mouth. I tell them how I chew my top lip until it bleeds, as I have no warning sensation in it. I tell them how I can't breathe through my left nostril. I tell them how my face aches. The bones ache. The metal aches. How when I am cold the metal in my head feels the cold and sends uncomfortable sensations through my head.

Now we are done with the injuries and they want to know how the accident has affected my life emotionally.

'It sounds like from your description of the number of times your father has been here since the accident, he has been supportive in the sense of being present when you are about to undergo a surgical procedure, something like that, being physically present with you?' the suit says.

'Yes, he has been physically present with me.'

I think back to the fight we had prior to my surgery. I think of how painful this has been for my family to endure.

'What I am hearing from you, there is still a tension there because it's difficult for him to deal with what's happened?'

'Yes,' I say. He is my one and only parent and I feel like this accident is causing a bridge of doubt between us. He needs me and I need him. I don't want to talk to these men about my relationships. I don't want them to know about my parents' divorce and then my mother's death.

I panic again when I am asked, 'Was there a boyfriend relationship before the accident that was affected by your involvement in the accident?'

I thought it better to say 'yes' than 'no'. I think that I must mention the romantic exchanges. 'There was just about to be one. Yes, and it was affected.'

'And who was that?' he asks directly.

'Oh, I don't want to say now. It's not important.'

'We won't pass along to him your perception of where things were before,' he persuades.

I hesitate and look at George. He nods his head as if to say, 'Tell them.'

'His name was Jason.'

'And what is his telephone number?' they ask. I try to avoid giving it to them but it is soon spoken from my lips.

'Don't ask him about it, OK?' I say. This would be embarrassing. What would they say to Jason? He would have no idea what they were talking about. I feel ridiculous. What if I had imagined his advances, his flirtations, his interest?

Again, it is 6.00pm and I am finished. My depositions are over. I am empty of any more information. There is nothing more about my life that they could ever need to know. I think every little aspect of my dreams, insecurities, damages and relations with my family and friends has been picked clean. I am done. I'm going home.

Revelations

'This above all: to thine own self be true ...'
William Shakespeare

D̲r Parker wasn't a psychiatrist who would be recommended to just anyone. After asking my lawyers for the hundredth time if they could play me the tape of the police report of the accident, it is suggested that I seek outside help.

'I just want to know what I looked like and how it happened,' I argue. 'Look ... I can't remember it so can't I listen to the gory details?'

'Louise. If you want to hear about it, then why don't you see someone who might be able to help you remember it for yourself? I've seen you getting upset every time we tell you about it. I don't want to do that to you any more,' George soothes.

Dr Parker works out of his house. His home is a small flat situated in East Los Angeles. Junkies surround the park walls, waiting for their next fix. Gunshots are heard in the distance. I feel apprehensive about my visit. How did I know that he wasn't going to fall asleep and humiliate me?

After ringing the rusty buzzer, I am let in. I follow the windy staircase to his psychiatric lair. The room resembles a cluttered office filled with reading material. Dr Parker is an overweight, over-aged hippie. He wears brown cords and a flower power shirt, which had been tightly and, I'm sure with difficulty, stuffed into his belt. His smile is broad and so is the large leather armchair he sits in. I sit across from him and nervously fiddle with my eye-patch.

'I've really been looking forward to meeting you, Louise. I've heard wonderful things about your attitude and recovery,' he says.

'Well, then promise me you won't fall asleep on me,' I say, prompting my explanation of my last encounter with psychiatry. He laughs. I relax. I tell him about the accident and about my mother. He asks about my father. 'Can we talk about that some other time?' I beg.

'Of course,' he agrees. 'Do you have a boyfriend?'

'No. Not really. I mean there is someone I really like and I think he likes me but he hasn't done anything about it. He's called Jason.'

I tell him about all the times Jason has taken me out and how he'd insinuated things but, when it came to the crunch, a light kiss on the lips was all I got. The hour passes quickly and I enjoy myself. I enjoy my sessions with him more as time passes. I begin to unfold my life to this man who listens. I tell him of my fears and my strengths. I tell him of my inability to fully accept my disabilities and damaged appearance. This is what keeps me strong. The knowingness that I will be fixed and attain my dreams. I *will* work again. I *will* take the eye-patch away from where it is now embedded.

It is 6.30am when the loathsome ring from the phone wakes me. Upon hearing Jason's voice through the receiver, I am propelled into a wide-awake state.

'Jason, what's wrong? Is everything all right? It's so early. What's going on?' I stammer, wiping my eyes so that I can see more clearly.

'Well, Lou, I was hoping you could tell me actually,' he says. There is silence.

'What are you talking about, Jas?' I say, a little nervously.

'I got a call from a lawyer this morning at 6.00am telling me that I have to come in and do a deposition for your case. I was hoping you could tell me why, as I'm a little confused as to why they would want to see *me*.'

I don't know what to say. The blood rushes to my cheeks causing a crimson blush. I'm at a loss for words. Nothing will come out to explain my stupidity in mentioning his name in the deposition. Now I'm going to have to come clean and tell him that I think, in some schoolgirl way, that I could be in love with him, or at least I have a huge crush on him and spend endless hours fantasising about how he will finally kiss me.

'Well, erm ... I think that would be because erm ...' I begin, hoping that he will finish the sentence for me. He doesn't. He is waiting. 'Well, they asked me if I was ...' I pause, I wonder how I'm going to say this without feeling stupid and extremely embarrassed. 'OK, I'll say this really quickly. They asked me if I was interested in anyone before the accident and if the accident may have changed any situations at all, and I said you. I'm sorry.' I don't sigh. I don't breathe. I hear a giggle from the other end.

'Jason? Are you laughing at me?'

'Yes, I'm laughing at you. You owe me one, big time, Lou. You better help me out with this then,' he says.

'So you're not mad?'

'No. I'm flattered. You know I feel the same way,' he says, not realising that his sentence has changed my life. I want him to repeat the '... I feel the same way'.

'Well, when do they want to see you?'

'Monday.'

'But today is Friday.'

'Exactly, Louise.'

★ ★ ★

I found myself a little confused when, after Jason's deposition, he shared with me that he'd had to have a stiff drink before going in. Also, he stated firmly that I mustn't read the manuscript. He'd been questioned for seven hours. Seven hours of mental anguish over the life of a woman whom he'd met only the year before. He was suddenly involved in a court case as the lover that never was. When we met to discuss his thoughts, I anticipated his words of love for me.

'What can I get you to drink? Vodka with lime?' he asks, scratching his messy hair around his scalp.

'Yes, please,' I say eagerly. I watch him waltz over to the bar. His slightly overweight and boyish body sends thrills through me as I think of lying next to him naked. How easy it is for my mind to imagine these things with Jason. I light up a cigarette and position myself on the chair, in my seductive way. My most seductive, considering how I felt these days. He was walking back over to the table. My excitement was being contained. The cigarette was being smoked quickly. He sits down. He leans close to me and reaches his arm across my chest for the cigarettes. I giggle and look into his brown eyes anticipating his next move.

'Lou, I need to talk to you,' he begins.

'I know,' I pretend, trying to put out my cigarette and almost setting the dirty ashtray alight. 'Hold on,' I panic, squashing the lit cigarettes into each other. Then I look back at him. I see he is finding my little battle amusing. Then his voice is serious.

'Listen ... when I first met you, I thought you were great. You were funny, good looking and great to hang out with.' He takes a long drag. Too long. I am waiting for the next line. 'Anyway, it was at a time in my life when I was trying to figure some things out. I was seeing someone and she was living in London, as you know. Anyway then you came along and confused things.'

I couldn't say anything. I didn't want to breathe in case I missed something. What was the punchline? Where was this going?

'Anyway, Lou. My point is, and this is really hard for me to say as I do have feelings for you, and if I were going to be with any woman it would be you. The thing is, Lou ... oh, how do I do this? I'm gay.'

Silence.

Silence. Silence. Silence. Complete embarrassment. Humiliation. World shattered. Devastation. OH MY GOD!

'I know,' I say. I didn't know what else to say to hide my humiliation. All the evenings I had thought about nothing more than Jason. All the hours I had fantasised about our first kiss. Our children. It was all gone. Taken away with a quick gust of wind.

'You know?'

'Well, yes. I kind of guessed a while ago. I just thought it was a little strange after all the things you'd been saying to me and then you not following through with them.'

I had no idea where all my words were coming from but wherever it was, it was working. He smiled at me.

'Unbelievable. And here I've been, stressing out about telling you as I have these feelings for you and I am attracted to you, and you knew. I can't believe it.'

I almost went as far as to tell him I was a lesbian, to make him feel more comfortable. Then I decided I probably don't need to go that far. I look at him. I stare at him. The mouth that is not interested in kissing me but someone else. Someone of his same sex. Wow. He didn't seem gay at all. Jason was a lad. How did this happen? All of a sudden, I was a naïve child arguing with the new rules that had been laid down.

'Is there anything you want to ask me?' Jason asks kindly, concerned.

'Are you ever going to fancy the same guys as me? Will you ever steal my boyfriends from me?'

He laughs, which in turn makes me laugh. This had been one of the situations I always thought happened in soap operas. Then Jason kissed me. The kiss I have been anticipating and dreaming of for the last year. Now I'm confused.

'Why did you do that?' I stutter.

'I don't know. I felt like it,' he says, almost too matter-of-fact. 'Come on, I'll take you home.'

In a funny sort of way, I felt closer and more comfortable with Jason now that he had told me he was gay. I felt that I should tell him. I did. We told each other how wonderful the other was. We told each other that we were attracted to each other. I told him that nothing would ever happen between us now that he had decided to fully 'come out'. He thought we should try once. I knew that it wasn't a possibility.

When I tell Dr Parker about my evening with Jason, he suggests that we have dinner. The three of us. I find this a little strange and am unsure of why I agree. I think maybe it will be fun to see Dr Parker try to assess Jason. The man he had heard so much about from me. I tell Jason and he is in agreement with me. The three of us meet at an Italian restaurant and are sitting at a table situated outside. A heated lamp is nearby to ease any evening chills. We talk. We drink. We laugh. And then, with no warning, my evening is shattered.

'So, Jason, Louise tells me that you've recently come out,' Dr Parker says as he lights another cigarette. I feel odd seeing him drink and smoke, seeing as he was one of my doctors. The mental one.

'Yep,' Jason says with a giggle, finding the doctor's interrogation amusing.

'But you're still attracted to Louise?' the doctor probes.

'Yep, I guess, but boys are really what I love,' Jason says.

'There is nothing wrong with bisexuality,' the doctor continues, giving me a look that reminds me of what people say about the sexuality of the good-looking guys in LA. I make my apologies and pay my share of the bill. Then Jason drops me home.

Late that night, I am lying across the couch pondering my life, when the phone rings. The voice at the other end is panicked and upset. It is Dr Parker. I sit upright and try to hear what he is saying between the sighs and what I think are tears. I rearrange myself again into a more comfortable, listening position.

'Dr Parker, please calm down. I can't understand what you're saying', I urge, finding it hard to be pleasant after the evening quandaries.

'OK, OK ... I couldn't think of who else to call and then I thought of you. I thought you'd understand. Please, please listen to me, Louise.' He cries into the phone.

'Of course', I say, unsure of why he needs to call me at 1.30am. 'Take a deep breath and tell me what's happened.'

He is quiet. I can hear him sniffing. He sighs. He breathes heavily and then again he is silent.

'Dr Parker?'

'Yes. I'm here. Uuuhhh', he lets out a deep sigh. 'I was in bed and then I woke up feeling that something was wrong.' I am listening, now a little nervous at what he is trying to tell me. 'So I got up and came into my office, and then I found her ...' He sounded choked and unable to continue.

'Found who?' I say softly.

'My girlfriend is dead, Louise. She overdosed on pills from my office. It's my fault, Louise.'

I am unable to say the right words, as I'm unsure of what those words are. Now I am silent. I feel a discomfort flow through me and the man at the other end of the phone. I had to speak. I had to find some words to comfort him.

'It is not your fault, Dr Parker. It isn't. You mustn't say that. If someone decides their time is up and they have that in their minds, that is a force stronger than any. If she hadn't found the pills in your office, she would have found something else somewhere else. You must believe me', I start consoling.

He sounds a little calmer, or maybe the shock has now sent him into a numb state. That's how I felt when Mum died. I went from the panic of what to do and what needed organising, to feeling completely numb and then disbelief.

'Can I read you the suicide note, Louise. I found it. Can I read it to you?'

He sounded like a man insane. Why would he want to read me the note? I was a patient of his and had only known him for a month. Before I could answer, he started to read. I listened to this woman's misery of her life. Her inability to see any direction or promise. Her refusal to see light at the end of the tunnel. Her pains and endurance. Her unacceptable family. Her wishes to ease the pain for ever. As he cries, so do I.

Nothing can hit you more than someone's last words or desires on this planet before they die. My mother's were, 'Oh my God, don't let me die', and this woman's in contrast were 'Oh my God, help me die.' Or the sense that she was dead already.

'I should go now, Louise. I should call the paramedics and get some help over here. Thank you for listening.'

He was gone. The phone was dead. I knew I had to stop seeing him. I knew that he couldn't help me with my problems. My problems were solvable through my own self. I will continue journaling.

Medical Mistake

'Let your tears come. Let them water your soul.'
Eileen Mayhew

Three months later

Another waiting room. Another doctor. Another day.

Last night I had drunk too much. Tilda and I went for supper. I needed to escape. I needed to giggle. The news from Jason, as much as I loved him, had sent me down. Then Dr Parker's telephone call had only added to my forming depression. Matilda had come to the rescue and I had drowned my sorrows in a few vodka cocktails. It didn't cross my mind not to drink. I ignored the doctor's warnings. I didn't want to live in fear of what could happen. So after I finished the first cocktail, I ordered a second and then a third. Now today, I am suffering. As my head throbs, the magazines lying across the small table do not appeal. Louise is with me today. She pulls aspirins from her purse. She offers them to me.

'No, somehow I don't think aspirin will cure this headache,' I say, rubbing my thumbs into the side of my temples. Going out and drinking wasn't the strong thing to do. I wasn't feeling strong. I was weakening through the exhaustion of keeping myself 'up'. I am still working for Steve and looking for a new acting coach; I've done the depositions and now am meeting with an eye surgeon. Along with that comes everyday life and my everyday pains.

The office is in a medical building close to my home. She performs surgery in a room adjacent to her office. She has been recommended to me. After this next surgical procedure, Louise is moving back to London. Her time in Los Angeles is done. Her school year is complete, as is her Hollywood dream. Mine feels like it's only beginning. This could be my last surgery. If this doctor fixes my eye, then I'll be ready to face my dreams once again. I am exasperated and fighting any signs of depression. This has been an arduous year and I'm ready to end it. I've been giving myself a hard time lately. I feel that I've no right to feel down. I have been testing my logical explanations as to why God would let this happen to me. My mind switches from strength to complete weakness and why me, hadn't I had a tough enough life already? Then my arguments of what I have, rather than what I don't have, come into play. The glass being half full rather than half empty. I have wonderful friends. I have a family who love me and support me. I have vision in one eye still. I have my legs to walk with. I have an opportunity to be fixed. I have had surgeons slave for hours to rebuild my face. My understanding is that I have chosen for this to happen. I have asked God to help me learn these lessons from this lifetime. I don't want to make any deals with God, but please let me have a shot at fulfilling my dream before anything else happens.

I'm in the doctor's office. She is browsing over my chart. Her lab coat is undone, revealing an olive silk shirt, with matching ironed trousers. I can tell she takes care over her appearance. She keeps looking from the chart to my eye and then back to the chart, on which she makes notes and markings on a diagram of a face. It is tainted with red marker pen by the time she is done.

'Well, well, well ... Haven't you been through it, Louise? Wow. You're very lucky to be here, huh?'

She slams the chart down on her desk, alongside the large-framed picture of her and, I suspect, her husband. He also looks like he's a doctor.

'Let's have a look then.'

She pulls her chair up close to mine. A huge apparatus of equipment is beside me. It is swung across to face me. I hesitate as my face is fixed into the face frame. The freezing metal sends dull chills through my jaw and cheeks. The last time my head had been caught in one of these pieces of machinery was when I visited Dr Kalb. I pray she isn't going to do the eye test with the air pop machine. I had flinched and twitched as a terrified animal on the vet's table, whenever Dr Kalb tried to. Then I notice the machine directly in front of my left eye is the air pop machine. I am brave. I don't moan. I let her examine me as if I were happy to be there. I make polite chit chat and then she tells me how my life is about to change.

'Louise, I don't see a problem with this. I think I can move your eye down so that it is visible and in the right place. I can do it in the next couple of days. I'll have to tighten the muscle and see what it's like once I get behind the eye, but if I were you, I would be very excited as I think this could be your last surgery.'

I wished that, in one breath of relief, I could have let go of all the pain and mental trauma I had felt in the last eighteen months. A celebration was in order. A large lunch and a large bottle of wine. Phone calls across the world to share my exciting news. My father is speechless. My grandmother is relieved. Kathy is crying. George, my lawyer, is working on my case.

Since the accident, I've had four major surgeries. This would be number five. My body is feeling it. My brain is feeling it. My moods are feeling it. I am up and down, up and down. I want to call all the agents I've met with and scream; 'I'M READY.' I'll be able to remove my ugly black patch. That will be strange. It has become a part of me. It is called sexy by men I meet out at parties and bars. It is noticeable. It attracts strangers to comment. It attracts bitchy women to comment. They spit in my face, at my differences. I have learnt to ignore them. To laugh at them. I have forgotten what it feels like to be normal. To look like the majority. I have become one of 'the others'. I have been through stages of freakishness. I have accepted this Louise. Acceptance was the first step.

Early in the morning, the cold weather prompted sweaters. These were soon taken off, as I have to change into my medical robe and wait for the doctor to come in and give me a pre-med. This particular morning, Louise is with me. Nerves have sent us to nonsensical giggles. I can't hang my clothes in the cupboard through my giggles. I am freezing. I keep complaining about the chills. We make brisk chilly sounds as we laugh in the changing area.

'Come in with me, pleeeeeeeease. It's OK .... I don't mind if you see my eye hanging out, Louise,' I beg, joking. As soon as a little man in a lab coat and rubber gloves enters, my joking ceases. As does my heart. It still does that even after all this time. Shouldn't I be a little braver by now? I question myself. I quickly look over to Louise for strength. For a reason to feel OK. Not to worry. We hug. I start to cry and then I remember – this is my last surgery. I remember my nightmare is over and I will once again be whole. Then my head reminds me that I have always been whole. Why is it that if something is wrong with the outside, we feel imperfect? Is this not only the housing for our souls? Before long, the IV is stuck into my arm and I am once again unconscious.

I am awake. I am at home. A tap at the door reminds me I'm not alone. Louise and her blonde, bouncing curls show their face. Her voice is soft and her eyes concerned.

'Do you need anything?'

'No,' I yawn and stretch, careful not to knock the bandage across my eye.

My eye feels sore and my face is tight. Louise holds out the orange bottle of painkillers. I take one. The tightness loosens. Not only in my face, but also in my mind and in my back. I am free again. Free to feel nothing. No pain. No sadness. Just painkiller land. This is a land I am blissful to be in. Again, I fall back to sleep. Hours pass and I awake with a dull aching pain in my left eye. I want to look at it. I want to see me again.

Hazy from my nap, I stand in front of the bathroom mirror. It is time to clean my eye. I am seeing the doctor in the morning and have had instructions to remove the bandage gently and clean any unwanted gunk from around the eye. Then place three drops of eye solution into the corner of the eye. I carefully peel away the tape. It is pulling on the area around the recent procedure. I am excited. The bandage is off and in the bin. I am ready to look. I'm so excited that I have a drum roll in my head. I turn my view to my face. Everything seems to be moving in slow motion. Noises are loud and slow with an added echo. The ointment is ready. The gauze is waiting. My moment is here. I am ready to look. I feel the anxiety moving through my stomach, up my oesophagus and into my throat. I open and glare. Move closer. I can't see her clearly. Hold on to the side. I think something's wrong. Hold on tighter. I peer closer not sure if what I have seen is real. The eyelid is hardly open. Maybe it's this way because of the bandage. Open it. I try to lift it with my fingers. It's difficult to move. I try to lift it with my eye muscles. I cannot. When I raise the lid with my fingers, I gaze at the eye itself. It is filled with blood. There is only a tiny piece of the pupil visible. It is hardly noticeable. This can't be real. I run out into the sitting room crying out Louise's name. She appears almost instantly from her bedroom, hearing the panic.

'What is it? What is it? Are you all right?' Her eyes are bright and wide.

'Look at my eye,' I scream, pointing my hands at my eye.

She comes over and rests her arms on my shoulders to steady her as she looks closely at my still, damaged eye. She doesn't say a word. She just stares at it. I am anxious. I am trying to stay calm.

'Well ... well ... it's fucked, isn't it?' I state. I can feel the tears coming to the surface, ready to flow.

'Maybe it's meant to look like that until she sees you,' Louise tries to say but I can tell by the tone and the stammer in her voice that she knows as well as I that I have a problem.

'My eye won't open, Louise. I can't open my eye again.' I am pacing.

'Calm down. Look, let's wait until you see her tomorrow before we make any assumptions,' she says.

'OK. OK.'

I don't want to believe that it's worse than before. I choose to take the waiting until tomorrow option. I cannot concentrate on anything that evening. I can't sleep and I am too agitated to watch television. I sit on the phone. I talk to friends. I bitch and cry. I have a bath. I can't relax. I walk the corridors of our apartment building. The neighbours annoy me. I return to our rabbit hutch and flop on to the couch. Louise tries to cook me dinner. I'm not hungry.

'Can't I call the doctor now and see if she can see me tonight or at least talk to me?' I cry.

Louise nods her head, but when I try the office it's a machine. I go to a birthday party to take my mind off the bloody mess. I drink brightly-coloured cocktails to hide my revelations. I go home. I fall into bed and then I'm once again clouded with darkness. Finally, I cry myself to exhaustion, and I drift asleep.

The following morning is here. I'm back in her office, in the examination chair. I am alone. Alone with the thoughts spinning around my head which now feels like a blender. I am still unable to open my eyelid and the placement of the eye hasn't changed since last night. What has changed is my attitude. I am no longer excited. I am no longer happy. I am flat. When she arrives, I do not smile. I do not speak. I look at her as if she were the devil. Deep inside, I am praying that she is going to smile and tell me that in a few days it will move.

'Hi, Louise. How are you feeling?' she begins casually as if nothing were wrong.

'It hasn't moved. The eye hasn't moved. The eyelid is unable to lift. It hasn't worked,' I immediately inform her.

She comes over to me and bends down, slowly peeling away the new tape I have covered the bandage with. As she peeks at her recent work she sighs, 'Oh no, it hasn't, has it? Oh well ... let me think.'

Oh well, let me think? I repeat in my head caustically. I feel as if I am in a comedy.

I then slide into a black hole. There is no light in my hole. Only darkness. Storms surround the hole. Storms of whispers of death and disappointment. 'You are never going to get anywhere in your life,' is shouted across the bleak hole. 'It is time to give up hope as it is getting you nowhere. It is time to be realistic and forget your dreams. They are gone along with your chances of change.'

I lie in my room and I cry. I cry for my mother. I cry for my childhood. I cry for my fears. I cry for my stupidity. I cry for my dreams. I cry for myself. I don't answer the phone. I can't speak to anyone, as I know I need to be alone. I feel as though I must be doing something wrong. Maybe I'm not being realistic and I should start listening to those who love me, who are telling me in the most careful way that I need to change my directions. I have thought about this and it doesn't seem an option. I can't think of anything else that would fulfil me. I cry myself to sleep again.

I am in the office and Steven is waiting for me to take dictation. I don't want to be here. I want to be at home crying some more. It's good for me to be out of the house, my depressed head is taking a break. I can't let him see how miserable I am, although he can tell. He has looked at my eye and not known what to say. My father sighed and said, 'I'm sorry, love. Maybe you should see if there is someone in England.'

I didn't want to go back to England. I still had a flicker of hope in one corner of my mind, thinking that something would change. I find my pen and notepad and start walking towards Steven's office at the other end of the long narrow corridor. The phone rings. I turn back.

'Hello, Louise, it's Amanda, your dad's secretary,' the voice says. Why was she calling me? I look at my watch. It's four in the morning in London.

'Is everything OK, Amanda?' I panic.

'Please don't tell your father I called,' she begins, 'it's really important you don't tell him.'

I co-operate and tell her that I won't tell him. Thoughts of him being sick are running through my worried mind. I can't take it. I can't take it if he's sick.

Amanda carries on talking. 'I have to let you know that I overheard your father talking to your lawyer today and it seems clear that you are going to lose your court case. They are waiting for the right time to tell you, so I wanted to prepare you.'

'What ...?' I stammer. I can't think. I hang up the phone unwilling to hear her pathetic information. My head can't think. My mind won't work. I can't breathe. I can't talk. I can't walk. I just stare. No energy left. A misery-filled life is hopefully about to end. I look at the window by the desk. I want to jump. To die. I am too tired. I can't take any more challenges. No light at the end of the tunnel. A big black hole, that is all. I want to scream. I have no energy to open my mouth. My mother, where is she? Dead. I want to be dead. I cannot pay the doctors' bills. I have no money. If I lose the court case like she says, I'll have over $300,000 in debts. I cannot start life again from this. My eye is shut. It cannot open. Am I supposed to put on a brave face, a positive smile? Oh, I'm fine. No big deal. It's just life. No. I cannot do that today. I have been living in a dream world. I've been thinking everything would be OK. My body is fizzing with nervous adrenalin. Uncomfortable tingles. I am breathing now. Quick and short breaths. Maybe I should stop. If I stop will I be sent back down to earth to finish this journey. To begin again as someone else who goes through pain. I choose to breathe. I run to the bathroom and when I am done I see the bowl is filled with blood. The stress has been causing haemorrhoids and they are meant to be clearing up. I am in my early twenties and suffering from stress that an old man or woman would have. I want to collapse on the bathroom floor and sleep. Cry and sleep. I look up to laugh at the sky above, but I can't find the humour. It has gone. Now I'm too tired.

I manage to walk slowly with great effort back to my desk where I slump down in the chair. Steven has been calling my name. I have not responded. I am staring at the wall. He comes over and, upon seeing me, rushes to my side. I am pale. I am in a trance. I murmur what has happened. I have to say it a few times as he can't understand my murmurs. He calls George Stanbury. They talk for a while. Steven explains my afternoon to him. The phone is put down and Steve looks at me concerned.

'George is going to come and take you home. He's going to talk to you, Lou. Please try and relax.'

George comes to the office and takes me for a drive. I am in shock.

'Louise, what she told you is untrue. There are risks with everything.'

He turns his attention from the road to check quickly for an understanding from me. I make a noise, an 'Mmmnnnn' sound.

'All I was telling your father is what I was about to tell you. The judge isn't sure if it is going to go to court. They are talking about settling out of court.'

He has my attention. 'So I would still get money to pay the bills?'

'Yes, absolutely, we're trying to get the most we can and that takes time. Everything is being assessed right now.' He looks at me again and takes a moment. 'Louise, I think you need to take a break for a while. Just calm down and do nothing. You have taken so much on. It really is time for you to rest.'

I look at him with disbelief. 'I have no money, George. I need to keep going. There is no time to rest.' I am once again sobbing. I want to scream. I want someone to take care of me. Where is my prince?

'Louise, if you don't rest then you won't be able to do any of these things. Believe me. Now take some time.'

He takes me home. I wander into my bungalow, where there is no Louise. Only yesterday she had moved back to London. Now I'm living with a woman named Alison. Alison is English, too. She seems lovely, although I'm sure she is a little perturbed about my situation and whom she is living with. I walk in, in a trance-like way. Alison is in the kitchen cooking. She is a chef. She pops her head around the corner and in a high-pitched, jolly voice cries, 'Hello, would you like some soup? I just made some.'

I stare at her blankly. 'No thanks, I'm not hungry.'

'Are you OK?' She is suddenly concerned.

'Fine. Really, just fine,' I reply. I don't want her to feel sorry for me or be pulled into the dramatics of my life. The phone rings. I pick it up.

'Yes,' I say blankly, with no intention.

'Lou, it's Nic,' the voice says.

'Nic?'

'Nic, your old boyfriend Nic ... Lou, are you all right?'

'Hi,' I respond, still with no energy.

'Are you OK?' He is concerned.

'No, not really. I'm sick of this life ... 'As I'm about to continue, he interrupts.

'I've been worried about you. I'm coming to get you and take you down to my parents' house in Malibu. You need taking care of and you've been doing too much. I'll be there in ten minutes. Pack a bag.' He is strong and I am listening.

I pack a small bag but, due to my mood, all the wrong things. Nic arrives and looks at my very pale complexion. He undoes my bag and while I sit on the bed, solemn and tearful, he goes through my things, finding what he needs.

We drive down to Malibu. It's dark outside and it's dark in my head. He is trying to make me smile. It's not working. The house is situated in the most stunning part of Malibu, right on the beach. I couldn't have asked for better medicine. When we arrive, I am handed a large goblet of wine. Nic sits me on the couch and lights a fire. My head begins to breathe a little.

'I have to be back first thing in the morning, I've so much to do,' I start to cry again.

'No, Lou. You're staying here. You don't need to go anywhere for the whole weekend. Let me take care of you, darling.'

Then he takes out my diary and, while ignoring my incessant arguing, cancels all of my appointments for the following week. He cooks me a huge bowl of pasta and we sit out on the deck by the beach, finishing the bottle of wine. It makes me tired and relaxed and able to fall into a deep sleep, worry free. The next few days are filled with long walks along the beach. We talk. We eat. We drink. I sleep. I'm nauseous, I am so stressed. I watch movies to escape. The slightest emotion sends me to tears. I slowly begin to unwind. The sound of the ocean is calming. Nic attends to my every whim and makes sure I'm comfortable. I hadn't realised how exhausted I'd become until I was away from it all.

Monday morning arrives and I'm sad to leave our hidden retreat. I feel better, though, and refreshed. Already, my mind is racing and listing ways to find a new eye surgeon. Back in my safe bungalow, I unpack and take a long, hot bath. I call Steve and let him know when I'll be back in the office. Alison gives me the soup she had saved in the fridge. I feel spoilt. I leave a message for Dr Kawamoto. I know he'll help me find someone to recover my shattered life.

Dr Rosenbaum

'The future belongs to those who believe in the beauty of their dreams.'
Eleanor Roosevelt

As I had hoped, Dr Kawamoto made the call. He set up the appointment. I feel a little apprehensive about meeting with another doctor. A little nervous about my capabilities to take any more disappointments. My father still urges me to be realistic and let go of my previous dreams. I can't fathom this thought. This is what keeps me alive. Anyone who has ever dreamed understands the power it has over you.

Dr Rosenbaum, I have been told, takes care of children. I can tell. I am waiting for the doctor. Ahead of me is a television playing *Bambi* from a video. This is a distraction. The room is sterile and the equipment looks sharp and shiny. Again, there is the large headset examining equipment which is easily swivelled to face the victim. In this case, me.

I'm feeling better from my short rest away. It's given me time to think. Time to re-evaluate and push myself back to determination. I don't want pity. I don't want my family and friends to be worried about me. I want them to be proud of me and say, 'She really did it ... I guess anything is possible.' That is what I really want. Most of all, I want it from my father. I don't know why it is such a deep need for me to have his approval. I suppose I want to make up for all the years that I only saw him on weekends. I want to show him what I'm capable of. I want to see his face glow with pride as I receive recognition for all of my hard work. These, too, are dreams.

Dr Rosenbaum enters. He's a short, Jewish man with large-rimmed glasses. He is gentle and thorough. Every question is answered. Every angle is covered. No smiles. Only concentration. He listens to my fears and he tells me the truth. He studies and measures the positioning of the eye and the eyelid. Even though I'm not happy to hear what he says, there is still a glimmer of hope. That means it's worth a try.

'Louise, I'll need to run tests. I need to see how much blood is getting to the eye. I need to see if it's worth the risk of doing surgery.'

As soon as I leave his office, I'm sent across the corridor to another laboratory. In here, I'm seated at a stool. In front of me is another strange-looking device, which I'm told by the helpful physician will be attached to my head. He says they are going to inject a liquid into my vein. This is going to make me feel suddenly nauseous. The nurse brings in a bucket in case I need to be sick. The injected liquid is going to turn my skin yellow. The machine is then brought up to my face and the laser projected into my eye. The number of working blood vessels, taking blood to the eye, will be detected from the fluorescent substance. I am lost in the description as soon as I hear the word nausea.

The test is done. I throw up. The results come back.

I am taken back to Dr Rosenbaum.

'Well, Louise ... a normal person has four blood vessels carrying blood to the eye. You now, it is apparent, only have one. This means that if we do the surgery and this last vessel is damaged, then your eye could disintegrate. I want you to think about this risk but I don't recommend it,' Dr Rosenbaum says in his professional tone.

I close my eyes to ponder my choices. Look normal or wear an eye-patch for ever.

'Disintegrate? You mean really disintegrate?' I ask.

'Not overnight. It would take about six weeks. It dries up and yes, disintegrates.'

I think about the positive things he has said – that he could fix my eyelid but that I could also lose the eye. I come to my decision. I wouldn't have come this far for it to go wrong now. I trust Dr Kawamoto's recommendation and if I don't take the risk, my dreams vanish.

'I want to go ahead and do it,' I say.

'But, Louise, if the vein is damaged, you'll need a glass eye.' He tries to dissuade me.

'I'll think about that when it happens.'

The surgery is set. Three months away. My eye needs time to heal from the last surgery.

Three months pass. I am ready, even though my family are strong in their convictions that I have undergone enough. They are tired of hearing my reasoning and sick of being worried. When I had told my father that if something went wrong I could get a glass eye, the phone had gone dead. I called him back to be told, 'Never say stupid things like that again.'

Alicia and Jason have opted to accompany me to surgery this morning. It is an early Tuesday morning, a clear-blue sky and signs of heat on the way. Alicia has become a dear friend and since Matilda and George have moved back to London, one of the reasons being earthquake fear, Alicia has taken over. Jason is an ever-present figure in my life and has grown to be one of my best friends. We have spent many evenings talking on the phone about each other's desires for the perfect man. As we enter the hospital, I remind Jason to call Alex and cancel the lunch appointment we had made. I had clearly forgotten I was having surgery. It had become so much a part of my routine that it was now interfering with my lunch plans. This is clearly a dry statement.

'Alex? Oh, that good-looking English guy that came round to your house last week?' Jason questions. 'Are you seeing each other?'

'No, of course not,' I deny, 'he was Charlotte's younger sister's ex-boyfriend and he's just moved here. He was given my number as a contact. That's all.'

I didn't think I was interested in him. I hadn't thought so when we had had coffee alone a few times. Then his friend came into town and suddenly I found myself missing seeing him alone. I put it to the back of my mind. Alicia squeezes my hand as she notes a look of fear and nerves slowly moving across my face.

I'm not so nervous about the procedure today. It is the procedure tomorrow that holds more of a challenge. Today, I will be unconscious. Tomorrow, I'll be awake. Today they will take the eye from the socket and work on the muscles behind the eye. Then Dr Rosenbaum will apply sutures (stitches). These sutures will not be trimmed. The threads will be left dangling from the back of my eye where they are attached to the muscle, to the outside of the top and bottom of my eye. Then tomorrow, while I am awake, the eye will be moved around through the pulling on the sutures. My explanation has been a very rough account of the version I received from Dr Rosenbaum.

Jason and Alicia tell stories and jokes to keep me distracted from the opportunity to think about what I'm doing today. I pray to God that this will be successful. I pray that my one vein carrying blood won't be disturbed en route. I pray for my mother to watch over me. I pray for the muscles to respond to the doctor's touch. The anaesthesiologist comes into the room. I leave my body once again and enter the dream world that I have recently become accustomed to.

When I wake up, I can't see through the Vaseline that has been rubbed over my eyes. My left eye feels sore and I can feel a bandage covering it, protecting it. I rub my right eye to try and get rid of some of the jelly that prevents me from seeing. As I become more alert, I see Jason sleeping in the chair to the left of my bed and Alicia contentedly reading a magazine. I try to speak. I croak. Alicia looks up from the glossy pages.

'Hey,' she whispers. 'How are you feeling?'

Jason stirs. His sleepy face turns to mine. 'You're awake,' he stretches.

We talk quietly while I am fed toast to make sure I can keep food down without being sick. When it is clear that I am conscious and full, I am allowed to leave. The nurse hands over an instruction manual, prescriptions, eye gauzes and phone numbers. I'm told to be in Dr Rosenbaum's office at 8.00am the following morning.

'It is very important that you rest, Louise. You mustn't rub or touch your eye. The sutures are very delicate and if they're moved then your eye will be moved, too.'

I understand. I am not looking forward to the visit in the morning.

'Can I have a Valium or something to take before coming to see Dr Rosenbaum in the morning, to calm my nerves?'

'No, Louise. He needs you to be alert.'

This wasn't the answer I had been hoping for. I wasn't very good at needles and eye-moving procedures. Not awake. Give me a general anaesthetic and I'll take the pain after, but not during. Please, not during. I knew the unpleasantries were only just beginning. I want to see under the bandage. To see if my eye is back. To see if the lid operates. I have to wait.

The next morning is here. I'm in Alicia's car. She is as nervous as me. I had asked her to sit with me while Dr Rosenbaum took the eye from its home and fiddled with the muscles. 'You don't have to look,' I said, 'I just need to have someone there.' Alicia agreed.

Today, I cannot watch *Bambi*. I'm too scared. Too scared to watch a bouncing deer run across the screen searching for her mother, or is that *Dumbo*? That will probably be playing in examination room four. I am pacing and then sitting and then pacing around the waiting room.

'Come on, darling. Try and sit down,' Alicia urges. Before I can sit again, the door to Dr Rosenbaum's office opens. I am signalled. I don't want to go in. I start to sweat. The excuses begin lining up in my mind as to how I can leave. I feel angry. Angry with myself for being so weak. Why can't I be brave? Why can't I just smile and say 'Go ahead, I'm fine with this.' Because I'm a baby.

I'm sitting in the chair. Alicia's on my right. The nurse is on my left. Dr Rosenbaum is directly ahead of me. He is talking slowly.

'It seemed to go fine yesterday ... the eyelid is working again ... Now please don't move, Louise, this is very important,' he says as he approaches me.

I see a silver pair of tweezers coming towards my left eye. I want to close my eyes. I am told I can't.

'I need you to look ahead with your right eye, Louise, and then do what I tell you ... OK, I'm taking off the bandage now ...'

'STOP,' I scream. The doctor jumps back.

'Louise, please, stay calm. If you let me go ahead, it will be over very soon.'

I am trembling. I really want to leave. I can't sit here while they take my eye out. I just can't do it. Alicia starts whispering words of comfort in my ear.

'Remember your dreams, Louise. Let the doctor do his work. Come on, look at everything you've been through.'

I listen. I try to breathe, although I'm finding it hard. I think of a song I can sing to myself and shout at the doctor again, 'HURRY UP. PLEASE, HURRY UP.'

I can feel the sutures moving my eye. It is the most uncomfortable and weird feeling. Not one that I would recommend.

'Look up,' the doctor instructs. I look up and he makes my eye look down by tugging on the sutures. This continues for what seems like a lifetime, but is, in fact, around ten minutes. Then the scissors appear and the sutures are cut.

The chair is raised. I can breathe again. A tissue wipes my sweaty brow. A mirror. I need a mirror.

'Can I see a ...' Before the question is complete, a mirror is handed to the doctor and held to my face. There is my eye. My beautiful eye. My damaged eye. My swollen eye. My blood-filled eye. It is visible. The pupil is visible. Not all of it, but some.

'I want to see you at the beginning of next week and then we can figure out how many more surgeries to do, if that is the case.'

I nod my head. I am exhausted from the morning's escapade. I need to sleep. I just want to leave before the attacking tweezers show their face again.

On Monday morning as I sit in Dr Rosenbaum's chair, my heart sinks once again. A ruler is held up to my eye to measure the adjustment necessary for the eye. It has moved back to almost its original damage point. Because I'm blind, it will not stay down.

'We could try again,' Dr Rosenbaum says, 'but I can't promise anything. It doesn't look optimistic.'

I tell him to shush. I won't listen to words of 'can't help you'. In order to get from A to B, a smile must be worn. Was I in denial? Am I ignoring the obvious? I am tired. So very, very tired. I want to sleep for a very long time. My body aches. My mind is having trouble thinking. I am snapping at people I care about because of my own impatience. Every time I go to get cash from the cash machine it says, 'Insufficient funds'. I am struggling to make ends meet. To find food to put in the fridge. To pay for the necessities and to stay positive about the rebuilding of my life. The financial strain is wearing on me. I want to be able to have one less worry. I wish the court case would end. At this point, the money doesn't matter. No amount of money can replace these losses or the time spent on recovering. These are all life lessons. I must look at them that way. Dr Rosenbaum is still awaiting my answer to the surgery question. Am I again to say, 'No, you WILL fix me'? As if pre-recorded on a tape, I say it automatically.

'I understand,' says Dr Rosenbaum. 'We'll try again in a few months.'

Back on Track

George Stanbury is serious today. We are approaching the time for big decisions. I have to be on the ball and awake. These decisions are going to affect the rest of my life. I'm keeping my head above water, hard as it is some days. I was still able to make Joanne laugh when I came into the office today. The jokes are always at my own misfortune. I have to make it that way. Now, seated across from George, I am more earnest.

'Louise, there's a lot to your advantage. It's just a matter of time. The news that the neurologist has recently given you about epilepsy is good. I mean, once again, if you have it as a result of the head injury, it's an advantage.'

I sit digesting the farce that my injuries are good news. I had just done a test with a neurologist where I had to stay up all night and then I was monitored in his office. The results were that because of the scar across my brain, there was strange activity. Activity I could outgrow but, for now, it had to be watched. I am sluggish today. My mood is cloudy and I don't have the mental energy to snap back or complain. Today, realism seems to be on my mind. This really is it. My life could be about to take a different direction. The eye surgeries aren't working. I'm finding out about new injuries every day. Everyone seems to be happy about my injuries, apart from myself.

'George? This is too surreal for me. The fact that every injury has its worth.' I pause and think. 'Tell me if this isn't a ridiculous question ... how much for the loss of an eye?'

Almost without hesitation, George opens a drawer to his desk. Out of the drawer comes a brown file. The file is opened and the pages are turned. He is murmuring the headings under his breath, 'Paralysis, Brain Damage, Loss of a Limb ... ah, here we are, Loss of an Eye.'

I am no longer shocked by anything. It seems that, in our world, everything has a price.

'$1.5 million.' He looks up at me.

I manage a deadened laugh. A laugh filled with disbelief that there is an answer to the question I had asked. I didn't want their money. I didn't want them to be able to tell me the worth of my life from a chequebook. I wanted some real people to be able to look at me and understand what has been smashed. I wanted someone to understand how, in one second, your life and its direction can change.

I shake my head and stand up. It's time for me to go. I have got my answers. In accordance, George stands.

'Louise, I know that upset you. I didn't make the rules. I'm truly sorry for your pain. I wish there was something I could do to make it easier.'

He looks down, finding it hard to look at me. I am numb. Numb to the extremities in my life.

'I'll have news about the case and if we're going to settle. I need you to think hard about all the offers that come this week. Please rest. I'm sorry your eye surgery didn't go as you had planned.'

'It's not your fault, George.' I turn to the door, picking up my bag and then looking back at the sad lawyer. 'It's just life, isn't it?'

I leave. I go home where Alison's cooking brings home memories of having a mother.

Later that week, I'm with another good friend, Lisa. All the friends I have made since I moved here have been good friends. The only people that can stay in my life are those that can take on my trials and instabilities. Because of this accident, they have been many. She has protected me from mean, unpleasant words that have been slapped on me in public. Only last night, she tried to punch a girl with overly silicone breasts who called me an ugly pirate who should let others go first in line. This was while I was waiting for the Ladies in a trendy LA restaurant. Lisa had heard the comment and was about to attack when

I quickly stepped forward to whisper the same words that Tilda had once used with me.

Today, Lisa is trying to distract me from my worries. As I'm telling her my plans for surgery in another few months, she begins to smile. The stunning actress suggests I go on an audition with her. An audition! Her large, oval, brown eyes widen as the excitement of her suggestion fills her with pride. She would be the one to build my confidence. Auditioning has become foreign to me. It's been so long. It has been something I've thought about but never realised as a reality.

'Don't be so ridiculous, Lisa. Have you forgotten who you're speaking to? Look at my face. Hello – eye-patch. I don't think so,' I say, completely flabbergasted that she would ever have suggested it.

'No, Lou, come on. They're looking for a group of girls. Just come for the fun. It'll be good for you.'

After a lot of persuasion, I decide to drag my girlfriend Debra with us. Debra, Miss Outgoing, is more than willing. This is from her training to be a pop star. Her incredible voice along with her facial features lead me to no doubt that she will book the job. I walk into the warehouse and my heart sinks as I encounter hundreds of beautiful young girls. All perfect. Beautiful hair. Two eyes. Symmetrical faces. Stunning pictures and loud laughter and chatter.

'Did you go on that Levi's job?'

'Oh yeah. I got it.'

'I'm going to the Caribbean next week to film the Miller commercial.'

'I just got a new agent.'

'My boyfriend is in a band,' and so on.

The chatter is enough to tell me I have no chance. I'm going to be laughed at. Memories of how I used to feel when I was at auditions come flooding back. The feelings of excitement I used to have. The thought that I had a shot at getting the job. I may be filming the following week. These thoughts are old. Now all I feel is insecurities and stupidity for coming. The ugly duckling, a story that fits my life at this moment. I wonder if I will ever be ready. I don't feel good enough. I feel too ugly. All my imperfections are in full view for all to gawk at. And they do. The girls stare at my patch. The little man wandering around with his Polaroid camera does a second take. Then he photographs me and, when he does, he says, 'Good choice, Jon Baptist will love it!' I go into the warehouse along with six other girls and we follow direction.

'I want you to scream like schoolgirls as you see the most beautiful man you have ever seen walking by.'

We scream and we pine and Jon Baptist does love it. The next day I get the call and I get the job. Along with Debra and Lisa. We are the principals. There will be eight of us. I cannot believe it. My friends cannot believe it. I'm going to be working in front of the camera again. A commercial. This is enough for me.

The night before the job, I'm too agitated to sleep. I stand in front of the mirror playing with my extensions, trying different angles to hide scars. I clean the patch and drink plenty of water. The secret to looking slim and having clear skin. I'll be able to call myself an actress again. Even if it was only for a day. I am to play a Catholic schoolgirl who is chasing a rock star from his limousine. According to the script, he's wearing Drakoir Noir and he smells incredible. I'll never know the beauty of the smell of the Drakoir Noir that is soaked on his masculine body. I don't care. I'm going to be working.

In a sound stage on the Raleigh studios lot, 50 screaming schoolgirls chase the perfect model who plays a rock star. The girls are Californian teenagers. And then there's us. I manage to be in the foreground in every shot. Debra and I make sure of it. Every time the director calls 'Cut', we run to the new position, pushing other schoolgirls from the front. This is working to our advantage until Jon Baptist pulls us aside. It is me he turns to. I am caught. I am embarrassed but this is over-ridden through my amusement.

'Eccchem, excuse me, Louise, yes?' he begins in his heavy French accent. 'It is great that you are in all the shots, but ... it looks a little strange for continuity if you are at every side of the car. It wouldn't matter if you didn't 'ave the patch but ... well, maybe you can take it off for the next shot? No?'

Unsure of what to do and whether or not I should tell him, I stand in silence. I am staring at him waiting for him to change the subject or say something to save me. He doesn't.

'I'm afraid ...' I begin slowly, 'it's just that I wear the patch for a reason. My eye is really messed up underneath.' There is silence. A silence I was becoming accustomed to. Oh God no, please don't let this be a problem. Just as I thought things were turning around. I'm immediately ashamed and ready to collect my bag and be thrown off the set. I wonder whether I should show him the damage. Is it necessary for him to see? Maybe I should just swallow my pride and know that I had tried and now it is time to go. Instead, he moves closer and studies my face.

'This cannot be true. I thought it was just a really cool look,' he says with a large smile.

I shrug my shoulders as if to say, 'I'm sorry.' The French director who resembles Kojak grabs my hand. I am taken back to the set. I finish the day's work and, before leaving, he comes over to me and says, 'Well done, Louise. That was wonderful. You are a very brave girl.'

The one-day's work, even if that is to be it for ever, has given me the taste again. The opportunity to feel alive. I am not ready to do other roles. This is the beginning of my confidence-building journey. It is a story to tell the doctors who had told me I would never work again.

The late afternoon offers a beautiful sunset and some quiet time. I'm not working for Steven today. I took the day off. I lie across the couch with my eyes shut. The pains in my left eye are subsiding as the muscles are relaxing and moving back into place. I have just finished another wonderfully inspirational book, *Creative Visualization*. I picked it up because on the back it talked about miracles. *How to make the optic nerve grow back,* it said. That was enough for me to purchase it. Alison is at her job where she cooks her amazing concoctions for the likes of Robert Redford and Barry Diller. When she comes home, I attack her parcels of left-overs.

I'm expecting George Stanbury. He has news he says. I'm over the news that the judge decided my case wasn't to go to court. That was yesterday. Now today, we have offers. I'm tired of being poor. I'm tired of not driving. I'm tired of having a truck filled with emotional baggage. Soon, the truck will be emptied and all I'll carry is a little purse of change. The change will be gold. The gold will be the strength I have from the experiences I have carried around and learnt from. I will have a perfectly positioned eye, an amazing man, a heart filled with love, an incredible career and giggling children. My incredible visualisation is interrupted by the knock at the door. I wiggle my bottom in the couch until I hear my back click, and then I stand up. I had drifted off while it had still been light and now my apartment is dark, only lit with the resonance of the sunset. I flick the lamp on.

George can hear me coming as my shoes cause an echo on the hardwood floor. I open the front door. George is there with a smile.

'Would you like to come for a drive?' he offers.

'Sure,' I reply and head back inside to grab my house keys.

Bruce, George's partner, is in the car already. I get into the back seat. As George starts the engine, I am handed an envelope. It is addressed to me.

'What's this?' I hold it up.

'It's from Rubin's insurance. It's their settlement. It's nothing to do with the dealership. But it's a start.'

I look back down at the envelope. I don't know what to say or how to feel. This is the moment I have been working towards since we began this case. It is now the summer of 1994. I had the accident in October of 1992. I am holding the first cheque in my hands. I am too nervous to open the envelope. This is the price to be paid for my losses and pain. This stood against everything I have talked about. I had to remember this wasn't my worth. This was the most we could get from the old man. I had been asked if I'd wanted to go for his home and I'd said 'No'. It was an accident. Why ruin his life? Enough damage had been done and, as I said before, no amount of money would pay for what I'd gone through or was going through or might never be able to do. The file lied. There was no price for the loss of a life, a limb, a brain and an eye. It was life. As long as my medical bills were covered and I could buy some food for the fridge. A car would be nice. And the opportunity to fix the rest of my face. Already I am shopping. I stop.

The car starts moving. I slowly undo the sealed envelope. I pull out the cheque from inside. I hold it in both of my hands. George and Bruce stay facing forward. And then I gasp.

In my hands, I am holding a cheque made out to Louise Ashby for $1,100,000.00. I have never had $10,000 and now I have a cheque for over a million. Then I remembered the lawyers seated in front of me were owed 33.5 per cent of that. Then I remembered that my medical bills would total in the end after the other surgeries I had planned, $500,000. But still, for now, I gawp at the cheque. I don't know what to do. I am having difficulty breathing. What do you do with that much money? I am 23 years old and find it difficult to manage $100. I would have liked to have gone for a celebration drink, but my ability to talk had disappeared. George understands. We manage a few words and then I'm dropped home with congratulations.

'We'll know about the dealership tomorrow. We'll call you,' were their parting words.

Back in the house, I'm alone. I am scared. I'm overwhelmed. I see the kitchen table and realise I need shelter from the feelings that are surfacing from the cheque. I gently climb under the table and pull my knees in to my chest. I begin rocking from side to side, the way I did to comfort myself after Mum died.

I don't know how long I rocked for. The tears kept coming. I was releasing all of the anxiety and anguish I had been holding in. I now didn't know how my life would be without these feelings. I had become so used to them. Then I thought about the most important thing of all – I didn't have to worry about money. I could eat when I wanted. I didn't need to work for Steven. I could join the acting class I wanted to join. I could breathe a little easier than I had yesterday. I could buy gifts for my family and friends. I could buy my father the suit I'd seen in Ralph Lauren to say 'Thank you'. I could have whatever I wanted. I could even go on holiday and sleep for months. But I'm too nervous to spend the money. I need help in knowing what to do with it. Again, I close my eyes and ask for the answers to be shown to me.

The next day, the dealership put in their final offer. I wasn't happy with it and neither was George. Initially, they had wanted to give me $1,000 per week for five years until I was 29. We'd said 'no' to that and now I had a cheque that was more acceptable. Acceptable to the courts. The money was deposited in the bank and each cut was taken. My anxiety was overwhelming and then the letter I opened when I got home from the bank sent me into shock. It was from the owner of the dealership.

He told me to be grateful.

Alex

My episode under the kitchen table has passed. I'm able to reward myself with my new-found financial stability. I joined a new acting class – The Howard Fine Studio. For the first time since I have been in Los Angeles, I am learning and enjoying my classes. I am not being tortured for my fate. It seems years ago that I felt the stress from the court case and my disfigurements. I am no longer working for Steve. I have a new car. This is the biggest gift I could have given myself. To be mobile once again. The car is a truck. A Jeep Cherokee. The fact that I am unable to remember the accident is only positive for me. I don't get nervous when I drive. I can leave my house when I want to, no longer having to phone around to find someone to come and get me. This is heaven.

I have been dating a little bit. I've been seeing a producer. I find his company entertaining. He takes me hiking after smoking a joint and then can't understand why I'm struggling to climb the mountain. He tells stories and keeps me entertained but then, after checking his diary, notices his very busy schedule. My time with him is limited. I can only have a few hours each visit.

Suddenly, my friends think I'm rich. When we go out for dinners and the bill arrives, faces turn to me. Only a certain few. The ones with no money that drink too much. I've been drinking too much, too. My celebrations from my settlement have so far lasted for three months.

I'm enjoying myself for the first time in a long time. Alison and I have been having parties at the house nearly every weekend. The producer tells me that I'm a party girl and then laughs. This upsets me. I stop seeing him or, rather, he stops seeing me.

A month ago, I was offered a line of cocaine. I had done it a few times when I was 19 and now it is showing its powdery evil face again. I try it. I like it. I am insatiable. I want more and more. I feel the freedom and confidence that I have lacked for the past couple of years. Our parties are no longer ending at 2.00am but 8.00am. It's the summer. It's a weekend. These are my justifications. The parties are lasting longer and getting wilder.

Then I am saved. Eye surgery is only a week away. I must slow down. Smoking stops the healing. The parties and the drinking and the drugs slow down. I go back to the gym. I am spending time with Alex. We are becoming friends. Alex is 6ft 2in, with deep, dark-brown eyes, dark-brown hair and a large mouth with large juicy lips. I am not thinking about him this way, though. Even though he's my ideal-looking man, he is out of bounds for me. I have to keep saying this over and over in my mind. 'Not for me. Not for me.' He makes me laugh. He makes me happy. He makes my heavy heart feel light again. When I am around him, I feel comfortable and as if I have known him for a million years. We spend time talking. We go out for coffee. Alex moved to Los Angeles a few months ago. He was one of the first to receive the dreaded call, that night on 5 October, when my life's direction changed. He was with Emily, Charlotte's younger sister. Their father had called to tell them the news. Alex had picked up the phone. He'd been told, 'Charlotte's friend Louise may die tonight!' I had met him a few months later when he and Emily came to LA to visit. I hadn't liked him. I'd thought him moody. I hadn't known he was merely tired. Now we were becoming inseparable.

Alison keeps questioning me. 'Come on, what about Alex? Lou, he's gorgeous. You both get on so well. Go out with Alex.'

'Alison, no. It's not even worth talking about,' I argue back.

Alex is forbidden. This is at the forefront of my mind.

I'm having surgery tomorrow. Alex and I are going to a party tonight. A party in the hills. It is Mike and Charlie's, old friends from London who live in LA now. Charlie, an aspiring rock star, has his band playing tonight. Mike is to become their manager. Mike, who had sat for hours at my bedside in the hospital and asked if I needed anything. Charlie, who I had been in love with years before at the sweet age of 15, as he sang along to the tunes we heard at friends' parties. Charlie, who strives for something the same way I do. We will overcome the obstacles. I can see it in his eyes. He has the same glimmer of hunger as me. No matter what it takes, we will always try.

Alex rushes round to open my door. He's driving my car. I want to relax. I am feeling nervous about having my eye surgery in the morning. Even though I have had it done before, I realise there are only so many times Dr Rosenbaum will operate before he tells me I have to have a glass eye. I don't let my mind go there. I can't. I've been informed of the actors and actresses who have glass eyes, but I don't want to be added to the list. I step out of the car and am immediately taken with the view. Los Angeles is sparkling. This is why it is called Tinsel Town. The entire city is electric. It seems almost magical. Mike and Charlie are living in a large house in the hills where the view is enough to transport you to a land where you can disappear in daydreams. The music is loud. The drunken slurs and chatter can be heard as they make their way to the street where we are both still standing. Alex is looking at me with a large smile. I wonder if there is ever a time when he doesn't smile. I have never known a man with as much energy.

We descend the windy staircase. I'm holding on tightly to whatever I can so as not to fall. We pass a kitchen on the way down. It is packed with drinking, flirting and scrambling for bottle openers. The floor is soaked in beer and cigarette butts. A large deck surrounds the house, on which the bar is set up, some barbecues and the band. This is a rock 'n' roll crowd. The girls are clad in leather and red lipstick. The men are almost dressed the same, only a few more tattoos and piercings visible. After saying our hellos, we search for somewhere to be still. A grassy bank by the barbecue seems the perfect location. There are a few hippie-looking men playing bongo drums nearby. We sit and, after having a sip of my beer, I place it gently on the ground beside me, careful that it doesn't fall. I remember I shouldn't be drinking.

'I'm just going to get a Coke,' I tell Alex, as he has just got his long legs into a comfortable position.

'No, don't worry, Lou Lou, I'll go,' he quickly says. As he begins to move his body, rather than standing up, it comes towards mine. I begin to panic. What is he doing? He lunges on to me and suddenly without hesitation, his lips are pressed against mine along with his body. It is clumsy. I am unsure of what to do. I am kissing him and I feel confused. I am confused with a feeling of 'Thank God he is finally kissing me', and then with guilt. I'm not sure whether to forget his past and enjoy this moment or whether to push him away. Instead, letting my head disappear into figuring out all the different solutions ruins me. I feel like I'm back at school. I feel the uncomfortable sensation of playing spin the bottle and, when the bottle lands on me, I want to run. Having only ever played once, this was enough. My mind has left the party. Come back, Louise, Alex is kissing you. I bring myself back from my childhood memories. Alex still lies across me. He is heavy. Everyone is looking. Get him off. Get him off. I hear Mike behind me.

'Is that Lou?'

This is enough for me to push Alex off.

'What are you doing?' I stammer, as if I hadn't wanted him to do it.

'I was ... Sorry,' he says, his guilty face suddenly blushing and looking hurt. I have just embarrassed him. I feel terrible.

'Come on. Shall we go?' I say. 'I have to be up really early for surgery.'

He stands up almost as clumsily as I do, and we leave. In the car, we listen to music. He smokes a cigarette quickly. Almost too quickly. I don't feel uncomfortable like I would with an unwanted date. I am merely confused. I'm thinking about Emily. I don't want to hurt her feelings. I don't want to intrude on her past with him. When he drops me home, where his motorbike is waiting, I feel nervous again about how we are to say goodbye. This time I lean forward and kiss him. I am in blissful ignorance to his past. Then he disappears on his motorcycle and I am alone. Alone with a head full of Alex and nerves for the morning.

Jason is at my house waiting. He's spending the night as he's taking me, once again, for surgery and then has offered to stay at the house and take care of me.

★　★　★

The hospital is the same. The doctor's the same. My tears are the same.

My nerves are the same. Once again, I drift away into a land of not-knowingness. This time, I am blissful to my dreams. I dream of my kiss the night before. I wonder why my stomach had flip-flopped when he held me. I start creating scenarios for our next meeting. Our next passionate moments and then ... I'm awake.

I can't see. I can't see. The room is fuzzy. Oh, it's the Vaseline trick again. A little rub and then all clear. Jason is awake, too. He is smiling his ever-loving grin. I want to tell him that I've fallen in love and then I kick myself. It was only a kiss.

'This time, we hope to see more of a change,' the doctor says.

Jason feeds me toast in the recovery room.

'As before, Louise, Dr Rosenbaum will see you in the morning. Now you know the rules. No scratching and no itching and no aerobic exercise.'

I laugh with Jason, 'As if I were thinking of doing aerobic exercise.'

Then we go home. Alex is waiting at the house. Then I realise why the doctor had said no aerobic exercise.

Jason takes me to my bedroom where he arranges the feathered pillows on my bed so that my head will be elevated. Where is Alex? While Jason has his head down, I sneak out to look for him. I find him in the kitchen making a hot drink. He sees me. He grabs me. We kiss again and again. I'm delirious. I feel like a child who is skipping around the room having being given the biggest gift of all.

'Lou?' I hear shouted from the bedroom. 'Come and get into bed.'

Now a naughty child, I run back to Jason.

Alex follows me into the bedroom where Jason has made the bed, adjusted for an eye patient. While I'm getting into the bed, Jason asks Alex to go into the sitting room with him. Alex winks at me and disappears. When he returns, he is giggling.

'What?' I ask,

'No aerobic exercise, Miss Ashby.'

Great – thanks, Jason, how embarrassing. This leaves when Alex gets on to the bed next to me and starts stroking my head.

'You're wonderful, Lou,' he says.

I want to cry. He is stroking my damaged head. Cringe. He's going to feel the bumps any minute. Breathe, Louise.

Dr Rosenbaum is more serious than before, it seems. Jason's holding my hand. I feel more pathetic than last time. Perhaps because I know what they're going to do. I lay my head back. I feel the tape being removed from the bandage and then I feel cold air around my eye as the bandage comes away. I think about how my father isn't here. I haven't asked him to be. I feel it was too much pressure after the past few times. It is a long way to come for him. He wouldn't be able to watch this. I remember how he had sat holding my feet the day that Dr Kawamoto sewed my eyelids together. I thought back to all the nasty things I'd had done to me from this accident. This was to be one of the more uncomfortable.

Then it begins. 'Look left,' and, as I do, my eye is moved right, through Dr Rosenbaum pulling on the sutures. I want to leap out of the chair. I want it to be done already.

'OK, ENOUGH,' I scream.

A repeat performance of the last time. This is noted. 'Not again, Louise. You have to be still.'

This time I have Jason whispering in my ear, 'Breathe, Lou. It'll be over soon.'

I wonder what Alex is doing right now. I wonder if he knows what I'm doing? I wonder if he is thinking of me. I feel a strange little flutter in my stomach as I think about him. This is a helpful distraction and keeps my mind busy for the 15 minutes that I'm tortured in the chair.

'OK, done,' Dr Rosenbaum says, and the hand-held mirror is brought to my face. There I am. My eye is down half-way. You can still see it is up in the clouds, but more of the iris and pupil are visible. I sigh. I sigh out all of my anxiety from the morning's pains and nerves.

'So, come back and see me next week and we'll take it from there,' he says. I give him a hug. He smiles warmly. That is surgery number six. I'm getting there. Slowly but surely. It's almost two years since the accident. It feels longer.

My life feels so different. I can see the signs of the collaborations of my surgeries. It is strange to see your face go through all the different formations that mine has gone through. It is incredible how the human body is able to take what it takes.

I check the messages on my phone when we are in the car. He has left a message. He will be at my house at 1.00pm. It is now 11.00am. I look at Jason and jump in my seat. He laughs at me.

'You're so pathetic, Lou,' he says endearingly.

When Alex arrives, I am tucked up in bed. I'm warm and comfortable and trying to hide the excitement I feel upon hearing his voice when he enters the house. I want to adjust my position. Maybe I should pretend to be asleep. It's too late. He's here. He's in the doorway. In his hands, he is holding a small bunch of brightly-coloured flowers. In the other hand are my eye solution and a clean gauze.

'I have come to clean your eye,' he tells me.

'Oh, doctor, really ...' I play along.

As he sits on the bed, I melt. I feel the sickness of how happy he's making me. His touch is gentle and, as he leans in close to my face while cleaning my eye, I'm not ashamed. I'm not ashamed that this man is able to study my scars. I'm not ashamed that he's cleaning the dry blood away from my eye. I want him to move his arm and kiss me and then, as if he's a mind reader, he does. Then the solution is thrown to the floor. With his foot he kicks the door shut. He kisses my face. He raises my T-shirt and slides his warm, large hand underneath and cups my breast. I can feel my breath becoming fast. Then the door flies open and we hear an almighty, 'OY. I'm not kidding. No exercise. Alex, I told you. Louise, don't do it,' Jason is yelling, looking very serious. 'This is serious shit, Alex. Her eye has to heal.'

'We were only ... we weren't doing anything,' I argue.

Alex sits up. 'Don't worry, man,' he says, 'it's OK.' Jason leaves.

Alex leans back towards me. 'Lou?'

'Yes,' I say, feeling that the brightness in my eye's about to blind him. I stare at him, ignoring the uncomfortable, heavy pain that is flying through my left eye. Ow, shit, that hurts. Ignore it. Ignore it. Look ahead. Forget the pain.

'I know this is really soon but ...'

OK, heart, slow down.

'I love being with you. I love everything about you. I love kissing you. I don't want to scare you. I hope it hasn't.'

I watch his face turn in the many directions of nerves and realisations as he professes his feelings for me. I feel the same. This has never happened to me before. Not like this. I have been in love before but this feels different.

'Let's go away for the weekend.' He is excited. 'Let's get in the car and drive along the coast and find somewhere to stay.'

He is spontaneous. Just as I am. Before I answer him, I'm already out of the bed, collecting things to take with me. First, I take a large painkiller from my orange bottle to ease the throbbing pain across my eye and head.

We appear in the kitchen where Jason is making a sandwich. He doesn't look amused when he sees the packed overnight case and the dribbled grin stretched across my face.

'What are you doing?' he says as he flings the knife on the plate. 'Lou, where are you going?' He leans back and puts his hands around his face.

'We're going to go away for a few days. Just to relax,' I say eagerly, too eagerly.

'Lou. I'm sorry, but that pisses me off. That is not going to be relaxing. You need to rest.'

'I'm not going to let anything happen to her,' Alex reassures.

Jason ignores us and picks up his plate. He moves into the lounge where he sits back on the couch.

'Bye, then. Louise, don't come crying to me if your eye is in pain.'

Jason's voice is but a mere hum. When we get into the car, I become serious as I remember Emily. This isn't fair. Maybe Jason is right and I should go back in. Maybe I should stop this before it begins. The thought of not going and of not being with Alex is unbearable. I was just beginning to have fun.

'Al? I need to talk to you about ...'

He kisses my mouth to stop me from talking. 'That's the past, Lou. She would want me to be happy. You make me happy. Please let it go.'

These are the only words I needed to hear from him. I knew I would have to talk to Emily. I felt it only fair that I talk to her about how and why it happened. Emily had been a good friend to me through my accident and had been to visit me in the hospital a number of times. More than Charlotte. I owed it to her to be an honest friend.

The trip to San Francisco, which is where we ended up after 12 hours in the car and four painkillers, was exhausting. When we arrived, there was nowhere to stay as we discovered a convention was happening that weekend. After driving around and stopping for dinner, we found a hotel in the middle of what seemed like crack central. I realised this in the morning when I opened the curtains in the hotel room and saw the view of a park filled with homeless and brown paper bags. Alex was incredible. He was taking care of me and, even though I knew it was sudden and very early to feel these things, I didn't want to be away from him for a minute.

Alex comes with me to see Dr Rosenbaum. The news is the same. The eye is down but has moved up once more. Dr Rosenbaum looks at me with the look that I don't like to see.

'Louise, I hate to say it but we have to be careful.' Pause. 'It is down. I know how determined you are to have it all the way, but I think we have to be realistic.'

'What about another surgery? How long should I wait?'

'We have options, Louise. There is the possibility of a glass eye. They are not as bad as you think.' He is covering my options and, when he talks about the glass eye, I feel my body sink into the ground. I will not let all this leave me with a glass eye. I have to try one more time.

'Please, Dr Rosenbaum. Just one more time.'

A deep, long, tired sigh. A shake of the head. He looks at me with his large, perfect, brown eyes and can see that I have to hear a 'yes'.

'OK. Come and see me in a few months.'

I knew that maybe I wasn't being realistic. At the same time, I knew I couldn't give up and let the medical doubts cloud my determination.

Headache

'We don't see things as they are,
We see them as we are.'
Anais Nin

Christmas fills me with warmth. This is my first Christmas with Alex. We've moved into a guest house in Beverly Hills. My sister, Abigail, is arriving to spend Christmas with us. I'm at the airport waiting for her. I am apprehensive about her meeting Alex. He means so much to me that, more than ever, it's important that he gets on with my family. Abigail has heard about him through my endless chatter on the phone. She knows I'm happy. Not only am I in love, but I've lost over a stone in weight because of it. My joy has led me to take more classes. I am inspired to do all the things I love. Alex and I have been going away at the weekends at any chance we can. This seems to be more often than not. We've been to San Francisco, Las Vegas, Palm Springs, the Grand Canyon, and Las Vegas again. We've been together for six months. I've never been happier.

The airport has the feeling of Christmas spirit. Families are arriving and leaving to be with their loved ones. I used to love Christmas more than any other time of year. That has changed now. My mother used to make us feel the world was ours. Anything we wanted, we could have. Now that we're separated, I knew that I would have to wait until I had my own family. I hoped this would be with Alex. He would make a wonderful father. My thoughts are interrupted as I see my grown-up younger sister coming through the gates. A large suitcase and various plastic bags are on the trolley. I leap out of the car, desperate to hug her. I run towards her feeling that I haven't seen her in over a year. I can't let go when I hold her. She has become thin and so tall. Abigail's face has become stronger and her freckles are still plentiful. She smiles broadly and then moans, 'I had a crying baby next to me all the way.' I take the trolley from her grip.

'Don't worry, we're going straight home.' I continue by telling her how luxurious our home is. I explain that I thought it best to collect her on my own and that Alex is at the house waiting for us.

While driving home, I feel a heavy sensation through my head and nose. I try to ignore it but it's sending the old creepy-crawly sensations through my cheeks and top lip again. Then a sudden, sharp pain shoots across my eye. I bring my hand up to my head quickly.

'What's wrong?' Abi asks, concerned.

I don't want to worry her and, trying to be sure myself that it's nothing, I say, 'Nothing. I'm fine.'

The windy streets of Coldwater Canyon take us to my new home. It's behind a large, rather unattractive, modern-looking structure. We drive up the steep driveway and park. The front door bursts open as Alex makes his presence known. He rushes down the short staircase to help with the bags and introduce himself to Abi. She's tired and tries to be as warm as she can. I usher her up the steps quickly, excited for her to see the house. As we walk in, the large sitting room with the large fireplace, which is filled with bright, gold flames, greets us. To the right of the doorway is a small, clean, marble-tiled kitchen. Then there is a carpeted narrow corridor. Along this and to the right is the luxurious marbled bathroom, then a little further is the guest room, which has French windows facing a back yard. At the end of the corridor is mine and Alex's room. This, too, is spacious and light. The warmth in the house is ever-present.

Abigail throws her things in her room and makes herself comfortable on my oversized Alice in Wonderland couch. I make a pot of tea. The pains begin again. I turn away to the window so as not to be seen. Alex notices. I tell him it's nothing. His reaction lets me know that he doesn't believe me. I glare at him. He knows to say nothing.

Abigail tells me stories of her life in London. Her new job. Her new man. Her new friends. And about Oliver. My favourite boy, my brother. I wished he had been able to come for Christmas, too, but he thought it best financially and for his father to stay home.

I'm listening to my sister and her tales of London. The pains in my head have become a consistent ache. There is a strange, sharp signal going through my nose. I'm trying to ignore it. I don't want to worry or fade in any way when it's Abigail's first night here. I haven't been ill in a long while and I'm sure that tonight's pains must be from excitement at my sister's arrival. I excuse myself and disappear to the bedroom where I fumble through my drawers to find a painkiller. The bottle is empty. The frustrations from the aches are making me moody. I need to lie down. I want to shut my eyes. Alex comes into the room and finds me crouched over the bed.

'What are you doing? Are you OK?'

'Yes,' I reply quickly, worried about Abigail being alone in the other room and sensing that something is wrong. 'I'm fine. Fine. Fine. Please ...'

'No, Lou. I'm sorry, but you need to lie down. Your sister will understand. I'll call the doctor.'

It felt safe to have someone who cared this much about me so close by. I was really worried about Abigail's reaction to my being sick on her first night. I shuffle into the sitting room where she is flicking through the hundreds of television channels. I sit next to her and put my hand up to stroke her hair. I'm aware of how sensitive she is and how she needs me to take care of her. She turns her tired face towards mine and smiles that familiar smile, 'Hello, Lou Lou.'

I squeeze her arm. 'It's so good to have you here, Abs.'

Then a shooting pain happens. I grimace. Abi notices.

'What's wrong? Is everything OK?' she says, concerned again.

I smile, but see this as an opportunity to explain that I might not feel up to going out tonight. 'We can order in and rent movies, though. Would you mind? Then I'll go to the doctor in the morning and he'll give me something for it.'

Abigail understands and says the fact that she's in LA is enough. I'm relieved. Alex comes in and signals to me to go to the bedroom. He mimes a phone to his ear.

'Louise. It's Dr Kawamoto. Alex told me what you're feeling. I'm sure it's nothing to worry about but I'd like you to go down to Cedars in the morning and get an MRI. Just to be on the safe side. It sounds like you have a sinus infection and because of the inside of your head being the way it is, the pains will be intensified ten-fold.'

I write down the directions for the following morning. He phones in a prescription for painkillers to the pharmacy. Alex, the superhero boyfriend, drives to the store to pick them up for me. The pain is eased.

I hardly sleep through the night. The pains are getting worse. The evening chill is causing the metal in my head to give me a headache, adding to the aches from the sinus infection. I leave the house with Alex early in the morning. I leave Abigail sleeping and put a note by her door.

At the hospital, we're taken down cold, airy corridors to the X-ray and MRI rooms. I can feel the echo of every sound in the corridor thunder through my fragile head. I have forms to fill out. Alex gives the nurse Dr Kawamoto's instructions. I'm taken to a room where I'm put in the claustrophobic MRI machine. I'm strapped face down and unable to move. The machine makes an electronic sound as I'm automatically moved into the tubing. The nurse talks to me through the microphone in the other room as she can sense my discomfort at having my head and body in a tube.

I have a new awareness. I can no longer get the common cold. For my colds, I'm being rushed to the hospital for MRIs. When would this end? I am embarrassed. I feel like a drama queen. I wait patiently in the tube. I close my eyes. I hope Abi is still asleep in bed and hasn't woken up upset that we left. I hope this doesn't take too much longer. Alex must be thinking, what kind of a crazy woman is he involved with? I come with so much baggage. How could he be happy? Stop, Louise. These are your hospital insecurities coming out.

I remember, once, when Matthew was flicking through a magazine looking at the beautiful models, I screamed at him. It was when I was still badly disfigured. It was terrible for him. I'd stood up and yelled, 'I'M SO FUCKING SORRY I DON'T LOOK LIKE A MODEL. I'M SO SORRY THAT YOUR GIRLFRIEND HAS A FUCKED-UP FACE.' That was a bad day. Even though my appearance has changed, it is apparent to me that the insecurities are still there. They had always been there. When I was at school, I always compared myself to the other girls. I always felt I had to be beautiful. Then, whatever I had was taken from me. When I was younger, I had nightmares that my mother would die, then she did. My head was off in a foreign land of fear now. It was because I was trying to breathe without panic in this machine. The reality that my inside would make my outside look better had become one that I treasured. The ten minutes that I was in the machine seemed like for ever. Alex is pacing the corridor. His heart is too large for his chest, I'm sure.

We sit and wait in the chilly corridor on a couple of wooden chairs for the results. A sinus infection is confirmed. More drugs are prescribed. We leave the hospital and return home to where I'm hoping my sister is finding everything all right. Before we go back into the house, we kiss in the car. His touch makes me feel more than it used to. Every day I spend with Alex, I fall more in love. I want my life to be with him. I have nightmares of losing him. I sometimes wake up in the middle of the night screaming. He wakes me from a bad dream of being without him. My fear of losing him is sometimes overwhelming and worries me. I'm sure that anyone who has lost a loved one feels this when they find someone they care deeply for. It's an automatic instinct. I can understand why some are jumpy about getting involved. We have to continue our experiences.

The day is spent at the house. I'm in great pain. The drugs aren't working yet. I don't want to mix them with painkillers at this point. There is tension. I cannot figure out if it's because Abigail wants time alone with me, or if she has something else on her mind. Alex leaves the house for a while. Abi stays in her room. When I beckon her out, she asks me politely to leave her alone. I'm weak now and too tired to argue. I fall asleep on the couch. When I wake up she is making tea and watching me. I smile over at her. She disappears back into her room. I call Alex. 'Please can you take Abi out tonight?' I feel the slur in my words. These drugs are strong. They're making me dizzy.

I persuade Abi to go out with Alex. Not much persuasion is necessary. Suddenly her glum face is happy. An evening out! This is what she needed. I can relax now. She'd been working hard in London and now needed to let go. Alex made me promise to page him if I needed to. I gave them a reassuring smile and they left.

I am alone. I feel like an old woman. I feel like a sick mother. My sick mother. Too sick to have fun. I flick through the channels. I turn the volume down. My head is still pounding. I drift asleep.

The room is thick. My heart is beating fast. I am sweating. I can't breathe. Panic rushes through me. My head is spinning. I'm having a reaction to the medicine. It must be the medicine. Where is everybody? Oh my God, I'm alone. Breathe, breathe, I must keep breathing. My nose is blocked. I am weak. My vision is blurred. I find the phone and page Alex. It is 11.30pm and I feel guilty. I'm intruding on their evening but *I can't breathe*. Alex calls straight back and says they'll come home. I keep apologising. He ignores me.

When they come in, I'm sitting upright on the couch. I am focusing on the television to keep my mind from the anxiety that has been coursing through my veins. Alex rushes over to me and feels my head. I try to smile but resemble a terrified bunny. Abigail shoots me a look, her face saddens and she goes to her room. I've upset her. I have ruined her evening. I want to go and say I'm sorry but Alex nudges me back into the comfort of the pillows he has plumped. After sitting with me for a while and stroking my hair, I feel a little calmer. He carries me to the bedroom where I fall asleep. Abigail has not been seen.

I feel better this morning. I slept through the night without waking. Alex is still sleeping, as is Abi. I want to take her out today and treat her to something. At 11.00am she's still sleeping. Then at 12.00pm there is still no sound. I knock quietly on the door.

'Go away,' I hear.

'Abi? It's me. Are you getting up?' I say quietly.

'I said, "Go away,"' she repeats.

I feel bad and turn the knob. She screams at me. I am shocked and stumble back. Alex comes running to see what the noise is about.

'I think I need to be alone with her,' I tell him. He leaves the house. I feel terrible that this friction has come about and don't know what I could have done wrong. I want to make sure she's OK. I leave her alone and go back to the couch. Before I leave, I tap on her door.

'If you want to talk, I'll be on the couch. Alex has gone out. It's just you and me.'

Time passes and then I hear Abi's bedroom door open and close. I hear the footsteps approaching. I sit still, not wanting to upset her. When I see her face, she is already upset. My sister's face is red and blotchy and it's obvious she's been crying for a while. I move towards her to hold her. She puts her hands up in between her sniffles.

'Lou, I'm sorry. It's not you. It's really not,' she begins. 'I can't bear it. I can't bear seeing you sick. Are you dying?'

The last words come out with another burst of tears.

I am shocked. It hadn't crossed my mind that she'd been thinking this.

'Abi, no. Why would you think that?' My voice is soft and caring.

'Well, you looked like Mum last night. Weak and sleeping on the sofa. It scared me and I got angry with you for feeling ill because I got scared ...'

'It's because of the accident, Abi.'

'But Lou, that was almost three years ago. You should be over it by now.'

I reach over for my sister. I understand all of her pains and doubts of love. She was so strong and so desperately in need of someone to take care of her. I had left her when I moved here when she was only 15 and now she needed me. As much as I needed her. We needed to understand each other. I understood her anger for the first time. I explained my injuries to her and how they were affecting my life but in no way was I dying. I was merely adjusting, and in time I would be better.

I had forgotten what it was like *not* to be the one who was sick. I had forgotten how hard it is to watch someone you care about in pain. I had become the one in the physical pain and, because it was now my life, I had adjusted to that. But now, listening to Abi, I remembered how torturous it was to watch our mother suffer. Even though she found her strength, our lives had to change. Now I had made my family's lives change. I realised how I needed to remember that. I wasn't guilty of anything but trying to understand. I couldn't adjust fate.

Patched Up

September 1995, London

My bed offers me comfort as I lie in, thinking about solutions to situations. These past eight months have given me more confidence as I progress in my journey to perfection. My eye, thanks to Dr Rosenbaum's last surgery a few months ago, is socially acceptable. The eye-patch is gone. I didn't want it to go. When the time came, it was hard to say goodbye. I was suddenly aware that it had become my identity. Who I was in Hollywood; the girl with the patch. It gave people a reason to come and talk to me. I was different. Now I was the same as everyone else.

For the first few weeks, I still held my hand across my left eye when I spoke to someone. Alex would nudge me, 'Lou, take your hand away, there's nothing to hide.' Then, slowly, my hand would move and I was sure that I was being assessed for damage. There was still something noticeable. There was a third of an inch of white showing under the iris. It looked like a lazy eye. This is nothing considering what it had been. I still saw all the imperfections, even through their rebuilding. They would never feel or look the same to me. As long as the rest of the world couldn't see the damage behind the mask, I was OK.

Now I am able to stay in touch with life. All lives take a whack. This time, I'm able to be there for someone else. I can feel his pain and fear. This morning, the news came.

The phone rang and I had a brief chat with Alex's mother. She didn't sound good. She sounded panicked. Alex took the phone. He stayed in the other room for a while talking and then, when he reappeared, I knew something was wrong. He had to go to London. His father was sick. He had cancer. I had to go, too. I needed to be with him. This was something I knew about and I had been in his position.

We packed bags and made calls. Alex is flying today and I am leaving tomorrow. I don't know how long we're going for, but I pack until after Christmas. My girlfriend Tamara is planning a trip to LA for a few months. We speak and I offer her my apartment and, in return, she offers me hers in London. This will be a base for Alex and myself. I am apprehensive about the trip. I pray to God that Sydney, Alex's father, makes it through this terrible time and I pray to God to take care of Alex and to give him strength.

When my flight arrives at Heathrow Airport, London, I go straight to the hospital. Alex is already there. I haven't met his father before. I have met Helene, his mother. I adore her. Alex greets me. He looks exhausted. He tells me the news. Sydney has stomach cancer and has lost a lot of blood. They have done several operations and are figuring out his chances. This feels all too familiar. I want to be strong and I feel that I am. I don't want my Alex to be put through the same pain that I was. Then I see Helene. She's not doing so well. We go outside for a cigarette and she cries. She's being strong, though. His family are finding it hard to look at Sydney, to see the machines and the blood. This is another feeling I'm familiar with. I want to meet the incredible Sydney that I've heard so much about. Alex takes me to the room. First he goes in and checks on Sydney, then I am given the OK.

Sydney Carlton was the kindest, most generous-hearted man I ever had the pleasure to meet. The instant I walked in, he made an impact on me. Not once did he feel sorry for himself, or choose to acknowledge his illness. He was concerned only about his family and friends' well-being. Even though exhausted from his surgery, he wanted to talk to me. He wanted to get to know me. He wanted to talk about things that were important to me. He was an angel brought down to earth to teach kindness and humility, of this I am sure. I could see why I was so in love with Alex. I could see where Alex got his incredible qualities. Sydney was a handsome man. His eyes sparkled and ran so deeply brown that I would melt into his words when he spoke. This wasn't fair. The questions and arguments I had never had with God before, I was having now.

We left the hospital and didn't sleep much that night. We stayed up drinking wine with Helene. We talked about Sydney and about Alex's plans to stay in London for a while. I said I would stay, too, at least until after Christmas. It was important for me to be with Alex. I didn't want to leave him.

My family was pleased to have me home, obviously not under the circumstances. My grandmother worried about me going through another family's pain from cancer after having already gone through it once. In an odd way, I felt like I was able to use my experience to help them. I knew the terminology. I began to understand more about my mother's illness and her reactions. I talked to Sydney about my mother's illness, only because he asked. I talked to him about anger and fear and why bad things happen to good people. What lessons we are meant to learn. He asked about my accident and even that experience could be put to good use. I started remembering things about Mum that I had forgotten. I felt close to Sydney even though I had only known him such a short time. Alex was being so strong and supportive for his family. He tried to do everything.

The Carltons lived in Hampstead. My mother died in Hampstead, at the Royal Free Hospital. I had never been back there. I had spent too many years there. Now, whenever Alex and I were driving home, I made him drive up the back streets to avoid the hospital. I caught a glimpse of the corridors of lights one evening and felt the tears immediately come to my eyes. Then, one night, I felt brave. My mother had set up a charity before she died – The Children's Leukaemia Trust. Her aim was to raise money to build a ward at the Royal Free for children. Recently, the ward had been built and was in my mother's name. No one in my family had seen it. We all let the memories of her death override our strength to visit the hospital.

This particular night as we are driving home, the fog outside and the corridors of lights again visible, I turn to Alex and say, 'Please take me there. I want to go and see the ward. I want you to come with me.' Ever since Alex and I had been together, I had always wished my mother could have met him. I knew she would have adored him as much as I.

We drove up to the hospital and, rather than being afraid, I was more excited. I wanted to feel the sensations I used to feel when she was there. I wanted the memories to come flooding back, even if it meant I would break down in tears. I needed to feel the loss of her again. I wasn't torturing myself, merely feeling the necessities of the closeness I had with my mother again. Alex held my hand. We always held hands. We made our way to the ward where my mother had spent so much of her last four years. I found the nurse who had helped to care for her.

'Louise. Wow, you look ... I heard about your crash. I'm so sorry. It's so good to see you ...' she gushed, genuinely pleased to see me. She told me she hadn't been up to the ward herself as she found it too sad. Then she said she would come with us and show me where it was.

I cannot explain sufficiently the feelings I felt upon entering this ward. Seeing the placard on the wall with my mother's name. Children running along the corridors, with their recently-chemotherapied bodies. Their balding heads and yet large smiles, filled with innocence and fighting their pains. I feel her all around me. More than anywhere, this is where I felt her energy.

'These children are alive because of your mother, Louise. Because of the money your mother raised they are able to have these air filters in the ceilings up here that take out harmful bacteria,' the nurse said. She was crying softly. I was crying. Alex was amazed. I felt like my mother was God. She had turned her illness into an incredible gift. I stood in the silence of the overwhelming energy I felt in the ward. I suddenly sensed the strength I had felt come into me the day my mother died. I knew that I was going to be all right and that her gifts had been passed on. Alex wrapped his arms around me and squeezed me, filling me with the safety of his love.

'Are you OK?' he said. 'She was an incredible woman, like you, Lou.'

I had never felt the honour of having the mother I'd had as much as I did at that moment. When we left the hospital, I felt complete and refreshed. It was a very strange sensation, as though she had been with me and spoken to me. I felt strong.

Knowing that we were in London for a while, I decided that I could take my first steps into getting my career back. I started making calls to agents. This time, I knew I wouldn't have to offer the *Star Trek* and horror movie option. I met with Janet Malone who, after a half-hour chat in person and explanations to her of my situation, signed me. I couldn't believe my luck. I had told her about the eye and she didn't flinch.

'We'll see what feedback we get from sending you out on auditions,' she said. I kept thinking something was going to go wrong. I wanted to leave her office before she changed her mind.

Sydney was home from the hospital and had a new set of doctors at a hospital in Fulham. Everyone was adjusting to the impact this was having on their lives. Alex was helping Sydney run the office and I was trying to be as supportive as possible. For the first time in years, I felt like I had a home in London again. I felt like Alex, Sydney and Helene were my new family. Sydney told stories and played practical jokes. Alex and him were a comedy duo. Helene rolled her eyes and chuckled. Years of the same antics, no doubt.

I took Alex to meet my family. My father adored him. My heart felt full. Oli enjoyed his new drinking buddy. My father and I were getting on again. I realised he hadn't been able to see me in the pain I had been in. One night, I questioned him about it. I asked him why he had never told me he was proud of my strength. I asked him why he thought I was weak. He looked at me in amazement.

'Louise, I don't know how you did it. I couldn't say that to you at the time because I thought if I did, then you might not feel you needed to be strong any more.'

He was a happier man now as well. He had a new girlfriend. Another young one! I wanted him to be happy and she made him happy. I could see it.

My first audition was for a commercial to be shot in Italy. I had to be a bride. I was nervous. I still felt unsure of my eye. I hadn't seen it on camera. I wasn't eating much because of the stressful lifestyle Alex and I were now a part of, so I didn't have a clothing 'what to wear?' drama. Everything I owned from the age of 17 now fitted me.

When I walked into the room and saw the camera, I froze. I searched the room for the lighting arrangements and to see at what angles I could hide my profile. What if they saw my dents and bumps? What if they started laughing at me and asked me to leave? I shuffled over to the marking on the floor and did the routine. Side profiles, look into the camera, say your name and who your agent is. I had read the short script outside and was prepared for my short acting moment. The casting director laughed at the right times. I felt confident about that. But then when she turned to her assistant, I was tempted to grab the tape from the back of the camera. I didn't want them to look at it and then notice things they hadn't seen.

Janet called me in the morning.

'Louise, hi, love. Listen, they really liked you at the casting yesterday and said you were right for the part.'

I listened attentively.

'But I'm afraid they saw a problem with your eye and so they've gone with somebody else.'

My heart stopped. My breath stopped. My life stopped. This was it. I had done all of this work on my face and still I was being rejected.

'Oh,' I managed. This was the response from the auditions that followed.

'How about another surgery? I think it's worth it. You're obviously talented,' Janet said one day.

'Right,' I said.

My father thought I should see someone in London. He made the appointment with a specialist at a hospital in Pimlico. I argued that the doctor wouldn't know what to do with me. If I had to have more surgery, then I needed to be with my regular doctors. We had a fight. I obliged him.

The waiting room was crammed full of people. The forms didn't have enough room for me to list all of my injuries and surgeries. I had to ask for more paper and was met with a very disturbing look from the attending nurse.

'Right,' she said in a 'doctor evil' kind of way.

I could see that my father was nervous as he kept rearranging the magazines on the low wooden table. Then they said my name.

We were taken into an ordinary doctor's office, no specialised eye machinery in sight. Mixed with the relief, was the question – why not? The doctor sat upright at his desk. His pen torch hanging from his top pocket. Then he looked at me.

'Well, look at that eye, then,' he said, almost rudely.

I was taken aback and couldn't force a smile. I turned and looked at my father with a questioning look of 'Where did you find this doctor?' My father glared at me to turn back to the doctor. I did and he was waiting for me to say why we were here. I began telling him the story and when I got as far as, 'I'm an actress so it's really important that my eye is in the right place,' he laughed and interrupted.

'Well, you'd better think of another profession, hadn't you? I mean, it's a tough business and no one's going to hire you with your eye like that.'

I looked around for the cameras. This must be a joke. Surely this doctor had not just been as contemptuous as I'd thought. But he had, and he was still staring at me.

Now my lack of inhibitions kicked in. I flew at him with my verbal abuse. I explained surgical procedures that he'd never heard of. I told him to take his indignant manner and use it with someone else as I had no intentions of having him come near me with his stupid pen torch and eye drops.

My father, completely embarrassed, kept urging me to close my mouth and hush the witch. But she was mad and she was out. We left the office, I briskly and my father apologetically. I had got used to this. Alex had to apologise for my behaviour a lot of the time, especially when I was hungry.

The news made it clear to me that I needed to have more surgery with Dr Rosenbaum. This meant that I had to think about Los Angeles. Christmas was a week away. We had been in London for two months. Tamara would be coming back soon. I had to think about my apartment in LA and the reality of mine and Alex's situation.

We sat down to talk about it. I knew Alex had to be in London. He knew I had to go back to LA to have more surgery. I couldn't stop crying. I didn't want to be apart from him. He didn't want to be apart from me. Helene asked if I couldn't move back to London for a while. I thought about everything I'd gone through in the past few years. I thought about the life I had built for myself in America. I thought about the dreams I had. I knew I had to give it a go. I needed to do it for myself. Not because I disliked London but because I had left on a mission in 1992 and my mission wasn't accomplished yet. I hadn't had a chance to start yet.

We decided that I would go back to LA in January. I would have the eye surgery and then come back for a while a couple of months later. Then Alex would come to LA for a month and so on.

The thought of being apart for months at a time seemed

unthinkable. I knew not to harp on to him, as his reason for staying in London was one I understood. He had his own pains to think of now. I had to be supportive and do what he needed me to do.

Christmas was beautiful. I fell more in love with Alex than ever before. We started talking about our future together. I loved his family and I felt that I had found what I wanted my in-laws to be. We talked about marriage. I cried at the prospect of us being apart while I was having surgery. I didn't want to leave him. I didn't want to leave Sydney or Helene. I didn't want to leave my family who I had become accustomed to being nearby again. My best friends were only a small distance away. Then I remembered my reason for going back and I knew I would return soon. March was the date we set for my return. Then my eye would be fixed and we could further our discussions about our lives together and what the future held.

Heartache

'I asked for Strength. And God gave me difficulties to make me strong.
I asked for Wisdom. And God gave me problems to solve.
I asked for courage. And God gave me danger to overcome.'
Anonymous

January 1996

The house is cold without him. I'm finding it hard to sleep. Alex is back in London and I'm here alone. I've never missed anyone as much as I do now. The bed feels empty and too big. I've seen Dr Rosenbaum and he doesn't want to work on my eye again. He thinks if he does, I'll lose it. The talks are back to having a glass eye.

I went out last night and got drunk. I went out with friends to escape from the decisions and feelings that were surfacing. When I spoke to Alex this morning, he got angry that I had been out drinking and wanted to know who with.

'Was it that guy who likes you there?' he had huffed.

He *had* been there and I didn't want to upset Alex by telling him. I tried to change the subject. To talk about something else. We had come up with an idea for a presenting show for me to do while wearing the eye-patch. We had written it together and a friend of mine was going to direct it. Alex was upset that he couldn't be here to work with us.

'Dad is doing well,' he tells me, 'he's being strong.'

I feel so far away. I want to reach through the phone and touch his face. I want him to know how much I love him and think about him. He knows. He feels the same.

As I thought about my plans to act with my eye-patch, I became frustrated. I knew I had to take one more chance. I call Dr Rosenbaum and book the surgery with his assistant.

'But, Louise, are you sure you want to take this risk?' she questions.

They had suggested a clinic in San Francisco where I could get a contact lens fitted for my eye with a picture of an eye on it. I spoke to the clinic. They said they couldn't help me because of the immobility of my eye. I had to have surgery. My grandmother and my father were less than pleased. My father booked a flight and said he would be here.

My father arrived. He's staying with me. I feel that he doesn't want to be here as much as he wants to be in London with his girlfriend. I feel that he's upset I'm having the surgery.

'I think this is silly, Louise. But you won't listen to me,' he says.

I won't listen to anyone. I have become stubborn and determined. I won't listen to Alex. He's upset that the doctor said there were risks and I was going ahead. I felt deep down that it would be fine.

My father drives me to the hospital early in the morning, where I know the routine. Change clothes, scrub face and eye area, take a Valium, get into the bed with the backless gown that freezes your bottom and lie in wait for the anaestheseologist to give the inebriating pre-med. I loved the pre-med. I couldn't feel any of my worries. I still cry when they come to wheel me away. My nerves would never leave my side. I would always feel my mother beside me along with my nerves.

I was lying on the cold metal trolley waiting to go into surgery. No one was around. I looked around the room. All I could see were sharp knives and tools. What were they going to be used for? I thought.

Then a nurse comes in. She is wearing a white gown with blood all over it. She has a large knife in her hand. I couldn't see her face. I start to cry. I told her I was scared and didn't want to have surgery. She pulls up the knife and cuts off my hand that is peering out from the covers. She says, 'Don't worry, I'm your nurse.' Then I look at her face and it is my mother. I scream and scream. I feel sick. I open my eyes and I can't see. The room is blurred. I scream again.

'Louise. Louise,' my dad says from the end of the bed, 'it's OK. The surgery went well. Dr Rosenbaum thinks you're going to be fine.'

'I can't see,' I say, trying to rub my eyes, relieved that it was only a nightmare I was having. Then I see Jimmy. My friend Jimmy is sitting on my bed looking at me.

'Hey, Lou,' he says, 'I just came down to check that you were OK.'

Jimmy, another new friend who offered only support. I smile at him. He knew the procedure. He'd heard about it and I think had been here before. I had to sleep off the anaesthetic and wait for my toast to arrive. This wasn't what my father had planned.

'Great, you're awake. So come on, do you feel ready to get up?' he says.

I am shocked. I'm still half-asleep. Was I being rushed or were my senses off centre? I had only just woken up. Jimmy looks at me and holds on to my hand with a comforting rub.

'I think she needs to sleep a little longer,' he says to my father.

'Well, I have to make a call to London. It's getting late and I don't want to miss her,' he responds.

I feel the blood rushing to my head. The hurt in my chest. I thought he was here for me and that I could have my father to myself, but it didn't seem so. His heart and his head were somewhere else. They were in London. I found myself appeasing him. I was in knots inside. I wanted to scream. I wanted him to tell me that he loved me and that everything else could wait. I wanted him to congratulate me on the last leg of my recovery. But no. He was up and looking for a pay phone.

'It's OK, Jimmy,' I reassure, 'I'm feeling fine.'

'Lou, don't knock the bandage and the stitches,' he reminds me as I am trying to move from the bed and into some clothes.

Dad and I drive home in silence. He's happy the surgery is over and I sense wanting to get back to London.

'Dad, if it is making you so nervous being here, then why don't you go home?' I say.

'There are no flights tomorrow. They're all booked.'

My mouth was agape. He had tried to get a flight. What was wrong with me? Had I been a terrible daughter? I called a girlfriend to help me collect my prescriptions. I couldn't ask my father to go to the pharmacy. I didn't want to burden him.

The next morning, Dad came in to check if I was awake as we had to go back to the hospital to have the eye stimulation procedure done.

I would never become accustomed to this. I was on the phone to Alex when he knocked.

'Don't worry, it'll be fine and I love you very much,' Alex said. 'I don't ever want to be without you again,' he adds.

Dad was standing in the doorway so I couldn't gush all my responses of loveliness. 'Never again,' I say.

Alex had gone a shade of green the last time I'd had this done. The doctor had removed my eye and then Alex's face changed colour and his body became weak. This didn't happen with my father. He was strong. He had seen too much before. Not just with me but with his mother and other friends who had been sick in some way. The threads are cut and I am done. It is over. The doctor smiles at me and sighs, 'It's done, Louise. It is over. No more surgeries. It's a miracle. If you hadn't made me do this, I wouldn't have. But it's worked and you're fixed.'

I search his face for sweat from the delicate procedure. It is dry, he is calm. He is a professional.

His words were the most overwhelming words I could ever have heard. Then, what I saw in the mirror confirmed it. The eye was bloody but it was in the right place. There was no more undercover white. Only the iris and the pupil. And then, as I looked from left to right, so did the eye. But it no longer looked up.

'Now, you can't look up any longer. I stopped that altogether. I tightened those muscles. This way the eye should stay down.'

I didn't try to move it as it was still sore from the operation. I trusted his words. I trusted his hands. I trusted my God and thanked him for bringing me thus far.

Alone, once again. My father has returned to his love. I am working on the show idea with Alki the director. Our minds are processing all the different ways in which we can shoot it. It will only be a ten-minute show. Friends are rallying round and want to be a part of it. I wish Alex could be here. We are filming in a couple of days' time. Tonight, I'm going out to celebrate. I don't like being at home alone at the moment. I miss Alex too much.

I am at a friend's house. A cocktail party. My drink is making me feel light-headed and good. There are beautiful people gathered. Do I once again qualify? A small group are discussing whether or not to buy some cocaine. I think about how it makes me feel. It will certainly take away my feelings of missing Alex. I just want to have a little fun. I won't do much as then I'll get depressed when I get home alone. Then my mind will think about Alex and his family in London. Then *the boy* walks in. The one that Alex dislikes. The one that likes me. He comes straight over to me. He is attractive. I look down at my glass. I mustn't drink any more. He sits down on the couch next to me. He compliments me. Then a friend approaches.

I am up. I am gone.

I return ready to chat. I don't care what about. I talk to *the boy*. I tell him about the show we are doing in a couple of days. He is laughing. It turns out he is a well-known actor in Germany. Having not been an avid viewer of German television, I am unaware. He wants to work on the show with us.

'But it's only very short and very, very silly. I mean, the humour is really stupid. There's no money,' I try and explain.

'I think it sounds great, Lou. I'd love to do it,' he says in his sexy German accent.

I'm so excited. I call Alki immediately and tell him the news. We start brainstorming as to how we could include him. He could be my long-lost lover, we decide. He will be obsessed with me and follow me around while I interview. It was done and it was written.

I got home late that night. I didn't feel well. I felt depressed about my consumption. I try to forget about it and sleep. I am unable to sleep. The drugs are working. The birds begin singing. I feel sick.

The phone wakes me. It is 10.00am. I am groggy when I pick it up.

'Hey, Lou Lou. It's Al,' the voice at the other end chirps. I stretch and sit up with my throbbing head, pleased to hear from him. I don't want him to hear the cigarette huskiness in my voice.

'How's Sydney?' I ask.

'He's doing OK,' he says.

I can hear that he's finding it hard. I'll go back in March. I have to be near him.

'How's everything going with the show?' he says.

I am relieved he asks. I want to tell him about *the boy*. I know I have to do it casually so he doesn't get upset.

'Well, I have really good news ...' I begin. As I am explaining the story, I am interrupted.

'WHAT? You saw him last night? Did you drink? Did you do drugs?

I know how open you are when you do that.'

I try to calm him down. 'Don't be silly. It's fine. But isn't it great news? He's going to do the show.'

The silence is long. 'Lou, if he does your show, then we're finished. He likes you. I know you, Lou,' he threatens.

'Don't be so pathetic,' I say, not taking him seriously. The phone goes dead.

Self-destruction

'Love yourself first and everything else falls into line.
You really have to love yourself to get anything done in this world.'
Lucille Ball

A year later

With new eyes, and a new confidence building, I am feeling nearer to the pursuit of my dreams. Nothing could hold me back other than my own insecurities. This is confirmed when a friend of a friend calls me to see if I want to audition for the new Michael Jackson video, 'A Stranger in Moscow'. I was only just at the point of holding my hand away from my eye, which I still felt was visibly weird.

Dressing for the appointment was easy. A waitress. Simple. Black skirt and white shirt. The problem arose as I arrived outside the white-bricked casting building on Ventura Boulevard. I suddenly felt nervous. Hot and cold and twitching on the left side of my face. What if my eye shows? I could always hide it by showing my other profile. I would feel so much more comfortable if my mask was on.

The casting director came out to the corridor where I was filling out the forms. Her warm smile soothed my erratic thoughts. 'Louise, why don't you come in?' I followed her into the brown-walled, dark room where a bright light and video camera were set up. 'Now you see this tray of drinks ...' she points to the set-up. 'I want you to carry that across the room with pain in your eyes.' The words couldn't have sounded any louder. Pain in my eyes. How could I hide my eye if I was looking directly into the camera? This is it. This is how it's going to be and now would be a good time to walk away. 'Just do it,' I heard myself whispering over and over again in my dull pained head. I knew I couldn't run. I had to do what she asked. I did it and I could feel the nerves itching and scratching to show their true form. To show the old disfigurements, to make the casting director cringe. I was made to do it again and again. Different angles and positions around the room. I felt I was being tortured. The following day, irony showed its glowing face as I heard the news that I had the job. How could a girl go through what I had been through and then get a job because of her eyes?

I'm in the make-up trailer. The lights are offensive. I'm tired. I had gone out for a little while last night. I didn't want to stay in. I look into the mirror. I look tired. I have been drinking too much. Way too much. I'm doing drugs, too. I know I am running. Running from everything. I haven't spoken to Alex since the day he hung up. He won't take my calls. My heart has been broken. I didn't feel it would ever be the same. Now I go out and party. I have cried more tears in the past six months than ever in my life before. Maybe they are not all for Alex, but they feel like it. I have been with other men. It's not the same. I only compare. Now I look thin and tired. I am trying not to go out so much but it is so hard to say 'no'. I don't want to stay home alone. I think about things then. I can't do that right now. I have to keep going.

My eye doesn't look good today. The lights around the mirror tell me so. I have not a trace of cover-up on. Today, I am a secretary. I chose this instead of the nun/hooker. I didn't feel the nun's rush to throw her habit from her head and dive naked into the swimming pool was an artistic choice for me. My manager suggested the secretary role. It's only five lines, but my first five in Hollywood. Today is a big day.

'I had a bad accident,' I tell the make-up artist, my insecurities and worries about her judgements on the possibility of noticing that I am not perfect are shown.

'You poor thing,' she says after taking a rest on the stool behind me to hear the wicked tale.

'I'm only telling you so you can cover up things,' I say, not wanting her to think that I am giving her the 'woe is me' yarn.

'Of course. Don't worry. There is not much to be done,' she reassures.

While I'm sitting facing the mirror, she works on my face. Before much has been achieved, the door to the trailer opens and another make-up artist comes in. Behind him is Eric Roberts, the lead in the film.

Nervous, I feel my body stiffen. I stare straight ahead. Eric sits on my left. My bad side. This means I can't see him unless I look at him through the mirror.

'Things are great. Things are great!' He finishes his conversation with his make-up guy as he sits in the chair ready to be made up. After he has got comfortable he turns his head to look at me. I continue looking ahead, feeling his gaze, knowing he's able to see my bad side. I think about the lighting. I try to think of something else.

'Holy shit!' he exclaims. 'They've done a great job on you.' Then he turns to my make-up artist. 'Good bruise.' Then back to me. 'Are you in a death scene?'

I realise he's talking about my eye. I'm horrified, humiliated and crushed. Then I remember this is me now.

'Actually, there's no make-up. This is me. I had a car accident,' I tell him.

Now he's embarrassed. He quickly apologises, raising his hands for his make-up guy to stop playing with his face. I realise I'm going to have to see Dr Kawamoto to have my eyelid worked on.

'You see this scar?' he says. 'I had a bad car accident, too.'

I sit and talk to him about my accident and he tells me about his accident. I really like him. He tells me he'd gone to RADA in London. He makes me feel good about my scars as he had them, too.

That evening, I go out to celebrate. Again, the liquor is flowing and the wraps are unfolding. It seems to have become part of the life I am leading. The crowd I am with do the same. As much as I try, I can't seem to get away from it. I don't want to get away from it. For now, it is making me feel good, as I don't have to feel.

Work is coming in. I do another small role in a movie. I do a couple of television shows. All the time, I continue drinking. I still felt empty inside. Even though I have done all this work on having my outside rebuilt, I am now ignoring my insides. I'm hiding behind the mask. Everyone thinks I am well. I am not. If I spoke to Alex, he would know. I am achieving my goals. I am dead inside. I thought I was having a good time. It was my way of escaping from the pain of my heartbreak and my past. My mental capacity to be strong seems to have gone to sleep. I had never asked for help and still don't want it. I want everyone to know that I am resilient to everything.

I stayed up all night when I received a call from London from a good friend telling me that Alex had been with someone. This made for another excuse to get high and stay up all night. I couldn't possibly let that reality sink in. Then we spoke. All the feelings were still there. I cried again. It was so good to speak to him.

When Alex called me from London to tell me that Sydney had died, I felt guilty for not having gone back to London. I wished I could have been there. I wished I could have said goodbye. I wished I could still be a part of their lives. When would this pain go away? I wanted things to be in perspective. It didn't happen. Instead, I started drinking more.

I began dating a man who enjoyed going out as much as I did. I loved him and he loved me but we both loved to drink and do drugs. I started to lose friends, people who had been so important to me. Alicia said she couldn't be around me. It was too sad for her. I thought she was wrong. I didn't understand. I was being warned to slow down. To stop the drinking. To ask for help. I couldn't. Louise had never asked for help. I was numb. I was numb to feelings now. Whenever something surfaced, it was pushed away with a drink or a drug, be it a line of cocaine or a joint. My headaches were getting bad. I started twitching. I thought it was because I needed more. I did more.

I felt appreciated for my generosity and parties. The weekends of debauchery. I had landed in Hollywood and was taking the wrong turning. Wrong for me.

Kathy and Steve had recently got back together and she was living in LA again. Then, the biggest shock of all came when Alex called me to say he'd moved back to LA. I had a boyfriend. I had a different life now. I was terrified of my feelings for him. We had seen each other but I found it difficult to let him see me drinking. I didn't know my friends in London were worried. I didn't hear the concerned pause when Wagi called at 8.00am and I was drinking wine with breakfast. I ignored Nico when he stormed out of a restaurant after telling me to slow down on the drinking. I had looked at him in disbelief – 'I only drink at the weekends.' When he left, I called him judgemental.

I broke up with my boyfriend after too many hangovers. I said he was the one with the problems. I was still going to class. I was still auditioning. I was still in during the week but, when the weekend came, the demons came out.

Then I began to notice and to dislike myself. I was finding it difficult to be with myself. It was as if I wished for sanity. My intake of drugs and alcohol was making me paranoid. My head was hurting. I felt like a self-destructive person would feel near to death and didn't seem to care. It was the darkness of the drugs. I needed to sleep more. I was becoming a different woman. I was losing the Louise that I thought I knew. I was losing the life I had fought for. Then once again, God rescued me.

An Angel Over Me

'I am me. In all the world there is no one else exactly like me.
There are persons who have some parts like me, but no one
adds up exactly like me. Therefore, everything that comes out of
me is authentically mine because I alone chose it.'
Virginia Satir

Abi arrives. It is January and I haven't seen her for two years. While I have been losing myself, she had been travelling around the world finding herself. She came with gifts. I opened the little parcels brought from India. The purple tissue paper came away and revealed two gifts that resembled the changes that would take place in my life. The first one was a wooden calendar of my life. Abigail had given the Indian man my birth details and he had carved my life chart. It could be hung on the wall. The second gift was a piece of oval-shaped ivory with a hole in the middle. It hung from a string rope.

'This resembles "new beginnings". We should hang them both above your bed and say a prayer,' she said.

We ascend to the bedroom and I hammer in a nail. I gently place the two meaningful gifts above where my head lies in the bed. We close our eyes and say a prayer. I say mine to myself. It is so good for me to have Abigail near me again. I needed her. I didn't want Abigail to hear how desperate I have become. 'Dear God. Please help me to change my life. Please help me find my way again. Help me out of this pain so that I may able to see straight and know that I have a future. Please help me stop drinking and taking drugs. Please help me to be me again and find the strength and determination that I used to have.'

I feel myself almost crying. Abigail looks at me with a soft look of concern and understanding. She reaches over and hugs me.

'It's OK, Lou Lou. Whatever it is, it's OK.'

My head is sore and my body aches. I feel like I'm coming down with the 'flu. Jimmy phones and says he'll come over and have dinner with us. We plan to watch a movie. This is a relief. I don't have the energy to entertain. My suntanned, rejuvenated sister understands. And that is the last I remember of this evening.

Abigail later helped me fill in the holes.

'It was just after nine. I was incredibly tired, still recovering from jet-lag after a lengthy trip from New Zealand. I hadn't seen Lou in a year-and-a-half, although we had chatted frequently during my travels. We decided that, in light of my jet-lag and a cold that Lou felt was coming on, we should stay in and chuck on a chick flick, munch on some goodies we had picked up from a deli on Sunset and smoke a joint.

'I should have seen something was wrong when we picked up the food. She complained of feeling really tired and she quickly lost her temper. Wandering back to the car, I remember feeling grateful that we had picked up her buddy Jimmy. I hadn't been with her for over a year-and-a-half and so I put the whole "out of character" behaviour down to the mad life she seemed to have been living for the past year.

'The idea of the freedom of expression is what drew Lou and her ambition. I thought her lifestyle of mad, famous, celebrity parties, drugs, alcohol and more parties lost in the hills seemed so cool. A quiet night complete with munchies was the plan for this night in particular.

'Austin Powers burst into song in a flash of electric colours sweeping his great set of teeth across the mega-sized TV in her plush living room. I was in heaven, bong in hand, tucking into a cheesecake and all this curled up next to my sister on her enormous couch. The room was dark. Jimmy seemed content packing the bong and occasionally looking up to see the two of us chilling.

'For some reason, the humour disappears now. Louise begins to shake. I thought she was being silly; after all, she is the prankster in the family. I laugh at her and say something like, "What are you doing?" Then Jimmy turned to me and told me she wasn't kidding around. I was frightened. Her hands were jerking around; her legs were shaking so heavily that the heavy couch was moving. She lay making hideous baby noises. She began to dribble and her eyes rolled up to the top of her head. I stood watching her eyelids smacking open and closed. All this and I had no idea what to do. Questions filled my mind. Jimmy kept telling me not to panic and that she was having a seizure. Hold on a second – she was having a seizure.

'"Surely we should be calling an ambulance, Jimmy ... she's scaring me ... what do I do? Christ, Jimmy, she's screaming."

'Four minutes later, she was still there, she was totally lost to me. I couldn't bear it any longer. I ran to the phone in the kitchen and dialed 911. My heart was in my mouth; confused and stoned, I tried desperately to give the ambulance crew directions to her house high in the hills. She lived in the middle of a maze. I had been there two days. I knew the basics but I was totally unsure of the way the crew had to turn. Grabbing an envelope from the counter, I found her full address and screamed at Jimmy – he told me to look after her. I felt ridiculous standing over her as she squirmed on the couch. All I could do was watch in disbelief. I started shouting at her, remembering that the sound of someone near always makes you feel more comfortable.

'The shaking slowed down and she seemed to stop. She was quiet. Lou turned to me, looking at Jimmy and me standing over her.

'"What happened?"

'Her eyes were blazing red and her body soaking wet with sweat. I told her she was OK. Everything was going to be fine; this was never going to happen again. I was pretending it was OK, pushing my fear and adrenalin back to where they had sprung from. Those dark corners of my soul quaked with worry. Finally, the silence is broken as she lies there sleeping and there is a knock at the door.

'It had taken them 25 minutes to get to us. I was furious and confused. Asking what was wrong on the doorstep, they walked in. We were relieved and slightly comforted that the professionals were here. She woke up as they began moving the coffee table away. The noise woke her up because she turned her face very slowly towards the ambulance crew and seemed to recognise them. It wasn't her. Lou disappeared again; a fearing-for-her-life look shadowed the soul behind this pained mask. Then it happened again.

'They forced her down and asked me to find any medication she may have taken. I flew up to her bathroom pulling bottles of pills in a rage into her handbag, snatching vitamins, anything, everything.

'Jimmy promised he would meet me at the hospital. I was shouting at her, "Stay with me, Lou, listen to my voice, stay with me. I love you, stay here and listen to me." I was screaming over the wail of the alarm as we raced through the busy streets to the hospital.

'We arrived and she was rushed into the emergency ward. Doctors started firing questions at me – what had she eaten? I told them she had smoked pot, I told them she was sick, I begged them for help. They wanted everything – her birth date, her age. There were six nurses holding her down as she fought to be free; more questions. I panicked, stopped listening to their questions and told them she had been in a bad car accident in 1992. I gave them the bag of pills and emptied out the contents of her bag into the sink ... maybe she had taken something ... find the answer, Abi ... look for the drugs. Somebody help her, she is in pain. Who are her doctors? Eye surgeon? Medication? Suddenly, control gripped me and I fired answers – opened her address book, reeled off names of doctors, their numbers and pagers. I tried to find an insurance card – where is it? Can't find it. Lou – stay with me ... LOU, IT'S GOING TO BE OK.

'It was late. Kathy had arrived. The doctors had made Louise as comfortable as possible. I was asked to take a break and get some air. My hand was wet with sweat from holding hers for hours. My voice was hoarse and now I had to phone her father in England. I had to tell him that she was really sick and in hospital again. Kathy saw my worry and through her tears she dialled him. I fled for air ... How did this happen? I don't remember how many times that night I prayed or how many times she disappeared. I can't even remember who the doctors were. Was it six or seven full seizures in three hours? Each seizure lasting under and over 15 minutes. I would have done anything to help her.'

I'm admitted to the hospital again, except this time I'm not pleasant. I'm unable to talk through the stutters and the trembles. I'm no longer in control of my body and movements. My arms are unsteady and physically shaking, as are my legs. My head bobs up and down and tears flow from my eyes. I am terrified. I'm dying. I can't let anyone see me like this. No one cares. I am in a state of self-piteous disgust and I want everyone around me to know of my pain. I've been here for days – how many, I don't know. I can't count. I can't even speak. I've been taken for numbers of tests. MRIs, EEGs and lumber punctures. The lumber puncture hurt. The needle was thick and obtrusive as it delved into my lower back to extract spinal fluid. I had heard them say 'spinal meningitis'.

Abigail is yelling at me to be strong. I am screaming at her to 'GO TO HELL'. I am stinging. I am filled with a rage, which is powerful and explosive. I have never felt anger like this before. I am burning inside like the centre of a flame. I am screaming at God to take me away. Hadn't I been through enough? I couldn't see that this was my doing and the neglect of my self. My soul was screaming to leave this maltreated body. I had been given a gift and I'd been abusing it. All the pain that I had induced throughout my life, all the times I hadn't said how I felt, all the times I didn't ask for help, they were all here bottled up and screaming for air. They had been suffocating and now they needed to breathe. The lid had been removed and the pains came out crying their different cries, hissing their hisses and seeping into the minds of anyone present. I was being stripped. Stripped down to the core. Suddenly I am blaming everyone for the pains in my life. Abigail is trying to calm me down again as I am throwing things around the room. First the phone, then the food tray and I'm searching for anything else.

'What's happened to you, Lou?' she screams through tears. 'I thought you were strong. This behaviour goes against everything you stand for.'

Her face is pinched and red, she's had enough herself. She has been compassionate. She has listened to it all and still I am not listening.

Her words sting.

'STRONG?' the witch in me screams. 'Strong? Do you have any fucking idea what it's been like and how hard it is to walk around every day and have people stare at you because you're a fucking monster. Do you know how much it takes to smile and not say anything? You have no idea. I haven't been a normal person in years. Don't you dare tell me how to behave.'

'I've had enough,' she shouts back and leaves the room, slamming the door behind her.

'You have to calm down, Louise,' Kathy says. She approaches the bed, a little hesitant, and then touches my sweaty forehead.

'I ... I ... I'm ... sc ... scar ... scared,' I stutter. 'Wha ... what's ... wroonngg ... with me?'

My head is feeling the chaos and is bobbing up and down, up and down. I am so so tired. I can't sleep. I've tried and my body has sudden jerky movements, which prompt me to stay awake.

When Alex comes in, I feel ashamed. I don't want him to see me in this state but it doesn't matter. I see the worry in his face. He looks tired. We are close friends through everything and I know he will take care of me. I have upset him. I have upset Kathy. I have upset my sister who has been overwhelmed with the shock of the past few days. But she has held it together and made necessary calls and arrangements. My father won't speak to me. This causes more venom to spit from my mouth.

'He doesn't love me,' I keep moaning.

My grandmother listens patiently as always, offering more words of comfort. She helps me to quieten the beast. I'm still scared. I still don't know how to say so. My fear is disguised as animosity. I keep complaining about the pain in my hand from the IV. When the nurse tries to change it, I cry for her to leave me alone. The doctors cannot find any conclusive diagnosis. They have run the tests and asked the questions.

When I've been there for eight days, a doctor appears with X-rays of my head. Kathy is there, anticipating his prophecy.

'Louise has a scar across her brain caused by the car accident she had in 1992.'

He points to the scar. I'd seen it before. My anger has abated now as exhaustion and tears replace it.

'Louise, the only conclusion I can come to is that you have been overdoing things and therefore irritated the scar on your brain. This will have sent nerve impulses which hence led to the seizures.' He pauses. 'Do you drink, smoke or take any kind of recreational drugs?'

I move my legs nervously under the covers and scratch my wrist where the IV has caused a red mark.

'Erm ... yes ... I ... I ... I've been ... d ... d doing ... a lot,' I admit.

He turns to Kathy and my sister who has now returned to the bleak hospital room. Then he looks back at me with a very serious look.

'Louise, if you drink or do drugs ever again, you will die. Your body and your head can't take it. This is serious. I'm not kidding around. You have had serious trauma over the years. This demands that you respect yourself. Take it easy. I don't want to see you in here again!'

Abigail and Kathy look at each other and then at me. The diagnosis had been given. I didn't have epilepsy, I didn't have spinal meningitis, I had a drink problem. I lie my head against the pillows. I feel the relief of the orders from the doctor. I feel for the first time that I don't have to pretend to be someone that doesn't feel pain. All the times I hadn't wanted to drink and hadn't had the willpower not to do so, had now become an order. Now I would listen. I knew that I would never drink again or do any other recreational drug.

I was human. It was OK to feel pain and to let people know. How many times had I heard my friends say to me, 'Louise, it's OK not to be Wonderwoman. You can slow down!'

Now I had no choice. God had taken care of that. It was time to listen. I knew my strengths and I was aware of what I had come through. I cry the tears that I should have cried a long time ago. For the first time, I feel a freedom from myself.

The Magic of the Mask

'Only those who dare, truly live.'
Ruth P Freedman

I live in a house on the corner where I had the accident. This leads me to believe that I have completed the full circle. A few years have passed since I left the hospital. My eye looks normal. I had the surgery with Dr Kawamoto and my eyelid is fixed. So many lessons have come to me from having been disfigured. Some people will never get it and why would they? They didn't live it. Only I can see the problems, or those that have been with me through my recovery. I took the doctor's advice and stopped drinking. I began asking for help when I needed it. I realised it was important and sometimes our lives can be so challenging that we need a little support. I sense a presence around me that I cannot explain. I know that I have become more than the woman my mother envisioned me being. I have worked with alternative healers, which I have found to be a large part of my recovery and healing. This becomes a very important part of my life having had so many medical procedures. Through visualisation and positive affirmations, we realise how powerful our minds alone are. Right now I am working with someone who is trying to regain the vision in my left eye.

One morning, I called Charlotte and told her I needed to see her. When I opened the door, I watched her cry tears of regret for not having been there for me. She explained the guilt she had felt for all those years. She apologised for not being there when I needed her. You never know that what can happen to change your life may only be minutes away.

I know my father is proud of me. For the first time, I am able to look back and make sense of things and understand the relationships that were affected from that ominous day.

What an incredible seven-year journey I took. I know now that anything is possible. I think of the times when I felt completely helpless and then how things came along showing me a reason to be positive. My face is no longer hidden. I no longer hide behind my mask – the mask that had become who I was. I now know that I can only take care of myself. I wouldn't have thought that the day would come when I would sit in front of a complete stranger and, having told them the story, have them say, 'What scars? I would never have known.' Once again I am a working actress and more doors are opening.

My dreams are unfolding and more are appearing. Through acting in television and film, I realise it doesn't complete me as I once thought it would. It doesn't make me who I am today. What does is my experience and how I can share that with you.

How Others Saw It

Recollections from those closest to Louise

Tamara Beckwith
(A Close Friend)

With naughty baby blues, razor sharp cheekbones, an enviable laughing elasticated mouth and childlike jumbo ears these features are somehow jumbled together to make up one of the prettiest faces I've known. Even from the naïve age of four this little girl named Lou was precocious beyond her years and I can clearly remember feeling that she had a mysterious air of pain and almost adult sensitivity wrapped about her like a little cloud even back then. Her wild and vivid imagination led to many wonderful sleepovers with us deep-sea diving with torches to the deep bottoms of our sleeping bags and crazy adventures around Wimbledon village on our beloved roller blades, skiing holidays were always tinged with Madam's drama and many siblings' unnecessary tears were shed as a result of our sheer mischievous natures combined to spell trouble with a capital T.

As an adult you realise there are surprisingly bad character traits about dear and old friends that you would simply not tolerate in a new friend, but somehow history with someone magically erases those little problems and makes the friendship tighter. Well Lou and I have been through tough times – admittedly mostly my fault (what a public confession) – and thankfully we both missed our history, our memories and our friendship enough to work through those troubles and I have to say that I feel privileged to be back in her life.

Lou's young life has admittedly been horrifically tinged with darkness and sadness but there have also been great moments of utter happiness and wonderment. Her life has been fast and furious, with great ups and terrific lows. Yet somewhere deep within her core she has a light that shines so bright and to me she is a model for us all in that whatever evil that seems so cruel and unfair in this life can be handled, can be dealt with and in some weird way a goodness can be gleaned from it.

Her strength is immeasurable, her joy for life infectious and her willingness to achieve against the odds remarkable. When reading her story you realise that yes, it is tragic, but please do not feel pity for my friend Lou. For she, like her beloved mother before her, is a true survivor of the first order and deeply loved by us all.

Abigail King
Lou's Sister

Courage
For Lou

Courage is something we all have inside us. It grows steadily as we walk this journey that is life. We reach for it when the travelling gets tough. On all our journeys, we find a time to call upon it. Louise's car accident was when she needed it most and I like to think that just a little bit of her courage has rubbed off on me. I am blessed to have her as my big sister and even more blessed to stand beside her.

In my short life I have also lost a mother who will forever live in my heart. Louise was there to hold me and comfort me following the formalities of such an untimely death. Together we have held each other's hand when doctors have told us news that has changed the course of our lives.

Fear, terror and bewilderment have ravaged our lives but together we have stood firm and stared them all in the face of adversity.

We have walked hand in hand through the endless tears we both seem to have cried for our past life and knew at the end of each mile we would need to tread bravely into a new and strange world that is ever evolving in front of us.

Though we live in different time zones thousands of miles apart, the bond that we share is forever growing. The pride I have for Louise cannot easily be put into words, but if you look you will see it in my eyes, if you listen you will hear it in my tone of voice when I talk about her daily, and if you're willing to look a little deeper, you will see it in my heart.

Louise has always known what she wanted to do in life. When she originally left for Los Angeles, she boarded the airplane with a sprig of courage, letting go of the past. I had to trust that she was going because she needed to, she was off to the City of Dreams.

We pay a price for getting our dreams if we are to be successful. Louise paid a high price.

I watched her leave the family house behind. She was a young girl filled with excited ideas and grit determination, almost bouncing with energy. I remember talking to her over the phone a few months later, about her new car and how fun it was to drive with the top down, with the sun shining on her face every day. On my first visit to Los Angeles, I saw a different woman lying in a hospital bed, thin and tightly curled up, bandaged thickly to hide the incredible swelling that doubled the size of her battered head. The scar across her forehead was heavily stitched; her face was purple and yellow from the massive bruising. I was drawn into shock, my own terror seized me, but when she turned her gaze to me, I saw love; more importantly, I immediately recognised her courage.

Over the years, she's become a face of courage. Through what seemed like endless surgeries, that courage has grown and grown. Louise is my big sister and, before the accident, I idolised her, but through watching her grow through the pain, fear and agony she has endured in her short life, she has become an idol of inspiration.

The sprig of courage she had many years ago has grown into a strong branch. I have watched her face this accident whilst writing this book and I believe now that it is finished she will be able to walk into the second chapter of her life free from the virtual prison sentence that began for her one early evening back in 1992.

We all have scars, some of them deeper than others. I now believe that it is those scars that help us become who we were always meant to be.

I love you, Lou.

Abi

xxx

Lauren
Lou's Sister

I was five years old when the accident happened. I woke up in the morning and my dad was gone. I was told he had gone to America to visit Lou. On the way to school, I remember my mum crying, but I felt too shy to ask why. That night, I was told Lou-Lou had been in a car accident, but she was with some good doctors that would make her get better, hopefully. At that age I didn't understand properly. Two days later, my mum joined my dad and Louise in the States. I went to stay at my best friend's at that time, Louise, for a week.

When my parents got back the following week, my dad showed me some pictures of the smashed-up car and Louise in hospital, it was then it struck — this accident was more serious than I thought. I just started crying.

A few months later, when I was told Louise was coming to England I was quite scared of what I might see. But I recognised her as soon as I saw her. I thought the only thing different was the patch over her eye.

Kathy Cooper
Lou's Surrogate Mother

When I got the phone call on 5 October, it was about midnight. The phone rang and we thought, well, we'll let the machine get it. Then we thought, if someone is calling at midnight then it must be important, so I answered the phone and it was Louise's father calling to tell us that she had been in a very terrible accident and was in the hospital; could we please go and be with her and he would be there as soon as possible the next day. Of course, I freaked out and handed the phone to my husband and started throwing clothes on and getting ready to go to the hospital.

When we got there, Louise was in surgery, and some of her friends were in the waiting room. We didn't see Charlotte; apparently, she had already been released, having been treated for minor injuries.

Dr Kalb came out probably around 2.00am or so to tell us Louise had come through the surgery but there was a lot of damage, particularly to her spinal cord from which fluid was coming out. He told us about her injuries and how grave her condition was and advised us to go home and come back the next day. I basically refused to leave without seeing her and making sure that she was alive and breathing no matter what condition she was in. So we waited a little longer while they got her out of surgery and into recovery and at about 3.00am we were taken in to see her. She looked pretty awful, as I've said to her, 'like a watermelon on steroids', and all I could think was that I wanted her to hold on until her dad got there. It was that bad. The doctors can only promise so much;

they can't promise that you're going to live. They can promise that they've done their job, and that you're stable and so on.

With everything that was wrong with her, the injuries and the leak from the spinal cord, the prognosis didn't seem to be very good. But despite being on a respirator all bandaged up and everything, just seeing that she was breathing and that her vitals were OK, we left and came back at about 8.00am the next day.

Lousie was in a room in Intensive Care and the nurse came in and I was sitting in there with her. At one point, she woke up and the nurse checked her eyes; the left eye was very, very bad, but I guess because of my experiences with people in hospitals, it wasn't as horrifying to me as it was to other people. She opened her eyes and recognised me through the one good eye and pointed her finger up at me drifted back to sleep again. She drifted in and out a lot. I would go out to the waiting room and give reports to whoever was there, and I kept talking to her whether she was conscious or not, telling her to hang in there until her dad arrived.

At one point, we got a Dictaphone and had everyone send messages to her which was really helpful. Louise recognised everyone's voices which was a good sign, because we knew that she wasn't brain damaged to the point that she didn't know who she was or who we were. That was a positive thing for us.

Louise's dad finally came. She was doing very very well. It was amazing how well her body was dealing with the trauma that she was going through. We were worried about how she would recover from such a trauma and we knew that she had to face a very long surgery a few days later, but she did very well when she really came to and was aware of what was going on. Her positive attitude was really what has helped her since then, as well as all the people there for support — her family and her friends came from around the world to be with her. That's how much everyone cared about her and I think that was a driving force, aside from her own will to live. She had so many people there to support her.

Her father arrived the next afternoon and, of course, he was just as worried if not more so than all the rest of us, but we knew that she had some really good doctors and we had a lot of faith in all of them. Her father knew Dr Hoflin, Michael Jackson's surgeon.

The next day, her father and I went over to her apartment. We felt like thieves ransacking her home but we had to find certain things of hers and we wanted to find a picture of her, one of her headshots for the doctors to use because we didn't want her looking like Michael Jackson, we wanted her looking like Louise Ashby. So we found a really good picture and stuck it up on the wall in her room. Her father tried to be positive during all of this.

She went into surgery very early in the morning and I remember the night before my husband saying to me that no one would be there with her in the morning before she went into surgery and I sat out on my front step and just cried that she was going to be all alone. I felt really bad because her father was in town and her stepmother and just the thought of her being alone before she went into surgery the next morning cracked me up. But her father got up really early and went over to her. It was a very tense day, just waiting and waiting, with the doctors coming out periodically but not often enough for us. Sometimes we would have to wait for hours on end to hear how things were going, and which doctor was doing which job, as they seemed to be doing their work in stages or in unison. The updates we got were positive, and everything was coming along fine.

The prognosis seemed good, once she got out of there and back together enough to set her up for her reconstrucive surgery six months later. Once she was out of the operation, she was into recovery.

Soon after her initial surgery, I remember Louise asking Emma for a mirror. When she saw her reflection, I don't think that she was horrified, she seemed to handle it well. She didn't totally break down and lose it. There was no, 'Oh my God, I look like Frankenstein.' As far as I recall, she dealt with it very well and having us there and being positive for her helped. Yes, she did look bad, but she didn't look as bad as she had done the week before. I mean, she looked one step away from death the week before and after the surgery she looked very well, considering.

She continued to handle things very well throughout her stay in the hospital and she was a pretty good patient — she didn't have much choice. I'd gone and bought turbans for her and, yes, they had parties for her in her room. Basically, my child was put on the back burner for two weeks so I was there for her as much as I possibly could be.

The family stayed around, friends came and went. Ben was still there when she came home from the hospital, as well as her grandmother and her sister.

She was well enough in the hospital to be released within three weeks. She went home to her one-bedroom apartment and her grandmother, her sister and Ben drove her absolutely nuts so she came to my house after that. Her dad was at our house, too. So she stayed in my study and that is when we started making up fairytale songs, 'Little Red Riding Turban' and, when we got her wigs, 'Princess Lou-Lou Hair of Many Colours'. Those were our first new names for her. We did her eye treatments and eye washes and looked after her and then she finally decided that enough was enough and her place was hers, so she called her visitors and said basically, 'Go to a hotel, I want to come home'.

She went home and started her recovery. She had good days and bad days. I would take her to all her doctors' appointments, hold her hand, ask questions and try to deal with the situation as best we could. She knew she faced a great deal more than what she'd already been through, and she also knew that she was a very lucky person to be alive. She had wonderful, absolutely wonderful doctors. Dr Kalb took a special interest, calling her his star patient — well, she's everybody's star patient.

Her attitude was mostly positive, although there were times when we would come out of the doctor's office and she would be very depressed. But she would pick herself up and realise that if she wanted to go on with life, then she had to face all the various procedures and get through them, so facing her operation in April, she did really well with that. She looked very good afterwards.

I then remained in contact over the phone and in letters for the next couple of years. She seemed to be doing very well with the other eye operations that she had. I came back in January of '95, when Louise had another eye operation that was to centre it and tighten the muscles.

I missed the actual surgery but was there the next morning to go to the doctor's office with her and Alex. Alex had been around for six months, so I don't think he'd really seen quite as much as I had. There he was, this big, strapping man holding Louise's hand and trying to be brave. When the doctor pulled her eye out of the socket, I didn't flinch, but Alex turned green and just about keeled over. Louise was very calm and patient; she had to sit still as it was a very important part of the procedure. Pull the eyeball out, tighten the stitches, snip them and put it back. It was quite an experience!

They did a really good job and she handled it really well. Since then, she's had another couple of procedures on her eye. She's had such a positive attitude throughout the whole thing. Everyone has their moments and, of course, she did as well, but the positive side of her won out.

But then we move to January of '98 when she started having seizures, an after-effect of a brain injury. She's fortunate that she managed to avoid them for so long, as they can happen at any time. She'd had five seizure-free years, which she'd faced with a positive attitude, and now she is handling this as well. At first, it was very hard because she didn't understand what was happening to her. It's now April, and she's still learning how to deal with it.

I think her drive and her ambition to have her life as she wants it is what keeps her going, even with the little set-backs here and there; sometimes they are big set-backs. She deals with them accordingly, freaks out here and there and learns how to cope with them. She's got a very strong resolve and not many people could have come through this situation as well as she has. I think she'll manage to get through this and be a positive influence to other people in a similar situation. Like when she had her seizures, we made up seizure songs and seizure jokes. Her sister, unfortunately, couldn't understand how we could be so glib about it but that was her way of dealing with it. If you can't find the humour in a situation, well, then it's all the harder to deal with. So we make jokes and that is part of her way of dealing with it and part of my way of dealing with her as her nurse and her surrogate mammy.

She's amazing. She looks amazing and even when she goes through bad times we always know that she is going to pull through and that she's going to make it and this isn't going to stop her. She's going to reach the stars.

John Ashby
Lou's Father

It was 5 October 1992, and I had a call from her friend's father saying that she'd been involved in a smash. Obviously, at first I thought that she'd just banged the car or something. It wasn't until I spoke to him at length that I realised that it was a major problem.

Then I rang the surgeon, Irving Kalb, and he told me what the situation was. Obviously, it was very, very distressing. He actually said to me, 'Can you get over here today because we're not sure that she's going to make it through the day.' So obviously my next thought was, 'How in the name of God do I get from here to there within something like three hours?' That means getting on a plane and getting there. The next couple of hours were spent ringing around and asking people to get me on a British Airways flight and I don't remember too much about the morning. I remember going to the airport and everybody being very nice, and getting the plane. The incredible thing was that Louise's friend Emma was there travelling over as well. The flight was 11 or 12 hours and I remember every hour seemed like a day and every minute like an hour which went on and on and on. I got a call from Irving Kalb literally five minutes before I got on the plane, and he said to me that Louise had come out of her initial surgery and that she was conscious and that her eye was responding to light, because they had already ascertained that there was a problem with her eye. He said she was still in a critical situation. Then I got on the flight to Los Angeles.

Some long-term friends of mine were there to pick us up and took me straight to Cedars and I went straight in to see her then. She was heavily sedated, and it was almost 24 hours since she'd had the accident. Her face was very, very heavily swollen and I think when she saw me there she must have thought, 'Why are they here, it must be something serious.' I imagine that's what goes through your mind. I wasn't really too concerned about what she looked like; I just thanked God that she was alive.

Then she was in the Intensive Care Unit I think for three days, and then she had massive surgery. I think it was on the Friday. That surgery went on for 17 hours. It was very fortunate for me that I knew so many people in Los Angeles and they really looked after me as there was hardly any time during that long surgery that there wasn't somebody in there whom I knew which was tremendous.

Obviously, I don't remember too much about the interim period. I was with Louise from the moment I arrived until the massive surgery; you know, going in and spending hours with her each day prior to the major surgery on Friday. I think by the time Friday came round, it was then a question of giving her her face back. That was when they really had to go in and restructure her face and future. All they did on the first surgery was to stabilize her. Once in the operating theatre, they established she had no cheek bone, her skull had been opened, there was scar tissue round the brain and those were the things they had to cope with. I mean, that is why it took so long, all the metal and restructuring her face and also finding out if there was any fluid leak from the spine.

Having come out of surgery, then having to cope with the turbans, the discomfort from her skull and everything, she has handled it brilliantly. It is an incredible thing, because my mother went through the same thing. She was in a car crash and they both handled the situation in pretty much the same way. They were both very positive about it. Louise was positive about it from the word go. I think the big problem, apart from having the physical pain and the physical disability, was when they shaved her hair off. You see, if you've got beautiful hair it's an aspect of femininity, and they took all her femininity away for a period of time. So that is a major blow for any woman and she handled it extremely well, incredibly well. Within a month, she had her wig, her eye-patch and she was out there. It was quite incredible.

When she got made up at first and the swelling went down — the swelling took a long time to go down – she looked amazing. Obviously, when she took the patch off the eye it was very, very receded. It was 3mm too far back and there was no pupil there at all, it was just white which was just terrible. That was October and she had her next surgery at Easter. That will give you some idea of how long it was.

I can't remember how many times I went over in the interim. I think I made another two trips. She came home for Christmas that year. I went out again in the February and then again at Easter time when she had more major reconstructive surgery at St Johns in Santa Monica to rebuild the cheekbone. They had initially stabilized it, but they had to rebuild the cheekbone, rebuild the eye socket and reposition the eye.

I remember going in to Post-op where she was recovering. She was still unconscious and I could see her cheekbone again. Now, bear in mind her face had gone back down by the time they had operated on her and had given her back her facial features. Prior to this, her face had just been one big lump of bone. I remember thinking, Oh, she's going to be so happy when she wakes up.

Well, of course, by the time she woke up four or five hours later, her face was like a balloon again. I reassured her and said, 'I've seen it, you haven't.' Sure enough, it did look good. Then the next problem arose – bringing the eye forward because it was still a little raised. There was still a lot of the white showing instead of the pupil, but that was much further on in her recovery.

Louise and I have always been pretty close. But there were things that she did and risks that she took when I would have said, 'Don't.' Like after the accident and the operation she went out and bought an old $500 banger and was driving around in it. So six weeks after the accident, she was driving around again in some old Cadillac with smoke pouring out of the exhaust.

It's hard to say how I've handled things. As I've said, the same thing happened to my mum. She went through the windscreen of a car, her face was smashed to pieces and she lost her left arm and she was eight-and-a-half months pregnant at the time. I remember thinking at the time, God, this is not happening to me again, and it was extra difficult because I was going through a marriage break-up as well so it wasn't the best of times

Obviously, thank God that it's all worked out and that she's reasonably healthy. On the other hand, you don't feel terribly grateful to

God because the past five years have been pain and torture for her. I mean, although there are great sides to things, there are down sides to things. So nothing is ever perfect.

But she never loses hope. If you knew Louise, she could be falling off a cliff backwards and she wouldn't lose hope. She'd think she was going to grow wings and fly away. She's the greatest optimist I've ever known, probably too much of an optimist for her own good.

Just as an example, they operated on her eye, just a simple, totally separate operation to bring the eyeball down. It was fine for six weeks and then it went up again and she said, 'Well, I'll have to have it done again.' That is a major decision when something doesn't work like that, to say, 'Oh well, I'm going to find someone who will make it work,' and especially when they say you could lose your eye. There was a chance that she could lose the blood supply to the eye, and she was prepared for that chance.

It was Louise's decision to say, 'Let's either make or break. Either I'm going to have a glass eye or I'm going to have this one looking relatively normal.'

Eventually, I went and visited the house of the man who had caused the accident. I went up there one night to find out where he lived, I couldn't help it. I remember driving back out to Woodland Hills — I had got his address from the attorneys. You feel so much anger, you feel, Who is it who did this to my daughter? What kind of people are they? What are they like? I went up there and parked my car down the road and I think I actually saw the car that caused the accident with a cover over it in the garage. I felt like going and torching it. Not really, but it's a difficult thing to describe. I never met him, but Louise did. It's just as well I didn't.

There are times when she thinks I don't really know what's going on. I know exactly what's going on. It's something that you learn to live with and it changed that day and it's with her forever, it doesn't go away, it's part of your life and everybody around you. All I can do is try and help her cope with it to the best of my ability and sometimes the best of my ability might not be to be demonstrative about things because I think its a fatal mistake for anybody to be demonstrative and make people feel sorry for you. Just be positive.

George Squire
(A Close Friend)

I remember I was living in the pool house in Bel Air. Craig had come round on the Friday for a drink and, in true Craig form, didn't leave. He was still there on Saturday or Sunday when Lou arrived in her new Mustang and we went up the road to the supermarket at the top of the hill to buy supplies. I seem to remember that we all partied that day by the pool and spent the night all huddled together. On Sunday evening, Lou left to go home and then on to acting class. Craig left soon after and I went to sleep.

A couple of days later, I had only really just arrived at work when I recieved a call telling me of Lou's accident. I remember speaking to Craig and arranging to meet him at Cedars-Sinai straight away. I left the office shocked and pretty worried as Lou was still in the operating theatre.

There were two people already at the hospital when I arrived. Craig arrived shortly after and we all spent a few hours trying to get information on her condition. They weren't telling us much. Louise was in surgery for about 11 hours. Once she was moved to the Intensive Care Unit, one of us managed to get in to see her by claiming to be her cousin, her closest relative at the time as her father had not arrived there yet.

I think it was a day later when I was finally allowed to see her. Her head was so swollen and wrapped up like a mummy and she was still poorly and weak but alive, and out of any immediate danger, which was good.

The next time I saw her was with Tilda. She was still so swollen yet she was already smiling and laughing painfully and showing her trademark sense of humour which pulled her through so well. That is when I gave her a cactus.

I do remember her laughing and joking all the time, which was her way of overcoming the shock of such a severe injury, but it was a bit unnerving at times as it seemed that she was trying to get back to normal too quickly. The doctors were amazed at how quickly and how well she was coping — it was a positive time, we were all, including Lou, so happy that she was OK.

Tilda and I moved in around the corner from Lou's apartment and we were so close that we were always popping in or going for lunch or taking Lou shopping. I remember eating a lot of Pavillion's orange chicken and Häagen-Dazs carrot cake ice cream. Even though Lou had lost her smell and taste, she still enjoyed the texture.

I remember Lou being concerned about her eye but she was reassured that in time it would be set right. There was also the frustration at being so swollen and at having lost her hair. I remember her turban and wig and, of course, there was the eye-patch. She had a major crush on Jason and he used to flirt outrageously with her, yet nothing ever happened. This confused Lou and made her concerned about her appearance but she has always been beautiful and still was then. Anyway, then he turned out to be gay and, boy, did I laugh!

As Lou recovered, she became understandably more anxious to have the corrective surgery on her eye. As far as LA life was concerned, Lou took it easy simply because physically she had to. When Lou did start going out, she was fêted by the crowd. People were constantly filling up her glass with vodka that she couldn't smell or taste. I remember finding her drinking a glass of water which turned out to be neat vodka and having to sit her down. Overall, Tilda and I were very protective of Lou and I would at least try to make sure she didn't over-exert herself at any of those parties.

Craig Lynn
(A Close Friend)

George called me at home in Venice Beach and said Lou had had an accident and was in hospital. I was concerned and left immediately on my motorcycle to meet George. On the way there, my mind was racing with every possibility, but we had no information on Lou's condition.

George and I arrived at the hospital, where there were lots of people around but it was hard to get information. Lou had hit her head hard in the crash and now was in a coma. This was shocking news. Lou was in Intensive Care and we weren't allowed to see her. Cathy, an old family friend, was the contact between friends and the hospital. Nico was there and making good use of his mobile.

We learnt of Lou's condition in part, here and there. I got agitated because I wanted to see Lou. If she was going to die, I wanted to have said my goodbyes to her, privately, next to her, to her spirit.

But because we weren't able to see Lou, I suggested to a few people that we make a tape of us talking to Lou together and separately so that Cathy could play it to her. Even though she was in a coma, I had heard that people could be reached and often reported remembering conversations and music that had been played.

When I was eventually allowed to see Lou, it was with a feeling of great relief that she was even alive. Lovely, funny Lou was alive. The initial shock of seeing Lou's injuries was intense. Scars, bruises, stitches and a very crushed left side of her face. I tried to be up and positive. Lou hadn't seen her face and was very upset about having no hair. She had a scar across her skull, from ear to ear. I tamely told her that her hair would grow back in no time. I had to leave for a meeting and promised to go back afterwards. Two-and-a-half hours later, I was at the door to Lou's room again. I went in and Lou gasped, 'What have you done?'

'You see, it's not that bad, Lou', I said, and we both laughed. My head was bald as well, a $5.00 shave at Ricky's barbershop.

I was very concerned for Lou, as we all were. After the hospital, there was a constant barrage of tests, doctors, extra operations, eye operations, plastic surgery, lawyers meetings, depostions — the pressure on Lou must have been pretty much unbearable.

After a while, maybe a year, more or less, Lou was back to her bubbly self, albeit with memory loss, blindness, loss of taste and smell — quite remarkable and couragous. However, I noticed that Lou was drinking and taking drugs too much, given her problems. I spoke to her and tried to warn her of the possible dangers. I told her to ask her doctors specifically about each element — drinking, pot and cocaine. I can't remember if anything came of it.

Another time in hospital I was in Lou's room when her surgeon came in to drain blood from her head. He pulled out a vicious monster of a needle, at least 9in, attached to a very long syringe. As he went towards Lou's head with it, I couldn't face it and had to leave. I was rapidly found by a nurse whom Lou had dispatched to fetch me back.

Lou had to give blood many times so that she had her own blood on hand for her many operations. I went with her the first time she did this and sat in the chair next to her, holding her hand and looking away from the blood at all times.

We would always laugh a lot in those situations with the nurses and doctors.

Ben
(Lou's Ex-Boyfriend)

I started seeing Lou in March 1987. We were both 16, too young, I suppose, to know about an illness like leukaemia.

I remember hearing that word mentioned again and again in conversation. I pretended, I think, to know what it was.

We were sitting in the Texas Lone Star in Gloucester Road that day. Louise was on her way to meet us. I was told she was being told the news as we ate.

'Leukaemia,' Louise's best friend said, 'do you know what it is, Ben?' Before I had a chance to answer, she continued, 'It's cancer of the blood.'

Now it all began to make sense. After all, cancer was an illness we were all familliar with. An intense pain, more like anguish, filled me. How would Lou cope with this news? How would it affect our relationship? What would happen now? All now, with hindsight, selfish questions, but we were young and so innocent. The question of death was still something none of us had had to deal with and, consequently, the furthest thing from our thoughts.

When I saw Lou she was still unsure of the full extent of her mother's illness. As it started to become clearer, I could see the frown on her forehead grow. Taking in so much was very difficult as such a tender age. She probably grew five years in that single day.

I saw Lou on and off for the next four years. We watched her mother fight this awful illness until her last day. I suppose, towards the end, our relationship had drifted. Lou was with her mother during all of her free time whilst trying to get her acting career off the ground. It was tough for her, but as time went by her resilience, patience and character all grew. Over this period, she changed from being an innocent young girl without a care in the world to a mature woman who had to take care of a family whilst her mother was in hospital. It seemed a tough task, but she carried it off with no complaint.

When her mother did pass on, Lou was by her side. I know from what she has told me that she got strength from her mother's amazing fight. Watching Linda was incredible now I think about it. She had such a young family. The worry of leaving them behind must have been terrifying, but she never once seemed negative. She really seemed to give the illness the best fight she possibly could.

So when the tragic day came, I truly believe that Linda passed on her strength and this has been the core of a personality that, subsequently, has had to deal with so much.

Less than a year later, Lou and I split up and she was living in LA. I was travelling around Australia. We were worlds apart but, as she well knows, she was never far from my heart. I was lying on a hostel bed somewhere on Sydney's coastline. Uncontactable, or so I thought, when a voice came over the tannoy: 'Ben Boultbee, phone call for you.' I sat up in bed knowing full well that this would probably not be a social call.

Gerald, a dear friend of mine, broke the news of Lou being in a car accident. I was shocked. I think I started packing my bags within minutes. That night, I was in Brisbane and two days later I was on my way to see Lou. I knew by this stage she wasn't critical but I really felt as a special friend I wanted to be by her side. I was fully prepared to deal with the worst, so when I finally saw her, my initial reaction was relief. Then she unpeeled the bandages showing me her head. She told me her sight in one eye had gone and her smell and taste. She smiled as she told me this. I smiled back but inside I sank. I found myself again asking the question, 'How will she cope?' but as I looked back at her smiling face, things had changed since I last asked that question. She was already fighting to put on a brave face. She has this uncanny knack of looking on the bright side of life in all situations.

Since then, Lou has been through five years of treatment. She's had to battle every step of the way. Her dreams and aspirations never seen to stray. She has always wanted to be an actress since the age of six and, after all this, she has in the last two years made great headway.

Oliver King
(Lou's Brother)

I was at Bradfield studying for my GCSEs. It was about 8.00pm and I was in prep when one of my colleagues walked in and told me I had an important phone call. It was Grandma and on picking up she told me that Lou had a been in a car accident, not stating whether it was big or small which has always angered me. She told me she didn't know much and that Louise was in good hands, the best in LA.

At first, I thought nothing of it as it is not every day an event like this takes place, especially so recently after the death of our mother. That night, I lay in my bed and the conversation with Grandma almost replayed through my mind and it dawned on me that something was wrong as Grandma didn't call me that much. It took me at least a couple of hours to sleep due to the recurring fear that my sister might be dead. I felt losing another very close member of my family was potentially devastating, not only to me but to Abi who was equally going through the tunnel of fate.

I didn't hear anything else of the accident from my Granny until the following evening when she updated me on Lou's progress. She told me that Louise had received attention immediately on arriving at Cedars Sinai and had undergone 11 hours' intensive brain surgery (I still hadn't been told what had exactly happened). She told me that Louise had survived the night — a good sign, but she was expecting a 24-hour operation that was to decide whether she lived or not. It was Louise who told me a couple of months later exactly what happened.

It was a couple of months before I saw her and I was very nervous on her arrival. I felt anticipation at seeing Louise and yet reluctant to find out what had happened. On seeing Lou, she was wearing a hat and dark glasses, looking completely different. It was quite emotional. I didn't want to cry. I was extremely happy to see her alive.

Karim Haliwagi
(A Close Friend)

It was early in the morning and I was told that Lou had had a bad car accident and there was a 50 per cent chance of her living. I went to Emma's house where it was chaos and I was given more information. There were eight of us there in a panic. The facts were very serious and the scary part was that we thought we were going to lose Lou. We were told she'd had 11 hours' surgery to save her life but didn't know if she was out of danger. I knew then I had to go to LA.

I was told on a Tuesday and flew out on the Saturday. My flight arrived at 10.30pm. I was so nervous that I had a few drinks before going to the hospital to try and calm myself down. I was extremely nervous at the prospect of seeing Louise. It is so easy to try and create an image in your mind when faced with such a traumatic situation but nothing could have prepared me for what I saw.

On arrival at the hospital, I was told I could not go into the ICU as it was too late. Emma was allowed, but not me. I snuck in through another entrance. I was horrified by what I saw. I had a lump in my throat, and my heartbeat rose by about 25,000 per cent. I couldn't believe this was my friend. I didn't recognise her. I was overwhelmed by the machines, tubes and medical equipment that was centered on her. To add to the shock, Louise got excited on seeing me, hence the heart monitor went into overdrive beeping way too fast causing the nurses to run in, so I had to apologize and leave hoping I hadn't added to the instability of her condition. Her head was twice its usual size, covered in bandages which hid her once beautiful face. Tubes carrying blood came out of the crown of her head.

A few days later, she was moved into a normal room and I was amazed that at no point did Louise show any self-pity for her condition. In fact, it was Louise who calmed everyone around her who was deeply affected by her condition. Lou's unbeatable spirit and attitude kept everyone in a buoyant mood, rather than dragging them down to the hell she really must have been suffering.

Emma Gold
(A Close Friend)

I was at home asleep and got a call at 6.30am from a friend who told me that Lou had been in an accident. She said she was in a really bad way, that she was with Charlotte and they weren't sure if Lou was going to live. I had to contact Lou's father, John. I was very freaked out after getting over the initial shock. I kept trying to call John, whose line was busy. When I got through, he told me he was flying out and I said I would fly with him, too. We were kept updated with news from the hospital. We knew it was touch and go whether Lou would be alive or not when we arrived.

I phoned all our main friends to let them know what was happening, and they all came to my house where we could all console each other.

I met John at the airport and we were both trying to be strong for one another. We got an upgrade and special treatment was given to us. It was the most horrendous flight and the longest ever. I kept going to the bathroom to cry without him seeing. It was a long 11 hours.

Steven Cooper came to meet us and took us straight to the hospital. We were taken straight into Intensive Care. I was very apprehensive about what I was going to see, but I put my feelings aside and knew I was there for Lou.

When I walked in, she was attached to every machine imaginable and her face was the size of a football. John was by her side. She opened one of her eyes and I could tell she was thinking, What the hell are you doing here? The waiting room was full of friends but they were not allowed in, only family and myself.

The first week I was by her side. She wasn't allowed the next operation until she was stable. I was there 18 hours a day doing nothing else. I stayed at her house. I took the book she had been reading. When I opened it up, a piece of paper fell out. She had been writing a letter to her mum the day before the accident. She had written, 'I really miss you and can't visit you at the grave as I am so far away, I wish I could see you again soon ...' It was unfinished.

I was reading her book to her before she became conscious; her dad was getting a coffee, when suddenly she said, 'Aren't you going to talk to me? You could at least read me the dirty bits.' The book flew out of my hands.

Louise kept asking for mirrors. The doctors requested one of her pictures from her modelling portfolio so they could see how to make her look again. The day of the operation was the longest day of my life. The doctor kept feeding me and John Valium. She was in surgery for 22 hours. One of the doctors came out and showed us X-rays and it was like a jigsaw puzzle. When she came out, they said it had gone well.

One of the joys of my day would be to help the nurses empty her tubes, not knowing what they were full of. Whenever I was back at her flat, the phone rang non-stop and I had to keep updating England on her progress. Then Wagi arrived which was a great relief for me as I got so stressed out.

When she came out of surgery she looked very different. I could tell it was her, but her face was very swollen, and one of her eyes was closed. I couldn't believe that they had shaved her hair off and opened her head from ear to ear, peeling her face forward. I was in awe of what the doctors had done. I was sure her mum had sent her back as there were still things she had to do.

Then Lou was moved into a private room out of Intensive Care. She still hadn't seen herself. The next traumatic thing for me to witness was her having the staples removed from her head which had been holding it together. That day, she asked me if I would help her into the bathroom to put on a turban to cover her head. We had still been avoiding mirrors but this time we couldn't. She was so drugged up that I don't think the full effect of anything she was about to see was going to sink in. Because we had tried so hard for her not to see herself, I was very nervous, but I knew I wanted to do it with her. The reaction was as expected. She was in complete shock. Her face was not the right shape, it was swollen and she had no hair and a monstrous scar. Obviously, we calmed her down and had to make her realise she was alive and that was the main thing. It's hard to explain, especially the extreme nature of her injuries. It was her face and it wasn't easy.

I was with her every day, 18 hours a day, and when I left and finally got on to the plane, I felt so guilty for leaving. I wrote her a card and cried properly for the first time at the end of my intense two weeks. It made everyone's problems so immaterial after seeing what Lou was going through.

In general, I think she has dealt with this amazingly well. I have enormous respect and admiration for her. I think she went through an enormous amount, she never slipped back and I always felt like she took on way too much. She always keeps persevering.

Frances Westover
(Lou's Grandmother)

I was rung by John Ashby and told there had been a bad car accident. Louise was in hospital, he said, she was unconscious and he was flying straight out there. I felt like it was the last thing I could cope with, what with the death of Lynda so recently. It was such a shock. I had hysterics. I was told it was critical and my thoughts were that this was the end. They didn't think she was going to make it.

Two weeks later, I flew out to see her and went straight from the airport to the hospital. She was now out of Intensive Care. Her head was bandaged, she was sitting up chatting and laughing. I never saw her head.

Acknowledgements

There have been many people who have come and gone in my life. Each person has taught me a lesson from which to learn. For all these lessons, I am eternally grateful. There have been men and woman who have helped to save my life, to rebuild my face and my future. To these men and women, I am eternally grateful. They are Dr Marshall Grode, Dr Kalb, Dr Alessi, Dr Kawamoto and Dr Rosenbaum.

I want to thank John Blake for giving me the opportunity to share my story. I wish to thank my mother for giving me the gifts of strength and determination. For showing me how to love and to be loved. I wish to thank my father for standing by me in times of hardship, even though it was hard for him to see me going through the pain. I wish to thank my grandmother for having words of wisdom and courage and always being at the end of the phone. I want to thank Abigail and Oliver for being such strong and determined people whom I love very much. I thank Lauren and Jonathon for their gifts of laughter and innocence. I want to thank Grandma Marjorie for sharing her experience with me at a time when I needed to hear it, and for her strength and courage. I want to thank Kathy Cooper without whom I would never be where I am today. I thank you for your gift of love in my recovery. I want to thank George and Tilda for driving me everywhere I needed to go and for their wonderful and silly jokes, which made me smile. I want to thank Craig for shaving his head and showing me the importance of friendship and loyalty. I want to thank

Emma and Wagi for being two wonderfully amazing friends, for flying across the world to be by my side, and for saving me with their smiles and laughter at times when I needed to laugh. I want to thank Belinda Norcliffe, Hatty Madden, Louise Golley, Tamara Beckwith, Debra Anderson, Sara Jane Gaslee, Sophie Stevenson, Jules Stevenson, Charlie Gardner, Mike Strutt, Alicia Gordon, Alison Attenborough, Steven Cooper, Jason Garrett, Camilla Storey, Sean Borg, Morgan Eldgridge, Donna Richards, Edward Laurie, Emily Chatton, Jackie Bregman, Simon Main, Marc Marmel and Nico Golfar for being in my life and offering me the support that they did. I want to thank Nicole for being my pillar of strength. I want to thank George Stanbury for being a great lawyer and a wonderful listener. I want to thank Kamala Lopez, Romy Ivsic and Tristine Rainer for sharing their amazing writing talents with me and in helping me to find my voice as a writer. I want to thank Ben Boultbee, Matt Baker, Alex Carlton, Nic Spikings and Judd Dunning for being the loves in my life and for their understanding of my crazy life and head.